"IT IS A NEW KIND
OF DIASPORA"

Riccardo Steiner

"IT IS A NEW KIND OF DIASPORA"

Explorations in the Sociopolitical
and Cultural Context of Psychoanalysis

Riccardo Steiner

London & New York
KARNAC BOOKS

First published in 2000 by
H. Karnac (Books) Ltd., 58 Gloucester Road, London SW7 4QY
A subsidiary of Other Press LLC, New York

British Library Cataloguing in Publication Data

A C.I.P. for this book is available from the British Library

ISBN 1 85575 250 6

10 9 8 7 6 5 4 3 2 1

Edited, designed, and produced by Communication Crafts

Printed in Great Britain by Polestar Wheatons Ltd, Exeter

www.karnacbooks.com

ACKNOWLEDGEMENTS

The paper on which the book is based was originally read at the first Congress of the International Association for the History of Psychoanalysis, held in Paris in May 1987, and was published in the first issue of the *Revue Internationale d'Histoire de la Psychanalyse*. The English version, which I have now completely rewritten and greatly expanded, first appeared in the *International Review of Psycho-Analysis*, *16* (1989), pp. 35–76, and was also read to the IPTAR in New York in November 1987.

I take this opportunity to extend my thanks to Pearl King who, at the time I began researching for this paper, was the Honorary Archivist of the British Psycho-Analytical Society; to M. Molnar of the Freud Museum in London; and to the Sigmund Freud Copyrights in Colchester for their assistance and for having given me permission to quote from the letters used in this book. To Andrew Paskauskas I owe more than one extremely useful quotation from *The Complete Correspondence of Sigmund Freud and Ernest Jones 1908–1939* (1993). I am also particularly grateful to the late Ilse Hellman and to Dr Josephine Stross for all their help.

I would also like to thank Jill Duncan, Executive Archivist of the British Psycho-Analytical Society; Adriana Poyser, to whom I owe a special debt of gratitude because of her patience and intelligence in editing the manuscript; and Klara and Eric King, for their skill and patience in the production process of the book.

Cesare Sacerdoti wanted this book and made it possible for it to be published. He knows why I am particularly moved by his care. We both know what the Diaspora meant for us and our relatives.

CONTENTS

PREFACE

As part of a broader research on the cultural effects of the "new diaspora" in Great Britain and in other countries as far as psychoanalysis is concerned, this book traces some aspects of the politics of emigration of German and Austrian psychoanalysts during the Nazi persecution.

Given the fundamental role played by Ernest Jones in that particular set of circumstances, and given that both Anna Freud and Ernest Jones were very interesting individuals, both in their intellectual and in their "institutional" stature (as one might call it, considering the role they played in the way psychoanalysis developed), it would seem to me that the Ernest Jones–Anna Freud correspondence during that period is an exceptionally important source for anyone who wishes to understand the significance of what I refer to in this book as "the politics of emigration".

The Ernest Jones–Anna Freud correspondence is an extensive exchange of letters, begun in the late 1920s and continued until Jones's death in 1958. Of these letters, about 220 were written between 1933 and 1939, concluding with a letter from Anna Freud to Jones dated 20 January 1939 and sent from her home at 20 Maresfield Gardens, London NW3, where she had found refuge, along with her father and family, a few months previously. In this same house, Freud was to die in September 1939, and it would remain Anna Freud's London home until her own death in 1982.

Space is limited here and leaves no room for lengthy methodological digressions. However, I need to remind the reader that this book cannot be other than a partial coming-to-terms with the issues under discussion. One of the major limitations is that I have been able to rely only on the material that is available in London. Using correspondence between Anna Freud and Ernest Jones, and that between Jones and A. Brill, Sigmund Freud, and others, as well as other documents, all deposited in the Archives of the British Psycho-Analytical Society, the book focuses mainly on the emigration of German and Austrian Jewish analysts to England, although the documents used allow the reader to get a very clear picture of the complex problems related to the same emigration to North America and other countries during the 1930s.

The correspondence held in the Archives of the British Psycho-Analytical Society is by no means complete. In fact, many of the letters—Jones's as well as Anna Freud's—are missing, as are letters from other correspondents. It is more than probable that these and other material concerning the issues discussed here may be found among the numerous letters belonging to Anna Freud and others that, along with the originals of the letters Ernest Jones wrote to Anna Freud after 1945, have found their way to the Library of Congress, Washington, DC, and to other U.S. libraries. It is probable that additional data might well be uncovered by those who have access to these. However, without wanting to appear overly presumptuous, I am fairly confident that I have succeeded in providing a first, rough idea of the politics of emigration as they were conceived and put into practice in London in the years in question. I would not wish to cause any methodological perplexities, but I do not believe that the uncovering of other documents would seriously alter my reconstruction of events, at least as far as Jones is concerned. Having said this, there is no doubt that if new evidence were to be uncovered, it would help to complete the picture.

"IT IS A NEW KIND OF DIASPORA"

To articulate the past historically does not mean to recognize it "the way it really was" (Ranke). It means to seize hold of a memory as it flashes up at a moment of danger. . . .

W. Benjamin, "Theses on the Philosophy of History", 1970, p. 247

CHAPTER ONE

Introduction

In this book I would like to draw attention to what one is able to unearth when one studies the letters between Anna Freud and Ernest Jones, and especially those written between 1933 and 1939 and centring on the problems that were generated by the persecution of the Jews and the forced emigration of German and Austrian psychoanalysts during the Nazi era. Initially, they discuss the problems encountered by those psychoanalysts who lived in Berlin during the early 1930s; they then move on to consider the plight of those who lived in Austria, and who, after the *Anschluss*, found that their already precarious situation had become totally untenable.

From these letters one can learn to appreciate the tactics that were adopted and the dexterity with which issues were handled in psycho-analysis at a more general level. However, these "stratagems" also have to be seen in the light of the particular way in which the relevant psychoanalytical institutions were managed and the characteristics they assumed following the racial persecution by the Nazi establish-ment of those Jewish psychoanalysts who were then living in Berlin and in Vienna. These issues are all brought to light in the Ernest Jones–Anna Freud correspondence, as both of them faced the difficult and often painful task of interceding on behalf of their friends and colleagues and of also helping to ascertain the most viable and the most appropriate emigration channels for those who were becoming the victims of the ever-growing persecutions.

This becomes even more evident when one compares their letters with some of the other correspondence quoted in this book. By drawing the reader's attention to what may at first appear to be the insignificant details of the personal lives of the people mentioned in this correspondence, I would hope to bring to light some of the factors that gave to this "new kind of diaspora"—to cite the biblical words adopted by Anna Freud on 6 March 1934 in an unpublished letter to Ernest Jones—the characteristics it assumed. In certain respects, all these elements were to have a profound effect on the history of the psychoanalytical movement, in each and every country where psychoanalysis is practised today. And to some degree the observations I make above with regard to the Jones–Anna Freud correspondence will be seen to apply to the other letters quoted in this book.

Apart from the more evident constraints concerning the disposition and availability of the correspondence as described in the Preface—constraints that can be described as "objective"—I wish briefly to draw the reader's attention to a much more general problem. The restricted nature of this book is also due to a much more complex series of factors, the most important being the confines imposed by any collection of letters. Letters are testimony to a specific, but limited, period in time, and their content can by no means be considered to be objective, or non-partisan. Thus they need to be constantly interpreted and re-interpreted, which obliges one to conclude that, as in other areas, a definitive historical interpretation of such correspondence is not wholly possible. Furthermore, history is not based on written documents alone, and none more so than the history of psychoanalysis.

There may be readers who think it rather naive, or indeed ridiculous, of someone like me—a psychoanalyst, and somewhat footloose—to begin by quoting from Bloch, from Fevre, or from those who have followed in their footsteps. However, allow me to pay homage to a historian who was to pay in person for his devotion to his profession; to a man who, as a Jew and a convinced democrat, was to suffer as a direct result of the Nazi persecution. In my view, Bloch's famous work is one of the most important human documents of twentieth-century historiography. From Bloch's *Le Métier d'Historien* (1954), I quote below a passage that speaks of the way historical documents should be considered:

> Notwithstanding that which seems to have been believed by the early critics, historical documents do not arrive here and there in the light of day as an effect of who knows what inscrutable wish of the gods. Their presence or their absence in the Archives of a Records Office or a library, depends on human factors which are by no means impenetrable to analysis . . . that which comes into play is nothing more nor less than the passage of the memory across the succeeding generations.

For many reasons, I find myself in complete agreement with this statement. But I will come back to this a little later. For the moment, let me also cite the affirmations of G. Le Goff, the medievalist and astute theoretician of contemporary historiographical methodology, for he makes a subtle distinction between monuments and documents, and he takes up the age-old discussion regarding their significance, to arrive at the conclusion that the historical document is a monument that must be ceaselessly subjected to judicious re-interpretations.

> No document is innocent. Every document is a monument which one needs to know how to take apart, dismantle. The historian must not only know how to discern the falsity of a document or evaluate its credibility, the historian must know how to demystify it. . . . The document is the result of an entire montage, both conscious and unconscious, of the history pertaining to a particular epoch, and of the society which has produced it. The document is the result of the forces brought to bear by the preceding historical societies, whether wittingly or unwittingly to produce and transmit a certain given image of themselves. . . . [Le Goff & Nora, 1974]

I wanted to refer to these statements, even if only very briefly and in passing, because it is only by taking these basic theoretical points into consideration that one may begin to make some sense of the "monument-cum-document" that the Ernest Jones–Anna Freud correspondence represents; and the same could be said of the other letters to which I refer. There is, however, one further difficulty to bear in mind, particularly for those who have to face such problems as are directly associated with the history of psychoanalysis, its institutions, and its leading personalities, and who, at the same time, also have to try to understand, if only in part, the interaction between its history and the events that take place within a much wider historical sphere. One need only think of the sort of problems that the Jones–Anna Freud correspondence poses in this respect. Needless to say, my comments apply, in one way or other, also to all of the material in this book. I must say right away that this correspondence undoubtedly raises a whole series of extremely interesting questions, even at the level of traditional research on the history of ideas, if one may be allowed to refer to it in this way.

For instance, just consider the narrative discourse, what the correspondence narrates and how it narrates it, and all the issues that may be raised in this regard. Naturally, one cannot say that Anna Freud's letters were specifically situated in a set tradition—nor were Jones's, for that matter. But for those interested in such details, it might be of relevance to note that Anna's letters were at times written in English and typewritten, and that at other times they were written in German, either on headed notepaper or on blank notepaper with her name printed at the top of the page. Yet on other occasions her letters were hand-written on pages taken from a notebook, sometimes lined, sometimes unlined. This was generally the case when she happened to be away from home, accompanying her father on one of his numerous visits to hospital for the various serious and not so serious surgical operations for cancer of the mouth; and it is beyond doubt that this passing from the typewriter to the hand-written letter would sometimes, though not always, lend a more familiar and direct tone to her writing, especially in the spring of 1938, during the Freud family's last impossible months in Vienna. However, these minor details aside, one must also ask oneself what the probabilities were that Ernest, Anna, and their colleagues were writing with a public in mind, or with a view to publication at some future date.

This raises one further question—one that we can no longer avoid asking, particularly when we consider the close filial relationship and the intellectual and professional collaboration between Sigmund Freud and his daughter and the important bearing of such a long relationship, and bearing in mind the role played by Jones, and *his* relationship with both father and daughter: to what degree did Jones and Anna Freud intentionally write and say what they did? What did they wish to leave recorded as understood, and what issues did they deliberately avoid mentioning or leave as understood in a consciously camouflaged and inevitably distorted fashion? To paraphrase, somewhat light-heartedly, the title of an interesting essay by Umberto Eco (1979), one must at this point also consider the problems associated with what one might define not so much as *"the lector in fabula"* and the role this entails, as *"the lector in fabula epistolarii"*, or the reader— myself, in this case—in the *"fabula"* of a collected correspondence, and the role he assumes when he has access to the sum of the various parts and the multiple combinations of roles that this type of narra- tion of the history of psychoanalysis makes available to him.

Pushed to the limit by racial persecution, by all the legal restric- tions imposed on their persons, including the confiscation of property and savings and such like, all those belonging to Freud's circle faced the same destiny. From the members of his immediate family based in Vienna to his psychoanalytical "family" living in Berlin, Budapest, Prague, Holland, Sweden, Italy, and France, to those living in Britain and America, all were suddenly to find themselves propelled into a colossal institutional, personal, psychic, and emotional maelstrom. Each of these psychoanalytical families or sub-groups already had its own history to tell, of cultural and historical differences, of different traditions and schooling; and sometimes the disparities were quite considerable. The diaspora subjected one and all to the sufferances of emigration, cultural deprivation, fragmentation, disorientation, and more or less forced acculturation (following Wachtel, 1974, I use this last term with a certain degree of caution, as each case is particular to itself). For a variety of reasons, all of which are of central importance to this book, not all of those who left Vienna, Berlin, Budapest, and the other cities of the Reich emigrated to London or to New York. Many of these refugees would eventually end up in such countries as Pales- tine, South Africa, Australia, New Zealand, and even Ceylon. One could say that, almost in accordance with some geometrical formula, the diaspora resulted in distances being tragically multiplied across the full extent of the earth's surface.

But these problems and the questions they raise aside, there is one other "specific element" to which I must now return as it is virtually impossible to ignore, given that it is an essential aspect of the study of psychoanalysis. This is the role that was played by the unconscious in those who became involved in the politics of emigration and the role that was played by their conscious and unconscious personal motivations. It is extremely difficult, if not impossible, to write about this historically. Yet, paradoxically, the unconscious is part of this history and needs constantly to be taken into consideration, particularly when one considers those problems that are specifically associated with what Granoff (1975) in France has rightly called *"filiation"*—that is, the special emotional bonds or rivalries that are created by analyses, by schools, and so on. It must be remembered, however, that in the study of this correspondence one is not dealing simply with one set of *"filiations"* but, rather, with multiple *"filiations"*.

Just how complex this issue is becomes apparent when one reflects on the fact that, if one takes into account the refugees themselves and those persons who came to their assistance, several hundred psychoanalysts were affected. It becomes even clearer when one considers the enormous unconscious problems inherent in a salvage operation of the type that was put into motion to save Freud and his psychoanalytical "family" and to safeguard the interests of the various institutions, the national and local psychoanalytical societies, and the International Psycho-Analytical Association (IPA)* in particular. These were problems specific to an élite group, so to speak, especially when one compares them to the whole phenomenon of the mass emigration of Jews during those years. If one reflects on what was to become one of the better-known consequences of these events—namely, the forced emigration to England of Freud, his family, and his colleagues—one need only consider the mobilization of Anna Freud's conscious and unconscious anxieties, in particular concerning members of the Viennese and Berliner circles who were associated with her and her father. One might also wish to visualize the types of anxieties that were mobilized in Melanie Klein and many of the members of the psychoanalytic circles in Britain, on their having to come to terms with the prospect of living one with the other within the British Psycho-Analytical Society (I come back to this further on). The same could be said for all those analysts who emigrated from Central Europe to North and South America, to Australia, and so on—and just think of the implications of this on future developments and events.

One is also obliged to admit that the *"filiation"* factor is an element present in the psyches and in the work of all those who study documents such as these. Nor would I exclude myself from the effects associated with *"filiation"*, not only in my role as historian but, more

---

* For reasons of clarity, after the first instance all references to the Internationale Psychoanalytische Vereinigung appear as IPA (International Psycho-Analytical Association), although at the time German-speakers would have referred to it as the IPV.

significantly, also in my work as a fellow psychoanalyst, and one hitherto greatly influenced by the teachings of Melanie Klein and her school of thought. I wish to mention these facts as I have to reiterate the need for one to bear in mind constantly that, by its very nature, this kind of research is necessarily "open" and "approximate". The research itself began in a specific moment in time, in a "here and now" that is nothing more than the establishing of a personal question mark over the past and the future.

I have already mentioned the large number of letters and other documents to which I will have to refer. However, what must be borne in mind is that it would be well-nigh impossible for one to approach such issues as the problems associated with the emigration of psychoanalysts from the "old continent"[1] if one did not take into consideration, together with its specific and élitist characteristics, the more general context in which this emigration took place and the great many problems that were created as a result of Jews emigrating from Germany, Eastern Europe, Austria, and central European countries generally, to Great Britain and to America.

Not being a specialist in this area of historical research, I have obviously had to base the major part of my observations—apart from the occasional piece of information that I personally have unearthed —on second-hand sources and on pre-existing material, and this is particularly so with regard to the immigration of Jews to Great Britain and North America. Furthermore, it has not been possible for me to enter into the complex issue regarding the official Anglo-American historiography of the Holocaust. This area has been very efficiently investigated by Dawidowicz (1975, 1981), who has ably demonstrated the extent to which the Holocaust has been virtually ignored by official historiography. Nor will I be touching on the problem regarding the so-called revisionist historiography, which tries to deny the existence of the Holocaust *tout court*. Indeed, given that so little can be gleaned from official historiographical sources, the sources I have tended to draw upon are the product of researches carried out mainly by Jewish historians. In this book I will give a brief outline of German and Austrian social and political history from 1933 to 1938, closely relating it to the emigration of the Jews. Whilst I do not intend to explore anti-Semitism and its social and psychological causes in German-speaking countries and in Eastern Europe (Bunzl & Marin, 1983; Friedländer, 1993; Goldhagen, 1996; Hilberg, 1985; Spira, 1981), I will have to touch upon the issue of anti-Semitism in Great Britain, and, in so doing, I will need to keep in mind the problem as it arose in North America.

It is important that certain dates and statistics should be borne in mind, as their effect is quite evidently reflected in the correspondence between Jones and Anna Freud, and between Jones and his colleagues. For reasons of brevity, I will touch only very briefly on the way in which these historical events—particularly the various episodes leading to Hitler's rise to power, its consequences, and the events that brought about the *Anschluss* with Austria (Carsten, 1986; Pauley, 1981)—were evaluated, constantly pondered over, and analysed by both Anna Freud and Ernest Jones. One would have to write a separate book if one were to attempt a detailed study of the ways in which they reacted to the events that were taking place and to what followed, especially if one were to compare Anna Freud's and Jones's comments with the observations on these same matters in Freud's correspondence of that period with Jones, M. Bonaparte, M. Eitingon, A. Brill, and S. Zweig, among others.

Space restrictions notwithstanding, it is still worth while making an attempt to understand how certain of the major protagonists of psychoanalysis—such as, in addition to Freud himself, Jones, Anna Freud, Eitingon, J. H. W. van Ophuijsen, Brill, O. Fenichel—reacted when faced with the savagery of the *Macht* and *Real-Politik* of the *"Hitlerei"*—to use the terms used by Freud in a letter to Jones dated 14 April 1932 (Freud, 1993)—or when faced with what I would call the manifestation of the death drive in the course of those socio-historical events. The ways in which they interpreted events and the consequences of these events determined the advice that was given on the co-ordination of emigration procedures, prompted the call for urgent action when the situation demanded it, and influenced the time-scale of the emigration.

In spite of the specific characteristics of the psychoanalytic movement during those years and bearing in mind all the scholarly work I have just quoted, it is my belief that, as far as the Jewish emigration issue is concerned, there is a direct parallel between events as they are narrated by historical sources and by most of the credit-worthy writings on this subject, and the chronicle that one is able to trace in the collected letters of Jones and Freud's daughter, and in the other archival material quoted. Such historical writings include Wasserstein's *Britain and the News of Europe* (1979, 1999), Sherman's well-known study entitled *Island Refuge* (1973), and more recently London's work

(2000).[2] On the emigration of Jews to North America, one ought to note Neuringer's important contribution entitled *American Jewry and United States Emigration Policy 1881–1953* (1980) and Breitman and Kraut's *American Refugee Policy and European Jewry 1933–1945* (1987). Another work to be considered would be Wyman's *The Abandonment of the Jews* (1984). These works give a very clear picture of the time-scale of the emigration problem and provide details on the three major emigration waves, including specifics on the number who emigrated from Germany and Austria during each of these phases. Neuringer (1980) makes a statistical comparison between the first departures from Germany in 1933–34 and 1935–36 and the mass departures from Austria in 1938 and 1939. All these statistics bear a direct relationship to the events described and commented on in their correspondence by Anna Freud, Jones, and their colleagues.

In order to understand the time-scale involved and some of the objective reasonings that lay behind a psychoanalyst seeking refuge in one particular place of exile rather than another—that is, what caused a certain person to opt for Britain rather than the United States or some other part of the globe—one needs to be aware of some bare facts: that Hitler rose to power in 1933; that in the same year the Nuremberg laws (which defined "Jew" and systematized and regulated persecution and discrimination: all Jews were deprived of their civil rights, and marriages and extra-marital sexual relationships between Jews and Germans were forbidden under pain of imprisonment) were promulgated; and that in 1935 the Nazi government introduced even more draconian measures to deal with its Jewish population in Germany. One must also bear in mind the uncertain situation in Austria at the time, that events were swept along by turbulent social and political factions violently in conflict one with the other, and that this led to the Vienna uprising of 1934, to the defeat of the Austrian social democrats (Glaser, 1981), to the assassination of Dollfuss (Botz, 1980; Carsten, 1986; Gardner & Stevens, 1992; Jelavich, 1987), and, ultimately, to the triumph of Austro-Fascism. The short-lived Austro-Fascist rule was immediately followed by the *Anschluss* in March 1938, in part in consequence of Mussolini's decision to withdraw his protection from Austria and create a new alliance with Hitler. With the *Anschluss*, the Nuremberg laws, regardless of whether or not they had hitherto been applied to the letter (Walk, 1981), came into force for Austria's Jewish population (Gedye, 1947; Moser, 1975). Approximately 180,000 Austrian Jews were now in

Hitler's direct domain. Drawing on Sherman's (1973) study, one can say that approximately 140,000 Austrian Jews left the country between 1933 and 1939 (see also Tartakower, 1967). During this same period almost 230,000 German Jews emigrated from there.

One must also remember that Nazi Germany had introduced laws on emigration and immigration (Lacina, 1982), and that similar laws were also applied in Austria, initially by the Austro-Fascist regime and, after the *Anschluss*, by the Nazis (Botz, 1980; Schwager, 1984). These regimes also exacted a very high price in monetary terms for the right to an exit visa and an emigration permit. However, one must not forget that both Britain and the United States also had their own laws on immigration and emigration (Breitman & Kraut, 1987; London, 2000; Neuringer, 1980; Strauss, 1983; Wasserstein, 1979, 1999). I will not comment here on the laws as they stood in other countries, as the great majority of psychoanalysts hoped to seek refuge in either Great Britain or the United States. It is also very important to be aware of the pressures that were brought to bear on the respective governments of these two countries by public opinion and, not least, by the various Jewish associations in both Great Britain and the United States at that time. In this respect, one need only consider the powerful influence of such organizations as the Anglo–Jewish Community and the Committee for Refugees, and their efforts to have the Jewish immigration quotas increased when the already precarious situation of the Jewish communities in Austria and Germany had become completely untenable.

There is another, perhaps less obviously tangible factor, and for this very reason one much more difficult to document, but of enormous future import nonetheless. Each of these possible places of refuge had its own peculiarities, its own institutional infrastructures, and a cultural climate specific to it. There were also differences where psychoanalysis was concerned, even between Great Britain and North America, determined by the culture specific to each, and the different way psychoanalysis had been conceived in these two countries. Furthermore, notwithstanding the fact that there may have been a shared understanding on the nature of the unconscious, the way in which psychoanalysis had developed in Britain and in the United States was not an exact reflection of psychoanalysis as it was conceived in Vienna or in Berlin (Coser, 1984; Fermi, 1968; Fleming & Bailyn, 1969; Gardner & Stevens, 1992; Hale, 1978; Jahoda, 1969; Mühlleitner, 1992; Mühlleitner & Reichmayr, 1995, 1998; Steiner, 1985).

In this context, and as far as Britain is concerned, I would refer the reader to the contents of an article published by Anderson in 1968. In spite of its dogmatic excesses, this is a work of considerable interest, particularly with regard to psychoanalysis. In it, the author makes a comparative study of the distinguishing cultural features indigenous to British and American society, respectively. He points out how a culture so deeply traditional and based on long-standing academic and scientific institutions as is that of Britain, with its late-positivistic and empiricist trends, was of considerable appeal to a certain category of intellectual refugees, such as Mannheim, Popper, and even Wittgenstein. On the other hand, those potential refugees who were either highly politically involved or from a Marxist environment— from Brecht's Germany or from the Frankfurt School of Fromm, Adorno, Horkheimer, and Marcuse—had earmarked America as their proposed destination. However, Anderson's analysis does not account for the fate that would befall those same refugees after they arrived in the United States, nor does he consider the after-effects on psychoanalysis, or on such persons as Reich, Fenichel, and various others from similar cultural backgrounds (see Jacoby, 1983; Mühlleitner & Reichmayr, 1995, 1998). Indeed, the correspondence I quote in this book might even provide us with additional information and shed further light on these issues.

I return to these matters later on in this book, as I consider them well worth pursuing. What the reader—psychoanalyst or not—must keep in mind are the more or less unconscious aspects of certain ideological differences and the effects of these. In this respect, I would refer the reader to Cohn's research on the "protocols of Zion" (1967) or to the more recent and remarkably interesting study on the ideological history of anti-Semitism by Gilman (1985), who examines the more or less latent historical anti-Semitic tendencies in those countries that had agreed to accept an immigrant Jewish presence within their national confines. Historical sources generally agree that, regardless of the fact that a Fascist party existed in the country at the time, Great Britain was in fact one country where Jewish immigration was relatively tolerated and where immigrants were treated with some generosity, notwithstanding the serious social and economic difficulties provoked by the Great Depression and the very high unemployment that followed. Yet Wasserstein (1979, 1999) is very critical of Great Britain and accuses it of having been anti-Semitic. In a book that has just been published, London (2000) has written what is, up to today, the most comprehensive study on the complex policies of the immigration of the Jews to Great Britain in the 1930s. Even London stresses that anti-Semitism was quite diffused in Great Britain.

The socio-economic situation during the 1930s entailed various restrictions being imposed by the British Government as far as its immigration policies were concerned, and these became effective across the board, regardless of social status or of whether or not the individual applying to enter the country was Jewish. Although on a different scale, similar problems were to affect those Jews who emigrated to North America, as we will see later.

Furthermore, in addition to the various institutional and cultural pressures with which the refugee psychoanalysts had to contend, one must also remember that this specific category of refugee would have belonged to the liberal professions, and the immigration laws regarding these persons were even more stringent. This was especially true for the medical profession, where openings to immigrant professionals wishing to practise medicine in Great Britain were very limited, even once individuals had fulfilled the requirement of re-sitting all the medical examinations necessary to qualify and practise in their particular field. The situation in North America and in other countries was not very different. I return to this issue later on, when I examine the controversies within the International Psycho-Analytical Association on these same matters and the difficulties faced by Jones, Anna Freud, and others in countering the ostracism suffered by those analysts who, having emigrated to the United States, for instance, did not hold a recognized medical qualification to practise. I will also look at the difficulties encountered by the immigrant analysts in Great Britain, who not only found themselves in similar circumstances, but who also had to contend with a lack of patients. All this obviously added to the émigré professional's already difficult situation.

If we restrict ourselves to Great Britain, it is hardly by chance that in Sherman's (1973) work on the immigration of Jews to this country he should want to be quite emphatic in drawing the reader's attention the anxious preoccupation of the British Medical Association, who were concerned with the possible consequences of large numbers of fully qualified emigrant doctors suddenly arriving on British soil from Germany, Austria, or other countries. As Sherman put it,

> When Lord Dawson, the President of the Royal College of Physicians, called on the Home Secretary in November 1934, for instance, he conceded that there might be room in Britain for a few

refugee doctors of special distinction, "but" as Lord Dawson himself added, "the number that could be usefully absorbed or considered capable of teaching us anything could be counted on the fingers of one hand"! [p. 124]

According to Dr J. Stross[3]—the paediatrician who, in place of M. Schur, accompanied Freud on his journey of exile from Vienna to London (personal communication; Jones, 1953–57; Schur, 1972)— there were certainly no more than 100 Jewish refugees who were medically trained and who were accepted as qualified to practise in Great Britain by the British Medical Association in the years between 1933 and 1939.

There are other factors to be taken into consideration which, although seemingly of minor importance, nevertheless help to complete the overall picture of the emigration situation as it was then. For instance, in Berlin, Budapest, Vienna, and elsewhere, there were considerable difficulties in securing the notorious "visa" or "work permit", which, among other things, also entailed endless and spasmodic waiting in the corridors and in the offices of the Gestapo and of the various consulates and embassies. The procedure was very well described by Anna Freud herself, when she discussed the ordeals of those aspiring emigrant psychoanalysts living in Vienna at the time (see chapter six). She gave a particularly powerful and moving description of these events when, in London in 1979, she spoke on the occasion of the centenary of Jones's birth. Referring to the floating vessels of human misery anchored in harbours and to the thousands of Vietnamese refugees who were at that time laying siege to the ports of the Vietnamese coasts in the hope of being able to board a ship or obtain an embarkation permit, Anna Freud instinctively drew a comparison with the very similar plight of the Jewish refugees during the Nazi persecution, all desperately awaiting exit permits and entrance visas to the United States or to the various countries in free Europe; and, as she pointed out, for many of them the failure to obtain these papers was tantamount to being sentenced to death.

Not to be forgotten, however, is the help that was offered by the Jewish communities, both in Great Britain (London, 2000; Sherman, 1973; Wasserstein, 1979, 1999) and in the United States (Neuringer, 1980; Strauss, 1983), in guaranteeing the sustenance and the well-being of Jewish refugees in these two countries.[4] For, as Dr Stross also pointed out to me, the refugees were prohibited from taking with them any monies or articles of value, such as jewellery, although up until 1939 they were still given permission to have their household belongings transported with them from their homes in Germany and Austria—as were Freud and his family, as we will see.

It is only by bearing in mind these circumstantial details, here condensed quite considerably, that it may be possible to understand, at least in part, the letters exchanged between Anna Freud, Jones, and their colleagues in the years between 1933 and 1939. It is only in considering the interaction between all these factors—taking into account the specific problems related to the internal history of psychoanalysis and the way the unconscious expressed itself in the tensions, the rivalries, and the theoretical differences between the psychoanalytical organizations in Berlin, Vienna, London, as well as in New York and in other American cities where a local psychoanalytic institution had been set up, particularly among the psychoanalytical protagonists referred to in the correspondence—that one may hope to succeed in clarifying these complex issues.

By following this particular line of research, it is my hope that the reader will be convinced of what I said earlier about there being a clear parallel between the general problems surrounding the forced emigration of the Jews during those years and the problems encountered during the forced emigration of what were in the main Jewish psychoanalysts. With one major difference, nonetheless—unlike the majority who suffered in the Holocaust, very few psychoanalysts, comparatively speaking, met their deaths in a concentration camp. In this respect, one might hazard to say that their being aware of the dangers of protracted indecisiveness (although the situation with the Freuds in Vienna did become very uncertain indeed at one point), coupled with the help and the solidarity that was offered to them in those horrendous years by their colleagues in Great Britain, the United States, and other countries, is one of the most moving examples of the force of life against the death drive, at least as far as psychoanalysis is concerned!

Now that we have a parallel between the major factors surrounding the emigration of the Jews and the circumstances surrounding the emigration of psychoanalysts during the same period, we can envisage more clearly the circumstances in which, following Hitler's rise to power and the sequence of events that immediately followed, Anna Freud, Jones, and their colleagues began to discuss the plight of psychoanalysis in Berlin. The Nuremberg laws had just come into effect. A few months later, these laws would convince Eitingon to leave for

Palestine. One of the consequences of his departure was that Boehm was left in control of the Berlin Psychoanalytic Institute, which meant, in effect, that it would now be impossible for a Jewish psychoanalyst to hold an official post within the Institute (Brecht, 1993; Cocks, 1985; Lockot, 1985, 1994). This situation, in turn, provoked the resignation of some of the Jewish members of the Institute and prompted a number of them to leave for parts unknown—and, as if on cue, those Jewish psychoanalysts who would later form part of the first emigration wave from Germany, which began in the last days of March and continued into April and May 1933, began to be referred to in the Anna Freud–Ernest Jones correspondence. Their names also began to appear in the letters between Jones and van Ophuijsen, Jones and Brill, Jones and Eitingon, Jones and Freud, and so on. One must also remember that in May 1933 the official burning of Freud's works took place in Berlin.

CHAPTER TWO

The first emigration wave (1933–1935) and the first *"Sorgenkinder"*

Uncertainty and confusion in Europe and North America

*Jones's, Anna Freud's, Brill's,
and van Ophuijsen's efforts to help*

For a fuller understanding of the problems that this surge in emigration would create and the proportions that it would assume (and which, a few months later, in a letter to Jones dated 6 March 1934, Anna Freud would refer to as "a new kind of diaspora", adding, "you surely know what the word means: the spreading of the Jews over the world after the destruction of the temple of Jerusalem"), one must remember that a number of analysts from Berlin and Vienna had already visited Great Britain and the United States and some had already emigrated there. By far the most famous of the immigrant analysts in Great Britain was Melanie Klein, who had come to London from Berlin in the mid-1930s (Meisel & Kendrick, 1986).[1]

Because matters were so complex, I think I ought to describe the effect that this first early immigrant wave of mainly Berliner analysts had on their American counterparts. Freud, Jung, and S. Ferenczi had all visited the United States in 1909, Ferenczi having revisited in the company of O. Rank and others some time later. Others, such as

S. Lorand, had emigrated to the United States in the 1920s; F. Alexander and S. Rado, both of whom had trained in Budapest and had then worked in Berlin during the 1920s, had moved to the United States by 1930 or thereabouts. Rado and Alexander, together with H. Nunberg, K. Horney, the lay analyst H. Sachs—who was to play an important role in helping lay analysts in America—and other fellow emigrants from Berlin, all began to assume a very important role in American psychoanalysis (Coser, 1984; Eisold, 1998; Fermi, 1968; Hale, 1978; Jahoda, 1969; Kurzweil, 1995; Roazen & Swerdloff, 1995). There is no doubt that these early emigrants played a considerable part in creating problems, tensions, and power conflicts at a local level, and at a certain point their actions led to strange alliances and to the establishment of groups made up of old emigrants from the Continent and newly arrived Jewish refugees from Germany, Hungary, and Austria, which caused hostilities to break out between them and the indigenous members of the various American psychoanalytical associations and local institutions, as we will see, in particular, in chapters four and six. In the New York Psychoanalytic Institute and the New York Society, however, some of the newly arrived refugees joined ranks with certain indigenous members and, together with some of the older generation of émigré psychoanalysts, attempted to ward off the rebellious or innovative tendencies of those who, like Rado, had acquired enormous power and control over the New York Institute during the early 1930s and later (Kirsner, 2000; Roazen & Swerdloff, 1995).

The history of this early emigration to the United States is therefore of great importance, and only by understanding many of the problems that arose from 1933 onwards are we better able to appreciate the reasons for American psychoanalysis and its various local institutions having been in such constant turmoil, particularly when one compares their situation with the relative stability of the British Psycho-Analytical Society, then under the strict control of Jones and its founders. It also helps us to understand the reasons for it still being a rather weak structure. Indeed, in the years between 1930 and 1933, Rado in New York gradually began to distance himself from Viennese orthodoxy. It subsequently caused him to leave the New York Society and found the Columbia Psychoanalytic Group (Eisold, 1998; Roazen & Swerdloff, 1995). However, the circumstances surrounding this case only became evident in the years that followed.

It is impossible here to give a full account of what happened in Rado's case, or of what happened to Alexander and the others, as it goes beyond the scope of this book, but a brief study of the correspondence between Jones, Brill, and others on Rado and the New York Psychoanalytic Society—which I have tried to summarize in note 2—should provide an approximate idea of events and of the climate of those years.[2]

Let us now focus on some of the details concerning the first German–Jewish emigration wave. As I mentioned earlier, the first signs of this began to be seen in March and April 1933—and, sure enough, for the first time, the names of certain individuals and the details of their circumstances begin to appear in the Anna Freud–Ernest Jones correspondence, as they do in many other letters too. In a letter dated 5 June 1933, Anna mentions the plight of E. Simmel and of K. Landauer, both of whom were experiencing serious financial difficulties. In talking about them, Anna refers to them as "*Sorgenkinder*": "children in need of care, and who are causing concern". This expression crops up very frequently in her letters, at least until her departure from Vienna to London some five years after this correspondence began. Her use of this expression would appear to be of particular significance, and one not to be ignored, especially if one bears in mind the comments I have already made in this regard, because it gives the idea of an extended family comprised of infants and children, older brothers and sisters, and parents whose duty it is to provide for them. Indeed, Anna's choice of words becomes all the more significant when one recalls that those to whom she referred in these terms were none other than adult psychoanalysts who, in finding themselves in very precarious circumstances, were being forced to regress, so to speak, to a state of dependency on Anna, Jones, and the Americans.[3]

Leaving aside for the moment the many possible connotations of the term "*Kinder*", to concentrate on the implications of the term "*Sorge*", which stands not only for the many anxieties experienced by the refugees, but also for the concerns of those persons who were in a position to help them to find a place of refuge—all of whom were members, and therefore a constituent part, of the psychoanalytic "family". The amount of information contained in the letters exchanged between Anna Freud and Ernest Jones, and in the letters between Jones and other correspondents, deposited in the Archives of the British Psycho-Analytical Society, could easily lead one into

interminable discussions on the subject, even if one were just to restrict oneself to citing the names of those mentioned, or if one were to
do no more than to follow the unfolding of their personal lives during
the numerous occasions on which these refugees were forced to move
from one place to another. Similarly, I would prefer for the moment to
pass over in silence a question that spontaneously springs to mind:
whether, at some time or other, Ernest Jones might not himself have
come to consider Sigmund Freud, his daughter, and their circle
of friends and acquaintances, his own "Sorgenkinder" (see chapters
seven and eight).

As anyone who has concerned himself with this type of research
will know, the sense and the meaning of the times in which these
people lived and moved is not only understood by studying the
chronicle of the more prominent personalities involved in this sad
story, but it can often be better appreciated by examining the vicissitudes of the many minor characters who also went through this same
experience. Had it not been for the circumstances of the time, the
names of some of these analysts would have remained totally obscure,
except for the fact that they appeared in the registers of the various
psychoanalytical societies in Berlin, Vienna, Budapest, and so forth.
In the correspondence between Anna Freud and Ernest Jones from
April 1933 onwards, and in the letters Jones wrote to Brill, P. Federn,
Eitingon, van Ophuijsen, and others to inform them of events as
they unfolded, we come across such well-known names as those
of W. Reich, R. Spitz, E. Fromm, F. Fromm-Reichmann, B. Lantos,
Landauer, T. Reik, and R. Benedek (see, e.g., Jones to A. Freud, 20
April 1933; Jones to Brill, 2 May 1933; Jones to Eitingon, 20 May 1933;
Jones to Federn, 20 October 1933). But in these same letters one also
comes across the names of F. Perls, F. Cohn, and S. H. Fuchs (who later
changed his surname to Foulkes) in London (see Jones to Eitingon, 20
May 1933) and those of F. Lowitzky, R. Oppenheim, L. Jekels (see
Jones to A. Freud, 20 April 1933), and the many others who had taken
refuge in Paris or who were passing through Paris at the time. In a
letter to Jones dated 23 August 1933, Anna sends him information
about those who had tried to emigrate to France and the difficulties
they were encountering, saying:

> "Aus Paris höre ich, dass in der allernächsten Zeit ein Gesetz gegen jede
> Einwanderung durchgebracht werden soll. Die Prinzessin ist jetzt übri-
> gens auch hier und berichtet, dass die Pariser Gruppe sich gegen die vier
> eingewanderten Analytiker gut benimmt."

[From Paris I am informed that very soon a law will be passed against any immigration. The Princess [M. Bonaparte] is moreover also here and tells us that the Paris group behaves well towards the four psychoanalysts who have immigrated there.]

Yet for the sake of historical accuracy one should also note that a few months later in Paris, as in many other countries, things did not look so well for the refugees. Just think of a letter like this from Anna Freud to Jones, comparing what was happening in Paris with what went on in London and even in Vienna. London seemed to have immediately accepted some of the German refugees (Anna to Jones, 27 November 1933):

"I also had a letter from the Princess M. Bonaparte about the new organisation of the new French group. . . . I feel that their behaviour toward the German emigrants is very disappointing. Why was it possible for you to give the emigrants their place in the Society so soon and why should they feel that they have to keep them at arm's length? The Princess writes that they cannot accept the medical people as members because they have no French licence. She says they could accept the lay people easily but they'd rather wait a little. But after all Rado, Alexander, Harnik, etc. were all Berlin members without a German licence; we also did not ask Frau Lampl-de Groot for her Austrian licence (she has a Dutch one)."

All this, according to Anna, seems to signify the same attitude of "distance from the IPA and lack of contact with it". In inviting Jones to try to mediate to help the German refugees, Anna added: "And is it not the main characteristic of an international association that there is an international bond besides the national feeling?"

And Jones had answered on 2 December 1933 that he fully agreed with Anna concerning the lack of commitment to the IPA of the French, but he also stressed—as would become one of his current motives of concern during those years—the need for a strong organization and leadership that would allow dealing with those delicate issues in a different way. The French were rather disorganized due to the lack of strong leadership. It would be most satisfactory, he concluded in a rather ironic mood, "if the Princess could be made both President and also editor of the *Revue* [Jones was referring to the *Revue Française de Psychanalyse* but probably also had in mind the example of himself as President and Editor of the *International Journal of Psycho-Analysis*]. It would be amusing to have a President who was a woman as well as being a lay analyst, though I feel the latter point would cause local opposition"!

The diaspora had indeed begun, carrying with itself all the contradictions, feelings, and problems it would arouse in so many countries and so many people who would try to help the refugees, often stretching what Anna called an "international bond" to its limits, because so many local and national interests would often prevail. And the names just quoted from A. Freud's, Jones's, and Eitingon's correspondences, not to mention those of many other people who were already engaged in travelling frenetically to and fro across Europe, not certain of what to do, trying to decide whether or not to leave Germany (and one must bear in mind that this was all happening in the first few months after Hitler's coming to power), give us a sense of the *Heimatweh* and the understandable desire of many of them to want to deny, at times, the extent of the risks they were running. Nevertheless, their plight must also be considered in conjunction with the difficulties they were already beginning to encounter in obtaining an exit permit. Furthermore, their dilemma was made worse by the fact that many of them only had a very rudimentary knowledge of spoken English, whilst others had none at all—a problem Jones would stress on more than one occasion in his letters to Anna Freud and others. I will return to all these issues in the concluding part of this book, with some moving quotations from the letters of some of the Hungarian analysts who had sought Jones's, L. S. Kubie's, and others' help to emigrate. I will also spend some time considering the importance of the stories recounted by some of the relatively minor figures involved in this tragic affair.

In a very beautiful book, written many years later (1984), Léon Grinberg and his wife Rebecca describe the psychological effects of emigration and exile, and many of their observations on their flight from dictatorial rule in Argentina could, in retrospect, apply to the psychoanalysts mentioned here, in that they, too, would have suffered the anxiety of loss and separation and would have had to acculturate themselves forcibly to a new environment. Nor should one forget that, as early as April 1933, Ferenczi was trying to encourage Freud and his family to leave for Britain (Jones, 1957, p. 189), but another five years were to pass before Freud would finally take a decision to do so and thus finally leave his "prison" behind him. In this respect, one must also bear in mind the significantly ambivalent reactions of those who remained behind towards those others who, having anticipated the events to come, had decided to leave Berlin and Vienna in those first few months.

What I need to emphasize at this point is that there was overall concern for psychoanalysis as an institution and the worry that its future might be placed in jeopardy if its members, already so fraught and anxious about the possibility of having to depart, were all suddenly to take flight. An important *Rundbrief*, signed by Anna Freud and dated 29 March 1933, gives an indication of the views of some of those who remained in Berlin. For although many had already departed, others, such as Simmel and Eitingon, calmly continued with their work.

"Wegfahren ist eine zu einfache Lösung und man lässt damit zu viel im Stich. Wenn man hinausgeworfen wird, dann bleibt einem nichts anderes mehr übrig."

[To depart is too easy a solution, and one leaves too much in the lurch. If one is expelled then there is no other solution.]

Anna then went on to inform her readers of the events taking place in Vienna, of the general atmosphere, of the enormous tension and uncertainty that filled the air. She then added that many of her father's friends had advised him to leave, but that he was staying put: *"er denkt nicht daran, ist sicher der Ruhigste unter sehr vielen Aufgeregten hier"* [He doesn't so much as think about going away, amongst all the excitement of many of the others here present, he is the most tranquil]. Only a few months later, Anna would even begin to criticize Eitingon. In a letter to Jones dated 23 August 1933 and written from Hochrotherd, where she was on holiday with her father and other members of her family, she wrote that Eitingon had been to visit them to explain the reasons for his having decided to leave Germany, and commented: *"Es ist war dass es ihm wenig zu wählen bleibt, aber es ist auch wahr, dass es sich damit isoliert zu einer Zeit, wo man jede Kraft in der Bewegung besonders nötig braucht."* [It is true that he has very little left to choose, but it is also true that in this way he will be isolating himself at a time *in which one needs to use all the available forces for the Movement*] (the international movement of psychoanalysis—emphasis added).

Echoes of these views are also found in a letter from Jones to Brill dated 25 September 1933: "Eitingon is now in Palestine on a visit. He returns to Berlin at the beginning of November for the purpose of clearing up his affairs and then returning to Palestine permanently. His relative isolation there will be a considerable loss to us, although actually there was a great deal of opposition to him in the Berlin group."

These extracts reflect the stance taken by Freud in the circumstances, for, on the one hand, they show a certain degree of scepticism, whilst on the other they serve almost as an admonition to those leaving the group—the Viennese particularly. Given the lack of documentation, it is difficult to establish with any degree of certainty whether, apart from all their other worries, some of those leaving Vienna in those first months of 1933 might not also have felt that they were unconsciously provoking further anxieties to add to those already existing, or that in taking their leave of Vienna they were somehow being singled out for their actions and were now being provisionally observed or appraised. Consequently, when on 27 March 1933 Anna replied to Jones's request for news of Jekels, one's curiosity is indeed aroused when one reads an observation such as the following: *"Jekels hat schon lange wünscht Wien zu verlassen; er glaubt wohl wie manche andere dass hier ähnlich gehen konnte wie bei den deutschen Freunden."* [Jekels had already expressed some time ago his wish to leave Vienna because he thinks that what happened to our friends in Berlin will take place here as well.] And to this Anna added, in her own handwriting: *"Wir glauben es nicht"* [We don't believe it].

But then Anna goes on to conclude her letter on a highly personal and deeply moving note, as will often be the case in the years to follow, especially after the Lucerne Congress, held at the end of August 1934:[4] *"Manchmal wundert mich dass auch in solchen Zeiten, wie die jetzigen der Frühling und der Sommer kommt, als ob es wäre nichts geschehen."* [I am sometimes left dumbfounded that even in times such as these spring and summer can arrive just as if nothing at all had taken place.]

The following letter is a further indication of the way things were being judged by Anna Freud and her family during those first months. In a letter to Jones dated 5 June 1933, having underlined the importance of keeping "track" of the refugees and having given Jones information about the various psychoanalysts who had left Berlin, she then refers to her brother Ernst, who had worked in Berlin and had looked after the interests of the psychoanalytic publishing house—*der Verlag*, as it was called. In thanking Jones for the help he had given Ernst, Anna then adds:

"I think he is too pessimistic about our situation here. What he has seen and heard in Berlin has caused that change from his usual optimism. I do hope we will be able to stay on. Anyway all my own wishes go that way. The only thing that would make me move is the idea that my father might be subjected to any indignities like '*Hausdurchsuchung*' [house search] etc. So far of course, everything is safe."

And, again, in a letter to Jones dated 11 January 1934, Anna Freud comments:

"*Meinem Vater geht es gut. Politisch beginnt es gerade jetzt wieder etwas unruhiges zu werden, wenigstsens schwirren wieder alle Gerüchte in der Luft herum die sich in der Weihnacht Zeit still gehalten hatten. Aber das alles gewöhnt man sich.*"

[My father is feeling good. The situation politically speaking is starting to become rather restless again. At least all the stories and rumours which were kept silent during Christmas time are whirling around again. Yet, one gets used to all this.]

Anna was, in fact, echoing, in part at least, her father's attitude during the first chaotic months which followed the Nazi regime's coming to power in Germany. Consider, for example, Freud's reply to Jones, who, on 1 March 1933, had written to him saying, "*You must be glad that Austria is not a part of Germany*". In his reply, dated 7 April 1933, Freud first expressed his joy that letters sent to England, "*unlike those to Germany* [were] *not exposed to the danger of being opened*", and then wrote:

"Despite all the newspaper reports of mobs, demonstrations, etc. Vienna is calm, life undisturbed. We can expect with certainty that the Hitler movement will spread to Austria, is indeed already here, but it is very unlikely that it will present a similar danger as in Germany. It is much more likely that it will be bound through the alliance with the other rightist parties. We are in transition toward a rightist dictatorship, which means the suppression of social democracy. That will not be an agreeable state of affairs and will not make life pleasant for us Jews, but we all think that legal emergency declarations are impossible in Austria because the terms of our peace treaty expressly provide for rights of minorities, which did not happen in the Versailles treaty."

Then, with great naiveté—which nonetheless was a very common factor among the Jewish community of Central Europe—and relying on a rather idealistic view of the actual power of the League of Nations, Freud adds: "Here legalized persecution of the Jews would immediately result in the intervention of the League of Nations...."

France and her allies, according to Freud, would have intervened immediately should Germany have annexed Austria, and should the Jews have been deprived of their rights! ... and he then concludes his letter[5] with what is a rather pathetic statement, when one considers, theoretically speaking, the claims and the observations Freud had already made about the general destructiveness and cruelty of humankind: "Besides, Austrians are not inclined to German brutality. In such a way we lull ourselves into relative security. In any case I am resolved not to budge an inch." He had also written to Marie Bonaparte along similar lines (see the moving letter dated 19 February 1934, quoted in Jones, 1957, p. 486).

And it is in Jones's answer to this letter where one is able to observe just how cautious he was in his correspondence with both Sigmund and Anna Freud—although one also has to take into consideration that the situation as it stood in those weeks might not have been very clear to Jones. Only a month later, his predictions, as far as Austria's destiny was concerned, appear to be somewhat different, as his letters to his closest friends testify; Jones would even anticipate the *Anschluss* between Germany and Austria. However, at the time he wrote to Freud on 10 April 1933, he still considered this highly improbable:

> "So far as I can judge, my opinion about the situation in Austria is the same as yours, though I should attach more value to the national-patriotic desire of the *Heimwehr* people to retain the personality of old Austria; they must have noted how swiftly Bavaria allowed herself to be swallowed by Prussia. I am in touch with the Austrian Embassy here and know how strong a fight they are opposing to the Nazi *Anschluss* movement."

The following letter should also give an idea of just how complex the situation was. This extract is from a letter Freud wrote to Eitingon in more or less the same months as his correspondence with Jones on the subject. Eitingon had written to Freud on 25 March 1933 to ask him about the situation in Vienna, to which Freud replied on 3 April 1933:

"Unsere politische Lage versteht hier niemand. Manz hält es für wahrscheinlich dass die Entwicklung ähnlicher sein wird wie bei Ihnen. Das Leben verlauft hier ungestört."

[Nobody really understands our political situation. It is thought probable that the situation will develop in a similar way as yours in Germany. Life passes undisturbed here. . . .]

Nevertheless, when reading this letter, one must also take into account that Freud would have been fairly reserved in his comments, as he knew that his letters were at risk of being opened by the Nazi censors.[6]

Incidentally, much pressure had been put on Freud's family in this regard. In Anna Freud's *Rundbrief* dated 29 March 1933, she in fact said that many people were trying to encourage them to leave Austria *"ehe es zu etwas kommnt"* [before something happens], though the problem was by no means a simple one (and this would be putting it mildly, considering the state of Freud's health, among other things! —see again Freud to Marie Bonaparte, 19 February 1934, quoted in Jones, 1957, p. 486). On the other hand, in his letters to Anna Freud, Jones takes care not to mention the situation in too explicit a manner; and when he does have to refer to it, he does so with a considerable degree of caution. For example, in his letter to Anna of 1 June 1933, in referring to Ernst Freud's idea of taking his father to Paris with him, Jones prudently remarks: "as far as my judgement is worth anything I should not think this at all necessary", although he might perhaps have had a plan of his own in mind, or he may have been fearing the consequences should the Viennese suddenly have arrived in London. He reiterated his views in a letter to Eitingon dated 12 June 1933: "Ernst wants to take Freud to Paris which I hold very probable eventually. I do not myself see the necessity for this in any case but that is a matter of opinion." However, some weeks before the above letter to Eitingon, in a letter to Brill dated 31 March 1933, Jones appears somewhat hesitant: "No doubt you are sharing our concern at present about the situation in Germany. The pogrom part of it is perhaps exaggerated, at least as regards its extent, but no doubt analysts will have a bad time economically. There is even some talk of forbidding the practice of it altogether."

As the weeks go by, Jones is much more open about the situation as he sees it. When he again writes to Brill on 2 May 1933, he states:

"The situation of the German analysts is pretty terrible. There are hardly any left in Berlin and I understand that no Jew is allowed to hold any official position in the Society there. Cries of woe reach me on all sides. Poor Landauer is stranded in Stockholm without any prospects whatever and so on and so on. Freud himself is behaving splendidly in the situation and still hopes *that Austria may not succumb to the Nazi menace though I think that is very doubtful.*" [emphasis added]

In reading this correspondence, one is able to appreciate the difficulties one encountered in the face of the unpredictable climate reigning in those first months, following Hitler's rise to power, even though in hindsight—and as has been claimed by certain recent scholars who have studied the period in question—the situation should have been crystal-clear from the outset.

One ought also to quote from another of Jones's letters to Brill, dated 20 June 1933. In this letter he wrote of the general situation, of the schisms within the societies of the IPA, and, as I mentioned earlier, of the need to keep the New York Society and the American Association united at all costs: "There remain only the British and Viennese as stable grown-ups and I am afraid the latter will go the way of the German *as soon as Hitler makes Austria into a German province which I think will surely happen sooner or later*" (emphasis added). This was written as early as 1933, quite some years before the *Anschluss* of 1938! Furthermore, Jones was to reiterate more or less these same views in a letter to Eitingon dated 24 June 1933, in which he again affirmed that he thought it probable that the situation in Vienna would become significantly worse.

There is no doubt that Jones was informed of the situation in his own way, also through his diplomatic contacts at the Foreign Office, and that as President of the International Psycho-Analytical Association he understood it as his duty to assume overall responsibility to safeguard the general well-being of his colleagues. In attempting to trace the origins of this particular aspect of Jones's "*Sorge*", one ought to mention that, from the spring of 1933 onwards, there is not one of his letters that does not, in some way or other, reflect his commitment and his responsibility towards his colleagues. For instance, he lost no time in asking both Anna and Eitingon to supply him with "*an exact register of those who have left Germany in order to know where they are going and so that efforts can be made to help them*"[7] (Jones to A. Freud, 1

June 1933; Jones to Eitingon, 29 May 1933; Jones to Eitingon, 12 June 1933). And Anna, whose Society in Vienna was beginning to host some of the Berlin refugees—Reik, Reich for a while, Simmel, and others—asked Jones to keep her informed too.

There is also a letter from Jones to van Ophuijsen, again dated 29 May 1933, in which Jones, with his usual acute sense of how things might turn out politically, reiterates the need for "a register" to be kept

> "of the movements of the emigrants. . . . I am trying to keep such a list myself. . . . One must remember that it might be useful to make that of the Viennese Society, for the same thing might happen there. My latest information from very good sources, is that a Nazi government will almost surely come in Austria before very long."

CHAPTER THREE

"What shall those members do?"

Jones's politics in 1933

"What shall those members do?" [van Ophuijsen]

"I hope very much that since writing your letter you have reflected more coolly on the situation and will not take any precipitate steps . . ." [Jones]

One nevertheless has to consider that, in those first months, and even later, communications between London and Berlin, Vienna, and the other psychoanalytic centres that were to become involved in the operation to rescue the emigrant analysts were not always very easy. Different people reacted in different ways and gave different interpretations to events in Berlin. Jones then had to evaluate and filter the information he received, and, having consulted with his various friends and colleagues, he had to decide what to do; sometimes he had to act very quickly. Nor should one forget that Jones himself would react in different ways to different people: I have already hinted at the difficult economic and socio-political situation existing in Great Britain at the time. This at times imposed considerable constraints on Jones's endeavours, as will become ever clearer in the extracts from his correspondence with Anna Freud, Eitingon, Brill, and others.

But one must also consider Jones's particular character (Roazen, 1976; Steiner, 1993) and the way he would deal with his own and other people's emotions. If the play on words did not sound so absurd, considering the tragic circumstances of the situation, one might define Jones as being a true representative of Imperial Britain, the standing of which is so well expressed in the song "Rule Britannia". Yet one may also want to make a further play on words and substitute "rule Britannia" for "cool Britannia"—and of this Jones's astuteness and the diplomatic and cautious way with which he faced problems would be a perfect example. As we shall see in a short while, his political acumen and his political endeavours were focused mainly on defending and preserving the Institution at any cost and in guaranteeing the survival of each and every psychoanalytical society that happened to fall on difficult times. Psychoanalysis was undergoing rapid but fragile growth, and preventing it from splitting, fragmenting, or disappearing altogether was something that had concerned Jones all during his years as President of the IPA, even before the crisis brought on by the advent of the Nazis.

It has to be said, however, that as far as his handling of the 1933–1936 crisis of the German Psychoanalytic Society was concerned, Jones's politics would sometimes lead to quite questionable results. Jones's prime concern was to ensure the preservation of the Psychoanalytic Institution, over and above the plight of its single members, and the cautious and hesitant manner with which he would sometimes evaluate the situation can be observed quite clearly when one studies the extremely important correspondence between Jones and his Dutch colleague, van Ophuijsen. I would say that his approach becomes particularly evident in the letters he writes in the year German analysts first began to emigrate. I hazard to say that there exists no better document to give the reader a feel of the more or less conscious personal motivations behind the emigration of analysts from Germany than the letters written by one of its key organizers. From them, the reader will also understand the objective difficulties that were encountered in organizing this complex operation as a result of the chaotic circumstances of those first few months. On 11 March 1933, Jones wrote to Eitingon, asking him for information:

"We are naturally concerned about the situation in Germany, especially from the point of view of our friends, and although it is no doubt difficult to write fully and freely, I should be nevertheless relieved to have some direct news from you. There is a rumour that the Berlin Clinic is closed.

"The situation is, I am afraid, unfavourable to the sales of the Verlag literature . . ."

This latter he added thinking of all the problems the *Verlag* had had to face and which Martin Freud had tried to solve, even before the Nazis had begun to make their threats.

The Jones we come to know in his correspondence with van Ophuijsen is quite different from the Jones who wrote to the Freuds —and, curiously enough, the leitmotif that emerges from these letters would also seem to reflect the worries that would dominate Jones's and his colleagues' thoughts all during the years in which they carried out the balancing act of endeavouring to protect the local institutions whilst at the same time trying to save their colleagues from the Nazis. This correspondence gives us a view of another side to Jones's character—that is, his flexibility. For instance, once persuaded of the gravity of the situation in Berlin, his decisiveness and his clear-headedness is quite remarkable. However, behind his statements the reader will also be able to glimpse the personal idiosyncrasies, the fears, and the motives behind some of his statements.

Van Ophuijsen lived in Holland at that time, and it was therefore much easier for him to travel to Berlin, even in those difficult months of 1933. He had also had the opportunity of meeting many of his German colleagues personally and therefore knew some of them better than Jones did. Van Ophuijsen thus became one of the main sources of information on events in Berlin in general, and in the first months after the Nazis took control of Germany, he was in regular contact with the Berlin Psychoanalytic Institute and his Jewish colleagues, Eitingon in particular. He was, of course, also in touch with Sigmund and Anna Freud and kept them up to date on the fate of psychoanalysis in Germany, and on the situation regarding those first émigré psychoanalysts. There is no doubt that both when the problems first surfaced, and later, when the situation became much clearer, van Ophuijsen reacted to events quite differently from Jones. Indeed, the Dutch analyst was very quick to recognize the danger facing the Jewish analysts in Berlin, and he was also aware of what this would have meant for psychoanalysis in German-speaking countries.

It is in the letters exchanged between Jones and van Ophuijsen in the first weeks after it was realized that the Nazi regime posed a real threat to psychoanalysis where one can observe just how distant and prudent was Jones's attitude at this early stage in their correspondence and how cautious he was in his letter to Brill. Van Ophuijsen, a very generous and caring but rather emotional analyst, lost no time in informing both Jones and Freud of the situation and in rather dramatic tones, as the letters testify. In his letter to Jones dated 26 March 1933, van Ophuijsen appeared to be particularly worried about Eitingon, the Polish Jewish President of the Berlin Psychoanalytic Institute, who seemed to be unaware of the dangers he faced. "He is looking for troubles or worse", van Ophuijsen stated. He concluded his letter with the information that, according to Dr H. Staub, whom he had met in Holland,

> "psychoanalysis will be forbidden! All younger analysts seem to have left Berlin and probably only Müller-Braunschweig and Boehm will stay. Dr Staub does not fear that the documents present in the Institutes would cause much harm. I am not quite sure they would not if the members would still have been there. Tomorrow I am going to try to send a letter to Eitingon through our Embassy in Berlin, as Dr Staub confirmed my fear that all correspondence is under constant supervision. I am going to ask Eitingon when he is leaving and where he is going. I will propose him to come to Holland first."

That same day van Ophuijsen had sent all his colleagues a *Rundbrief* in which he had stressed that the Berlin Institute, and psychoanalysis generally, were in jeopardy, and that if psychoanalysis were to be banned, there would be *"eine Haussuchung"* [a house search] of the Berlin Institute. The Dutch analyst stated that he was very worried that the Nazis might find material that could be used to harm both patients and analysts. He reiterated his conviction that Eitingon, who was either completely unaware of the risks or was denying them, was in danger

> *"als polnischer Untertan, als Jude, als Analytiker und nicht zuletzt als der Sohn eines Mannes dem die Stadt Leipzig sehr Vieles verdankt."*
>
> [as a Polish citizen, as a Jew, as a psychoanalyst, and also as the son of a man to whom the city of Leipzig was deeply indebted.]

However, in his reply there is no doubt that Jones's mood was rather irritated, and he wrote back to poor van Ophuijsen in the same grandiose, self-congratulatory, *"pax Britannica"* tones as those in a *Rundbrief* he had sent to his friends on 1 March 1933, in which, whilst expressing his concern for Verlag's future under a Nazi regime, he had praised Martin Freud for his good work:

> "I hear of turmoils in the groups at New York, Paris and Holland but hope that the other Societies are as peaceful as the British one. From England the chief news is that an extensive re-organisation of the medical curriculum is taking place, there is an urgent demand to introduce training in Clinical psychology . . . it is certain that psychoanalysis will receive a prominent place in this work and will for the first time be taught at all the Universities and Medical Schools in this country."

Indeed, Jones's replies to van Ophuijsen on 28 March 1933:

> "So it took a German revolution to disturb your sleep! At all events I am glad the silence is broken. You may imagine that we also in England are very concerned about the fate of our German colleagues, though my opinion is that you tend slightly to over estimate the dangers, just as Max grossly under estimates them."

Jones then gave his views on Eitingon's situation in Berlin, saying: "I can give a full diagnosis of his condition internally, but not externally. Externally I should think his life is not in danger." He then proceeded to explain his reasons for these views and also stressed that he was "sceptical whether it will be possible to forbid the practice of psychoanalysis, this being after all a medical procedure open to every doctor and one that could be controlled only with the greatest difficulty. It is more likely that they will forbid the sale of Verlag books."

Contrary to the information van Ophuijsen had previously given him, Jones said only H. Kaiser and J. Harnik, as far as he was aware, had left or were in the process of leaving Germany. He continued this letter to his Dutch colleague by giving his views of Eitingon's emotional state. It was, Jones thought, *"Verleugnung der Angst dabei auch der Gefahr"* [Negation of anxiety coupled with negation of fear], and he then proceeded to mention Eitingon's difficult relationship with his wife. In concluding his letter, Jones adds: "I should not consider it impossible that the Nazis would raid the Institute but I do not think any harm could come of it. They would never have time to read all the notes, and the names of the members are easily obtainable otherwise."

Note, however, how Eitingon himself would describe the situation in Berlin during those first weeks—both to Freud and to Jones. In a very moving letter to Freud dated 19 March, in which he talks of himself and of his work as the founder of the Berlin Institute, Eitingon asks Freud what *"Ich mit dem Institut machen soll oder richtiger wie ich mich all seines möglichen Schicksalen gegenüber verhalten soll"* [I should do with the Institute, and how I should behave *vis-à-vis* all its possible ways of ending up]. He then explains his plans concerning the Institute, should it be forced to close. He wants to be there until the last moment, should this happen. On 24 March 1933, in reply to a letter Freud had written to him with advice on how to proceed, Eitingon again went over the chances the Institute might have. By this time Eitingon had already thought about leaving Berlin and of handing the Institute over to Simmel, but he had serious doubts about some of the latter's qualities. It is curious, nevertheless, that in a letter to Jones dated 27 March 1933, he should still be describing his work and the situation in Berlin as being quiet. They were able to work as before, he told Jones, and, up until then, none of his colleagues had been *"behindert"* [hampered] in their activities. It was natural that many young doctors should be ready to leave Germany, he added. A letter he wrote to Freud on 25 March 1933 went more or less along the same lines.

Yet it was as a result of a *Rundbrief* sent by van Ophuijsen on 3 April, and of a letter written to Jones on the same day, where van Ophuijsen insisted that his Berlin colleagues were in real danger, that Jones would appear to have changed his attitude. In his *Rundbrief*, van Ophuijsen wrote that he had just returned from Berlin, and that the situation there was *"schrecklich"* [*frightful*]. He said that Abraham's widow, who was then running a hostel, and her daughter, Hilde, needed help—Hilde particularly, as she would not have been able to continue with her studies in Berlin. He informed his colleagues that many analysts had already left Germany, and he then proceeded to list them all! This list was probably the first to be compiled and the first to provide details of what was actually happening at the Berlin Institute. F. Boehm had gone to Riga; Cohn and Fenichel to Oslo; Harnik and A. Gross were going to Copenhagen; K. Lampl and his wife to the Hague; Simmel to Switzerland; R. Spitz was planning to go to Brazil, perhaps; Staub to Paris; A. Watermann to Amsterdam; M. Wulff to Palestine. . . . Van Ophuijsen adds:

"Ob Boehm zurückkommen wird is es fraglich; denn es wird geflüstert dass sein Vater doch jüdischer Abstammung sein soll! Simmel wird nich zurückkommen."

[Whether Boehm will return, is an open question, because there is a rumour that his father is of Jewish extraction. Simmel will not be returning.]

He then apologizes for perhaps having exaggerated the danger Eitingon was in but reiterated that the situation was very grave.

In his letter to Jones of the same date, van Ophuijsen explains the difficult position Karl Abraham's widow Ilse and her daughter were in and asks Jones whether there was any possibility of Abraham's daughter being able to complete her medical studies in England, and what a foreigner in England had to do to be able to qualify as a doctor. He was also asking on behalf of Dr H. Watermann of Hamburg, who wanted to sit his medical examinations in England before possibly going to South Africa to work. Van Ophuijsen concluded his letter by saying:

"Germany is at the present a hell for the German Jews and I can not see how long it will continue to be so. There is no visible sign of any reaction. The next step taken by the Nazis is, as I am informed by Dr Watermann though I did not read in the papers myself, that mixed marriages will be considered illegal from now on. Do write to me [underlined] or send an oral message to Abraham's daughter through a person you can trust. But if you write, you must be very [underlined three times!] cautious. You have not [underlined] been so in your last letter to Eitingon, it might have harmed him, as it is now absolutely certain as it was probable before, that his correspondence is under control."

As I said earlier, it was at this moment that Jones's attitude to the situation changed, probably as he had also begun to receive information from other sources, and requests for help. "I got your terrible letter yesterday," Jones replied to van Ophuijsen on 5 April, "and I had not realised the situation was so bad." He then asked van Ophuijsen for further information about the emigrants, because he wanted "very much to have a complete record of what has been happening". And did anybody know where Reich had ended up . . . ? (And in chapter seven we will see the kind of *"Sorgenkind"* Reich was to become for both Jones and the Freuds.)

But it is in the following comments, contained in the same letter, where one can really observe Jones at his "best", when, faced with the prospect of there being a sudden flood of immigrants whom he would not realistically have been able to help, he put his cards very firmly on the table, so to speak. Indeed, with extreme lucidity, he explains the problems and the difficulties a German Jewish immigrant would have to face. Apart from needing to be qualified to practise, and apart from requiring permission to remain "in this country", the main obstacle was the difficulty in finding work. . . . "We have several experienced members who find it difficult to live. . . ." England was not that different from other countries:

> "There is a strong feeling, voiced this week in Parliament, that we should revert to our traditional role of welcoming refugees from political persecution, as we did with the Huguenots and many others. On the other hand the unemployment, which is unprecedented, evokes a counter reaction against admitting foreigners. It is therefore hard to say, which of these two will influence the prevailing regulations. . . . *Fear can easily arise at the idea of immigrant hordes and this would naturally have a reactionary effect. Also England would be more likely to develop this fear in the case of people coming from the East than from the South. There is still some prejudice against German-speaking people and a vague association with Communism."* [emphasis added]

Jones then proceeded to give very precise details on the academic requirements for a person to qualify as a doctor in England if he came from abroad and had already begun his medical studies in his country of origin. The complications were quite worrying, and "I have not mentioned the question of lay analysts as you did not directly ask about it. But I am afraid their chance of earning a living here or of getting permission to remain in this country, is still less bright than in the case of a doctor."

Britain's liberal tradition meant that hospitality could be offered to all . . . but the unemployment situation . . . the Great Depression . . . the fear of huge numbers of immigrants . . . the vague paranoia of associating German Jews with Communism[1] . . . personal rivalries among the analysts . . . the hurdles to be overcome with regard to the technicalities of medical training . . . the complex problem of lay analysis . . . It is curious, and significant at the same time, that what we are faced with here is a condensed summary, or a rehearsal, if you like, of what was to become the blueprint for many of the other letters Jones and his colleagues would write (see, for instance, Jones to van Ophuijsen, 23 May 1933). Furthermore, not only does the above letter to van Ophuijsen seem to condense so many of the issues that were to become the focus of their many letters (see chapters four, six, seven, eight), but it could also be used as a paradigmatic example of the general immigration problem as it existed in those years. It is with some regret that one notes that scholars such as Wasserstein (1979, 1999) do not appear to have known about this and other letters written by Jones and colleagues on these issues, as their use would have helped to corroborate, and further highlight, the appalling Calvary suffered by so many Jewish émigrés, Jewish psychoanalysts included.

In the weeks that followed, Jones was to become even more closely acquainted with the sudden deterioration of the situation in Germany generally, and in Berlin in particular, including the plight of the psychoanalysts living there. Van Ophuijsen began to send him ever more detailed letters on who was leaving, on the situation of those remaining, and so on. When, in a letter to van Ophuijsen dated 3 April 1933, Jones expressed his sadness at the situation of Abraham's family and his wish to help Mrs Abraham and her daughter, saying how at least Karl Abraham had been spared the heartbreak of seeing how his beloved Prussia had behaved, his Dutch colleague and friend responded by supplying him with data on the situation of Jewish lawyers, by telling him of how Jewish doctors were no longer able to work in hospitals, and by giving him even sadder news of Abraham's wife and her financial problems. He also briefed Jones on those who had left: "Bernfeld left a few months ago"; nobody knew where Reich was (van Ophuijsen to Jones, 6 April 1933). A few days later he wrote again to describe the difficult situation of the Berlin Psychoanalytic Institute, and that it was increasingly becoming the focus of the Nazis' attention, who were suspicious of any "international relation" and were consequently intercepting all of the Institute's correspondence (van Ophuijsen to Jones, 8 April 1933).

Although the following letter was written some months prior to the one Jones wrote to van Ophuijsen cn 15 July 1933, at a time when Jones seemed not to be totally aware of what was to happen just a few months later, one will find in it this same mix of a wish to help and disenchanted realism. In a letter to Freud dated 10 April 1933, having thanked him for his offer to give financial help to Abraham's wife and having informed him of what he and van Ophuijsen were doing to assist Mrs Abraham and her daughter, Jones adds:

> "There are formidable difficulties in the way, both as regards admission to residence in England especially when earning a living, and even to leaving Germany. The German solution for what they regard as superfluous Jews appears to be not to send them away but to keep them in a cage until they starve. At the same time their guilt gives them a certain sensitiveness to outside opinion."

Nevertheless, in those days Jones was still moderately optimistic—or perhaps he was trying to avoid worrying Freud unnecessarily when he added:

> "I know for instance that an interview between Lord Reading [R. D. Isaacs, an eminent British politician of that period] and the German ambassador here produced a deep impression. Therefore the furore will surely die down. But in the meantime the positions in medicine and law will be occupied by Gentiles, so that the harm cannot be undone. There is an intense indignation in this country among all classes, and I should think also among many Germans. . . . Our Society is unanimous in wishing to help [the refugees] in every way it can."

Even as late as 10 May 1933, in a letter to Freud wishing him a happy birthday, Jones adds:

> "I fully realise the set back we have had, and that we even yet may not know the full consequences. But as you said, on your seventieth birthday you have no illusions about the extent of our progress and therefore can have fewer disappointments. I think psychoanalysis is more securely based in England than in any other country, and feel we can quite safely all adopt the motto 'slow but sure'."

Here again some of Jones's statements sound too optimistic, if we compare them with the extracts from his correspondence with Brill and Eitingon dated just a month after this letter was written.

At this time Ferenczi's death had suddenly became the focus of various letters, and it seemed to increase the sadness and the uncertainty of those months. Jones, for instance, comments to Brill on 24 May 1933:

"Perhaps they cabled to you that Ferenczi died two days ago and was buried today. I do not know any details. The shock of his news will surely bring back the memory of that inspiring figure we used to love. But in view of his deterioration of recent years we cannot honestly say that the event is a great blow to the international movement itself, although it doubtless will be one to the Hungarian Society. *Tempus fugit* and it is our duty to think of the future rather than the past."[2]

It is, of course, impossible to follow this correspondence in all its details, but I think it is worth mentioning another of van Ophuijsen's letters to Jones, written during those extremely chaotic weeks. In commenting on Ferenczi's death, which van Ophuijsen called "a sudden blow", he reiterates what he had said in his *Rundbrief*—that is, that should the German Society have been dissolved, something that had been voiced in the previous weeks, this would have complicated matters enormously (Brecht et al., 1993), and one needed to make plans to help colleagues in Germany. Van Ophuijsen's insistence on this issue seems to have been prompted by Jones's continued unwillingness (Jones to van Ophuijsen, 23 May 1933) to accept his colleague's view that there was a risk that the German members of the dissolved Society would cease to be "attached to the IPA"! Indeed, in his letter of 23 May, Jones had again stressed that "there was only the practical question of how to keep regular contacts" and had reiterated his previous concern that "all the members who leave their homes in Germany" should be asked "to communicate their address and future residence to me. I would then have a definite list". To which, on 26 May 1933, van Ophuijsen had replied: "I do not agree with you on the question of the German members. For as a matter of fact these will cease to be members of the Internation. Ass. the moment the German branch will have been '*behördlich aufgelöst*', officially dissolved." "And when so, what will you do?", he asks anxiously and rather polemically, as Jones, in van Ophuijsen's view, had not appeared to have realized the full extent of the impending disaster, "Or rather what shall those members do? By that time they will be scattered all over Europe, they will address themselves to you, to me or Anna Freud, and we may or may not be able to help them personally and on our own account, but not officially."

However, in his letter of 29 May 1933, Jones seemed to have become somewhat more understanding of the situation:

"Of course I should not oppose your suggestion about the German membership if it seems desirable. I only doubted if it were immediately necessary. After all", he added, with his habitual political realism, and taking his usual stance on the Institutions and their necessary role, "the German Society is still in being and will remain so *unless it is officially dissolved by the German Government.*" [emphasis added]

But matters suddenly became more complicated, even for the generous van Ophuijsen. Again, it is through his correspondence with Jones—and bearing in mind what was also beginning to take place in America—that one is able truly to appreciate the very bitter and indigestible pill the refugees would often be forced to swallow—and this was not due exclusively to the socio-political and financial situation of the countries to which they emigrated, nor to other difficulties, as outlined in the extracts I quote above from Jones's letters. (It must be reiterated that Jones's letters also show that he had not neglected to give thought to finding a solution for those analysts who may have been forced to leave the Institute, notwithstanding the fact that priority had to be given to the survival of the Institute itself.)

Rather, what at a certain point becomes apparent from van Ophuijsen's letters are the inner rivalries, the jealousies, and the competitive envy that would develop as a result of the arrival of these refugees, and the repercussions these hostilities had on the various psychoanalytical societies that, willingly or less willingly, took them in as members. Although one needs to consider the circumstances and acknowledge the difficulties of the situation, one must also stress that these tensions were not solely created by the defensive—or, if one wants to use this expression, by the narcissistic—reactions of the indigenous members of the various psychoanalytical societies, but that the refugees too had their characterological difficulties, which sometimes had very little to do with their condition *"Sorgenkinder"*!

But let us for the moment return to van Ophuijsen. At one point the Dutch analyst informed Jones that there were serious problems within his Society, as a result of his having helped the German analysts Landauer, Watermann, and Reik to move to Holland. This had made an already difficult situation much worse. The difficulties within the Dutch Society would eventually cause it to split, and a second Society, "The Society of Psychoanalysis in Holland", was created in November 1933 (see Brecht et al., 1993, p. 78). Again, we can see the strategy Jones would adopt. He immediately began to put pressure on his colleagues, in an attempt to prevent the Dutch Society from splitting (Jones to van Ophuijsen, 15 July 1933; Jones to Brill, 20 June 1933; Jones to Eitingon, 21 July 1933; Freud to Jones, 23 July 1933). But even more important and interesting than the fate of the Dutch institution are the reasons for the German analysts having been rejected by van Ophuijsen's colleagues, for these are emblematic both of the situation that was to arise in Britain in the years after Freud and his family emigrated there in 1938 (I go into greater detail on this matter in chapter eight), and of the enormous problems that were to be created by those refugees who chose to emigrate to the United States (see chapter two, particularly note 2; see also chapters four, six, and eight). These issues will become clearer when we look at the correspondence between Jones and Brill and the difficulties they encountered in the course of the first wave of emigration to America in the spring and summer of 1933 and no less during the one that followed.

In a letter to Jones dated 13 July 1933, van Ophuijsen informs him of the allegations being made by A. J. Westerman-Holstiyn, who was accusing Landauer, Reik, Watermann, and the other analysts who had been invited to Holland by van Ophuijsen of being "*ausländische Neurotikern*"—that is, "foreign neurotics". In his letter to van Ophuijsen dated 12 July 1933, Westerman-Holstiyn had called Landauer and Reik "*zwei Bomben*" [two bombs], and he had told van Ophuijsen in no uncertain terms that he considered the attitude of these new arrivals to be one of excessive criticism and superiority, in that they were claiming that the only truly classical analysts were those who came from Vienna and Berlin. There was havoc among the Dutch candidates and colleagues, and if these analysts were to remain in Holland permanently, van Ophuijsen said, this would lead to serious problems and would cause the Dutch Society to split.

Note also the incredibly offensive letters that Westerman-Holstiyn sent to Landauer in September 1933 and on 7 October 1933 (in Brecht et al., 1993, pp. 64–65). In Brecht et al., one can also find a letter from Landauer to Westerman-Holstiyn, dated 5 October 1933, in which he openly discusses the whole situation concerning the threat the Dutch analysts saw in the German refugees. It is important to note that in this letter Landauer also comments that although Westerman-Holstiyn had been rather insulting, he acknowledged that his Dutch colleague had wanted to emphasize his wish to help his Berlin and Viennese colleagues, and that he was *not* anti-Semitic. However, Landauer commented, he had also noted that the Dutch analyst had stressed that the indigenous Jewish community of Holland might react very negatively towards the émigrés if the latter did not behave as Westerman-Holstiyn had suggested.

In this letter to Jones, van Ophuijsen also stressed that he did not want to arrive at any compromise with Westerman-Holstiyn, and that he was prepared to accept the eventuality of a split occurring within the Dutch Society. Jones was not to think that being classified a "foreign neurotic" was just a slip of the pen, and van Ophuijsen spoke of his colleagues' "*Unverschämheit*", or impudence. He then asked Jones to send Westerman-Holstiyn's letter on to the Freuds and to Eitingon for their advice on the matter.

As we have already seen, Jones was, of course, much less emotional than was van Ophuijsen on issues such as these. It is interesting that in his reply dated 23 July 1933, Freud should tell Jones (p. 725): "I have read van Ophuijsen's letter to you as well as your reply. Your counsel to maintain diplomatic calm is certainly justified, but W. H.'s behaviour remains disgusting and may well embitter such a serious man as Ophuijsen. The poor exiles never have it too easy anywhere."

In a letter to Jones dated 23 August 1933, Anna Freud also stressed that both she and her father had taken the correspondence between van Ophuijsen and Westerman-Holstiyn much more seriously than had Jones. She also emphasized that, in a case such as this, she thought that "*mit Diplomatie im einzelnen gegen diese Stimmen nicht viel ausrichten kann*" [to use diplomacy against this kind of frame of mind would not achieve very much]. It is obvious that the Freuds reacted in a different way to Jones because Jewish colleagues were involved.

Central to these disputes was the refugees' attitude of "*bei uns war es besser*" [we did it better at home]. As we saw earlier, this problem would also recur in the United States and would, in essence, also be the cause of all the friction after 1938, following the arrival of the Viennese in London, between Anna Freud, her Viennese colleagues, and the British Psycho-Analytical Society (see Steiner, 1985, and chapters six and eight). In all cases, however, disputes would be further exacerbated by the rivalries and jealousies on the part of local analysts.

Jones's reply to van Ophuijsen's rather emotional letter is typical of the position he would take in such circumstances, and it helps us to appreciate what a skilled and truly realistic politician (in the Machiavellian sense of the term) he was at times. On 15 July 1933 he wrote to van Ophuijsen, saying, in a somewhat cool and distant manner, that his colleague's "state of indignation made your [van Ophuijsen's] letter rather less coherent than usual! . . ." Jones then informed van Ophuijsen that he had been in touch with Westerman-Holstiyn and that, in his view, the Dutch analyst's main concerns were with another matter: that of "what to do with Dr [E.] Perls who was in Amsterdam and was exploring the possibility to be trained in England". Jones insisted that he did not know all the background details to Westerman-Holstiyn's complaints but then added:

> "What you call a threat seems to be a friendly warning that some colleagues who feel more strongly on the matter than Westerman-Holstiyn himself, might vote against the acceptance of these two foreigners as members of the Dutch Society. . . . If the expression 'foreign neurotic' also refers to Reik I find it harsh, but not altogether untrue. Landauer is another matter, and I am quite unaware of any sort of objections to him."

As always, Jones tried to make a distinction between matters that were personal and those that concerned the Institute. However, do not forget his comments about Reik! . . . This is an issue to which I will have to return later, because it is obvious that Jones is here indirectly revealing his own criteria for selecting émigrés.

Yet the extract that follows is probably the most important part of Jones's reply:

> "It would be evidently very difficult to invite and support any foreign analyst against whom the bulk of one's colleagues had some strong objections but I cannot judge how best to deal with the problem without knowing the nature of their objections. I took good care in London to discuss the matter with our Society before dealing with any foreign applications. My situation proved to be easier than yours, inasmuch as all the members here unanimously welcome the immigration of any foreign colleagues that cared to come, provided of course that they were fairly warned beforehand of the difficulties and poor prospects in front of them."

Whether or not Jones's claims that the British Society would *"unanimously welcome"* the refugees were absolutely true would only be confirmed in the years to follow, but one must assume that these comments were but a wish-fulfilment on Jones's part, particularly when one considers that he himself had already begun his own assessment procedures to determine who was suitable for entry to Great Britain and who was not!! (See also chapters seven and eight.)

However, it is important that we note what he also said in this letter about the Dutch Society and van Ophuijsen's worries, as here one has a very clear picture of Jones's overall strategy (as mentioned earlier). In the following passages this is unequivocally spelt out: as always, the first requirement was the necessity to save the Institution, over and above the needs of any single individual:

> "I hope very much that since writing your letter you have re-flected more coolly on the situation and will not take any precipi-tate steps that would prove to do no good and might do much irretrievable harm. I am certainly in favour of *à l'outrance* when it cannot be avoided (e.g. Adler, Jung, and so forth) but it is rare to necessarily split a Society in two for this purpose. I was never convinced of the necessity of splitting the Swiss Society. Before deciding on the desirability of such a step I should certainly want to know more definitely the full nature of the grounds and the hopelessness of any other means of dealing with them. After com-ing to such a decision it would be then a matter of choosing the clearest issue on which to break."

Van Ophuijsen's reply, dated 18 July 1933, was nevertheless very clear, and in accepting Jones's remarks on the fact that his previous letter had been incoherent, he also added another extremely impor-tant point, which confirms the views I expressed earlier about the painful mixture of objective and often very subjective and danger-ously unmanageable reasons that made the immigration issue such a difficult experience for all those persons involved in it:

> "It would take too much time to explain in full the attitude of a large number of our members towards those German colleagues who want to settle down here. They are afraid to suffer both financially and narcissistically, inasmuch as those colleagues could hinder them to play the part they choose for themselves. All the reasons they give are rationalisations."

In my view, this exchange of letters needs no further comment, as I think most of the statements in them speak for themselves. But I could, of course, go on quoting from them and relate the sad way in which this correspondence on the problems between the emigrants and the Dutch Society ended. In fact, on 21 September 1933, van Ophuijsen wrote to Jones to announce that there was now the need to explore the possibility of creating a new Dutch society, one able to host Landauer, Watermann, and the other German refugee analysts, and he asked Jones whether he would be prepared to accept a new Society as a branch society of the IPA.[3]

Echoes of Jones's ever prudent and detached manner where van Ophuijsen was concerned are also evident in a letter he wrote to Anna Freud on 1 June 1933, in which he discussed van Ophuijsen's proposal that the German Society—or, rather, the members of the Berlin Institute—be enrolled in the Vienna Psychoanalytic Society. As he had already informed van Ophuijsen on 9 May 1933, Jones did not agree with this because, he said, he could foresee the risks, should the same circumstances occur in Vienna as they had in Berlin. Once again, we are able to observe Jones coming to the defence of the German Society and its right to maintain its own membership while it still could—or, in Jones's own words, "as long as the German society remains in being". Then the situation worsened. Indeed, in the autumn of 1933 Jones and van Ophuijsen would meet in Holland, where Jones had gone to meet with Boehm and C. Müller-Braunschweig. He had asked van Ophuijsen to be present at this meeting, which was held to discuss the situation of the German Society after it had become clear that Eitingon no longer wanted to remain in Berlin and had decided to emigrate to Palestine. Jones was very suspicious of Boehm at that time. He had already expressed his qualms about Boehm in a letter to van Ophuijsen dated 9 May 1933, saying: "Boehm is distinctly untrustworthy, he even consulted with the Nazi authority. . . ." He now says in a letter dated 18 September 1933: "Boehm wants to meet in Holland to discuss the reorganisation of the Society. You should be present as a *Beirat* [witness] in the Hague. I expect you share my suspicions about his political trustworthiness."

Incidentally, on the same day, Jones had written these same comments to a very depressed and pessimistic Freud.[4] Yet one must also say that Freud and Jones would both be diplomatic in their dealings with Boehm in the months that followed, as they would with Müller-Braunschweig.[5] In fact, Jones particularly, and to a certain extent Anna and Freud, too, would all support Boehm's activities and decisions from the moment he became President of the German Society in the late autumn of 1933. Jones would claim to be doing so with the future of German psychoanalysis in mind, and with the desire to protect the Jewish members of the German Psychoanalytical Society, as can be seen from a letter he wrote to Freud on 18 September 1933. His endorsement of Boehm would, however, place him in a rather ambiguous and difficult position.

Eitingon, on the other hand, had quite different opinions on matters concerning Boehm and Müller-Braunschweig—the contents of his letters provide us with a fuller picture of this extremely delicate and ultimately tragic issue. As early as 21 April 1933, in a letter to Freud, he had accused Boehm of having tried to manipulate the situation in Berlin in his absence. To have Boehm as the "*Vorsetzender unserer deutsche Institution*" [representative of our German Institution] "*ist natürlich ein Unglück...*" [is of course a misfortune], Eitingon comments in his letter—and we must remember that these views were being aired during the first months in which Boehm and Müller-Braunschweig were officially dealing with the first batch of restrictions then being imposed by the Nazis on the medical professions, and which effectively prevented the Jews from practising. The two German analysts were claiming to be exploring what could be done to save and preserve the Berlin Psychoanalytic Institute and German psychoanalysis in general.

Van Ophuijsen, for his part,[6] continued to stand firm in his defence of those Jewish analysts who had refused to accept the Berlin Psychoanalytic Institute being reorganized under the directorship of Boehm and other Nazi collaborators. In this respect, van Ophuijsen wrote a very moving *Rundbrief*, dated 24 December 1933; he proposed that, as had been suggested by the left-wing Jewish analyst Klara Happel (Brecht et al., 1993, p. 36), all those who were not "*so masochistic*" as to want to remain but had decided to leave the new German Society ought to be allowed direct membership to the IPA, at least until the next International Psychoanalytical Congress, when a proper decision could then be taken regarding the fate of these analysts, should they not have applied for membership with other psychoanalytical societies. Of course, Jones was opposed to this idea when he first heard of it, as there were no such provisions in the Statutes of the IPA and he was afraid that, if this suggestion were to have been put into effect, it would have created a quite chaotic situation (see Jones to Eitingon, 15

December 1933). However, he was later to change his mind, as can be seen in his letter to Eitingon dated 29 December 1933.

I will have to return to the German Society and its problems later on in this book, as I would now like to look at how Jones, in the meantime, had begun to try to assist the small number of German refugees whom he had helped to come to England in 1933. It is interesting to note that, commencing with a letter dated 20 May, Jones's correspondence now contained specific information on 5 of the 12 or more refugees who had appealed to him for help in emigrating to Britain. "Perls from Hamburg, Dr Cohn from Berlin and Dr Fuchs [later Foulkes] from Frankfurt, Frau Frankl and Frau Heimann" . . . "Gerd, Hilde and Frau Abraham . . ." read Jones to Freud, 3 June 1933; Jones to Brill, 20 June 1933; Jones to Anna Freud, 6 May 1933; Jones to Eitingon, 20 May 1933. In his letter of 20 May 1933, Jones informed Eitingon that Reich was in Copenhagen, and that Gerd Abraham was "a fine young fellow". In his letter to Eitingon of 23 May 1933, he stated that he considered Cohn "a capable analyst but made the impression of someone with insufficient adaptability to this country".

Cohn would eventually settle in England, at least for a while, although a letter to Jones dated 21 November 1933, from C. P. Oberndorf, the American psychoanalyst, reads:

"I have talked over with Dr. Brill the question of helping some analysts to come to America from Germany. It seems to both of us that Reik would be out of the question because he is not a physician and also because of his age . . . the name of Fritz Cohn has been suggested and if we can get in touch with him I should like to communicate with him."

To which Jones replied on 2 December 1933, saying, "Cohn is in England and seems settling down here". Jones seemed therefore to have changed his mind. He then asked Oberndorf to help Reik, in spite of the latter's bad clinical work, stating "He is better with books than people and might really do some valuable work", and he asked Oberndorf whether he might not be able to find Reik a post in the United States as a researcher, or perhaps an "assistant librarianship".

And another letter, dated 3 July 1933, to his colleague reads: "You might perhaps have heard that Dr. Homburger [later on he decided to call himself E. Erikson] of Vienna settled in Copenhagen last week. I am to see now more of your friends Drs. W. M. F. H. (*alle angenehme Leute: der Mann etwas schweigerisch*) [all nice people: the men are a bit taciturn]."

Considering the views he expressed in his letters to van Ophuijsen and others in those same years, it comes as no surprise to read Jones's comments to Eitingon[7] about these refugees: "such people are very welcome to us but the external situation is unfortunately very unfavourable". This, however, had not interfered with his efforts to help either Frau Heimann or Frau Frankl, notwithstanding the difficulties he was to encounter in finding them hospital posts. Indeed, by September of that same year, both had been given permission to practise as psychoanalysts (see Jones to A. Freud, 19 September 1933).

See for instance the letter Jones wrote to Eitingon on 21 July 1933:

"I am sorry that our two women colleagues here, who have made a very good impression, have been refused at the only women's hospital in Great Britain. Their immediate future is very dark, but we still have some plans that may find a way round the difficulties. F. [referring to Fuchs, subsequently Foulkes] also of Frankfurt has not yet succeeded at obtaining entrance to any hospital but he still has some chance of doing so."

Jones did not mention the surnames of his colleagues (Heimann, Frankl, and Fuchs) in his letter to Eitingon, as he was probably worried about the letter being intercepted by the Nazi police.

It is patently clear from the various comments in his letters to Anna Freud and from his lucid analysis of the general situation then pertaining that Jones's activities in those early months reflected in miniature both the hopes of the immigrants then arriving in Britain— Jews and non-Jews alike—and the difficulties they were having to face in settling. And a letter to Eitingon dated 12 July 1933 provides some idea of Jones's sense of realism and the extent of his political cautiousness, for he would not have wished to provoke false illusions and would not have wanted émigrés from Germany to arrive either at random or en masse:

"My standpoint is as follows. We cannot recommend anyone to come here because even if all the great difficulties are overcome, there is not enough work for our own people and the prospects of making a living are at present very poor indeed. Naturally matters might improve if the economic situation gets better, but one has no right to take the responsibility of advising people to face such a bad situation. On the other hand, if an applicant says he is faced with starvation and must in any case come, then we will certainly welcome him and help him to the best of our power. There is a very genuine feeling of sympathy among all our members and we are all prepared to make what sacrifices are possible, but we cannot create patients. Further it would be foolish for anyone to come without the means to support themselves without work for at least a year, and naturally they must learn English as early and thoroughly as possible. I am sure that the early arrivals will stand the best chance and do not like to think of what will happen to those who may have to come next autumn or winter. Again it would be inadvisable for anyone outside to come without making a preliminary visit here when we can give them all the necessary information."

On reading this letter, and if one thinks back to his letters to van Ophuijsen and others, it is obvious that Jones was not just expressing his personal opinion on the situation. However, as I have already hinted at earlier, one must always bear in mind that when it came to deciding how best to help those German colleagues who wished to come to England, Jones would play his safest card . . . and would favour one individual over another on the grounds that they were better suited . . . to life within the British Psycho-Analytical Society. Of course, he may not have been able to anticipate with total clarity the events of 1938, when Freud, his family, and the Viennese had to depart hastily from Vienna, and during which time Jones's "selection" procedures were forced to their limit. But I will come back to this point in chapter eight. There is no doubt, however, that in spite of his being so circumspect, there was a genuine wish on his part to provide all the help he could, and that he wanted to make good use of his special skills in this regard (see, for instance, Jones's earlier comments on Dr Cohn, Reik, and others). Indeed, it would appear that his comments were also dictated by the restrictions that were being imposed by the British Government of the day on the quota of immigrant doctors and other professionals in general being allowed into the country, in addition to the problem of the Jewish refugees, as studied by London (2000), Sherman (1973), and Wasserstein (1979, 1999). After all, in explaining the situation that would face medical students who wanted to apply for a post in a British hospital, Jones had stressed that, in 1933, there had been 700 applicants from New

York alone, and that these were having difficulties in finding places in British hospitals, and "they were nearly all refused".

This is the same man who, in a much earlier letter to Freud—on 19 June 1910 to be exact—had defined himself as lacking in originality, and whose prime ambition at the time was apparently *"to be behind the scenes"*. This was a person who, when comparing himself to Freud, was to add the significant comment that *"to me work is like a woman bearing a child, to men like you I suppose it is more like the male fertilization"*. Now the self-same Ernest Jones had found himself in a position of some power, where he could finally realize his dreams.

Behind the scenes, Jones, in full control of operations, began to throw himself body and soul into rescuing the refugees. In his position as President of the International Psycho-Analytical Association, he had the authority to liaise with all the various psychoanalytical associations abroad, he had access to both the Foreign Office and the Home Office, and he had contact with many of the Embassies in London. He therefore wielded considerable power and, as a result, was to play a quite significant part in the diaspora's final outcome. It is also interesting to note the spirit in which Jones operated. I have already mentioned his clear-headedness, his practical approach to matters, and his generally realistic outlook. Further evidence of this is contained in a letter, in answer to one from Anna Freud of 27 March 1933 that I quoted earlier (see chapter two). Jones comments here on her remarks about it being practically impossible, in view of the situation, for her to enjoy the arrival of spring. His comments are another example of the way Jones responded to difficulties. It also reveals just how impeccably British was his *"Sorge"*. In this letter, dated 2 May 1933, he wrote:

> "Your passage about spring, my dear Anna, touched me very much. Suffering and pain are forced on us very much nowadays by the state of the world, but I think we should try to fight against the feeling that we ought to involve ourselves in other people's suffering. We get involved enough through our sympathies without adding our moral compulsion as well. Surely it is our duty, if one wants to use such a word, to allow ourselves to be as little weighed down as we can possibly manage; in that way can we be of most use."

However, one ought perhaps to add that Jones was not a Jew, nor did he happen to be in Vienna or in Berlin at that particular moment in time. Nevertheless, his apparent aloofness did not prevent him from providing financial help to some of the refugees, as Freud and others had also done. In the case of Abraham's wife and children, for example, Jones had lent Hilde some money to run a small hostel in Berlin quite early on, before the Nazi threat had become so insistent. Incidentally, he was never able to recoup his loan because, as he put it in a letter to Eitingon dated 21 June 1934, "one of the first acts committed by Germany's idol whom Freud in a recent letter well styled 'the *Rauberhauptmann*' had been to confiscate all foreign possessions". In those early months he also offered to help Abraham's daughter, as can be seen in his letter to van Ophuijsen dated 5 April 1933, where he states "I need hardly to say that we should be prepared to give her a home if she decided on this plan and we could arrange for her analysis to be continued gratis in England".

Indeed, one could spend many hours in following all of Jones's comings and goings, in his effort to help those early immigrants. One would be able to observe the not inconsiderable pains to which he went to obtain work permits and to find suitable posts for them—but only after they had been interviewed by him and his colleagues at the British Psycho-Analytical Society—a not altogether pleasurable experience, by any means. One would also be able to appreciate the trouble he took to ensure that he was kept informed on the situation in Berlin by maintaining regular contact with van Ophuijsen, with Eitingon and others, and with those German analysts who would later collaborate with the Nazis and of whose behaviour Jones had already begun to be suspicious in the spring and summer of 1933.

One of Jones's principal sources of information, as I have already mentioned, was Anna Freud in Vienna. She kept him up to date with information on the various people and their situation, and she came to play an increasingly important part in his efforts to save not only the refugees, but also psychoanalysis in Germany. Indeed, Anna Freud would also keep Jones fully up to date both on her father's situation and on the events taking place in Vienna and within the Vienna Psychoanalytic Society. Finally, one must not forget Jones's involvement in the activities and the rescue of Verlag. It was whilst trying to solve this and other issues that in October 1933 he met with Müller-Braunschweig and Boehm. Incidentally, Jones considered Müller-Braunschweig to be less anti-Semitic than Boehm! But it is in a letter addressed to Anna Freud and dated 2 October 1933 that we find what appears to be a serious reconsideration, on Jones's part, of the two Aryan analysts. His change of heart followed his meeting with them on 1 October 1933.[8] This letter to Anna is of fundamental importance, because it helps us to understand the difficult and the rather ambiguous and questionable attitude that would at times characterize Jones's handling of the changes that were taking place within the Berlin Psychoanalytic Institute, which would eventually lead to its chaotic closure and to its absorption into the Deutsche Institut für Psychologische Forschung und Psychotherapie, controlled by M. H. Göring, which was also accepted, in part at least, by Sigmund and Anna Freud (Brecht et al., 1993, p. 140). Indeed, Jones's letter to Anna contains a by no means pessimistic report on the situation in Germany, despite the fact that Göring—a nephew of the Nazi government minister of the same name—was now in control of the Berlin Vereinigung. In fact, in this letter Jones got so carried away as to congratulate Boehm for having intervened and having saved many of the Jewish psychoanalysts from being sent to concentration camps in August and September of 1933!

As the contents of this letter are quite important, I will quote some of its more significant passages in full:

> "My visit to Holland was I feel very successful both in clearing up the situation and in advising about a number of difficulties.
>
> "After the interview my impression of the Germany situation has slightly altered and I do not feel that the people concerned are quite so villainous as it had been suggested to me here. Müller-Braunschweig was pretty objective. He showed no signs of any anti-Semitism, but evidently felt rather German. I suppose his leanings towards idealism draw him a little to that somewhat neglected aspect of Hitlerism. Boehm, on the other hand, was more sceptical about the Government but did show some indications of anti-Semitism, possibly associated with the unfortunate discovery of his unhappy grandmother. It would certainly be absurd to make them responsible for the fact that outer circumstances have unavoidably brought them certain slight advantages. I think Boehm's initial action was very debatable, though there were more good reasons for it than I had been informed of. His subsequent conduct was either externally forced on him by direct communications to the Institute or in other cases was in my opinion very wise in the circumstances. It certainly looks as if he must be given the credit for having saved Psycho-analysis in Germany

from a terrific explosion that threatened early in August. Had it not been for his prompt intervention then, and the very useful connections he happened to have in convenient quarters, there would have been a violent attack at that time which would have probably ended in the dissolution of the Society and Institute and the internment of most of its members in concentration camps. They have absolutely no choice about the *Gleichschaltung*; it is no longer a debatable question. I can understand that Eitingon feels regretful at this necessity though it does not explain his not letting me know about his decision to emigrate to Palestine. I take it that he had been tremendously upset the last time.

"The position in Germany in the immediate future will be as follows. Boehm will be President, Müller-Braunschweig Secretary and there will be no other officials or members of the Training Committee—the last because there is no one else fitted to undertake such work. Schultz Hencke, whom they do not regard as sufficiently reliable in his psycho-analytical work for this purpose, has unfortunately been given a permanent position as representing psychoanalysis in the new Fach Psychotherapie Kommission of the Government, which is conducted by a psychotherapist called Göring from Elbefeld who is a cousin of the famous addict. A definite assurance was given in Germany that the work of our Society and Institute would not be hindered (incidentally, psychoanalytical works are to be found in every book window), and there is no prospect of the use of psychoanalysis being forbidden. It is possible that von Hattinberg's being generally called a psychoanalyst has a little to do with this, though he has taken no step himself in the matter. His attitude in private concerns appears to be definitely friendly. There are now about twenty-one members and associate members who practise and intend to practise in Germany (not counting a few non-practising members). Nine of these twenty-one are lay analysts, a higher percentage even than in England, and there is no reason to anticipate any difficulty about their continuing to practise."

And, as Jones explained to Anna (over-optimistically, in retrospect): there were still more than nine Jewish psychoanalysts left in Berlin. He then concluded his remarks on the Germans as follows:

"My impression on the whole is that it is unduly pessimistic to think that psychoanalysis has been destroyed in Germany. It continues and will continue, though it has been forced to make a fresh start on a lower basis and with mostly fresh material. Unless any reason appears to the contrary I think our wisest course is definitely to support Boehm and Müller-Braunschweig in the honest efforts they are undoubtedly making to salvage the situation."

And there would still be a lot to say and to comment on in respect of Jones's activities on the international front, and on how, in his efforts to find the refugees a home, he would closely follow events not only in Germany and Austria, but also in Paris, Italy, Switzerland, and even in Spain and South Africa, as well as, above all, in the United States (see Jones to A. Freud, 19 September 1933). By 19 September 1933, Jones had already informed Anna of his efforts *"to convince"* Brill, as he put it, *"that a fund should be raised to pay the expenses of colleagues who wish to emigrate to America. I'm sure there is room for it."* But, he had then added, *"provided they do not settle in New York itself"*.

Indeed, note Brill's comments to Jones on 12 May 1933: "We are also very much exercised over the situation in Germany and I must take off my hat to England for her frank attitude towards the situation. I do not know what to do when I am asked by some of those people about coming to settle in this country."

Having told Jones that Dr Cohn (the same Dr Cohn mentioned in Jones's letters to Eitingon of 20 and 23 May 1933), a member of the Berlin Society, had written to him, Brill then goes on, along lines similar to the comments Jones was making at the time in his letters to Anna, to Eitingon, etc. with regard to the financial situation in Great Britain, to say:

"I wrote to Cohn that if he would be willing to settle in another city, there would be a good opportunity for his earning a livelihood here. New York has really enough analysts. In fact I believe we are beginning to be overcrowded. What attitude do you take in a matter of this kind? I feel that we ought to do something for those men who are stranded. I would be very glad to co-operate with you in any way you say. *We may perhaps be able to raise a small fund for them. Take that please with reservations because it is very difficult to get money here."* [emphasis added]

Also important is Jones's letter to Brill dated 20 June 1933 because, among other things, it shows the lucidity with which Jones could foresee the situation in general, including what would happen in the

United States. Having stressed the need for Brill to remain in control of the situation in New York, reminding him that "experience seems to show that analytical societies need a firm ruling hand", and having given the example of what had happened in Berlin after Abraham's death—"nothing but personalities, arguments, insults, etc."—Jones then adds: "This would certainly happen pretty quickly with the New York group which has so little discipline. *As you know, new arrivals in America develop a peculiarly rebellious psychology. It simply means that the son–father complex is still unresolved and keeps being imparted into all sorts of unnecessary situations*" (emphasis added). Jones then follows with some personal comments on Rado, who was causing serious trouble in New York, adding: "There is similar disunion and trouble in the French and Dutch groups and little is left of the Germany one." Then, after having mentioned the British Psycho-Analytical Society and his worries about the destiny of the Viennese, he adds:

> "All the more reason for the few stable elements to sit tight and hold the flag until better times come. This is all the more important in New York, both because there is bound to be a good deal of shifting from Europe to America and because New York must be the fulcrum for the rest of the States. . . . We are having a distressing time over here with the German refugees. I gather that none of them have money enough to go to America, so you haven't the problem. If any of you people are raising funds to help them, possibly some of it might be deflected to psycho-analytical directions. It would be very welcome for the purpose of supporting poor analysts until they get a footing in a new country. We are taking about half a dozen in to England, though I do not know how they will get a living. More are in France and the rest scattered over all sorts of countries. These are hard times, so we have to give the best that is in us."

CHAPTER FOUR

The refugees' American dream

"They could emigrate for instance to Buffalo, Detroit, Cincinnati, St. Louis . . ."

The letters from Jones to Brill on these matters also have to be referred to and quoted. For instance, Jones's letter to Brill dated 23 September 1933 is quite revealing of the strategic policy adopted by him towards those Central European colleagues who at that time were obliged to emigrate to America—and, as we shall see, although this letter confirms his wish to help, it also reflects his worries concerning British psychoanalysis (see chapter eight).

The letter comments on the information Brill had given him on Nunberg, who, according to Jones, was "a sound man and should do well in time anywhere if he can get a decent start". But note Jones's subsequent comments, as they are essential to understanding the shape that emigration to the United States was to take and the way in which this was engineered by Jones and by others, but by Jones particularly, because of his overriding interest in protecting British psychoanalysis. "Would it not be wiser for him and other future emigrants to settle somewhere other than New York?", said Jones of Nunberg's situation (something that Brill had already hinted at in his letter to Jones of the 12 May 1933, when talking of the first German emigrants then applying to go to the United States). He then added:

"They could emigrate for instance to Buffalo, Detroit, Cincinnati, St. Louis where there is a considerable foreign population. Though I expect one shouldn't talk too much nowadays about 'foreign population' because just as in England, the immigration had been so restricted in the last twenty years that the main bulk have been very much acclimatised. It think it is extremely important to try to help more of our German colleagues. . . .

"Many of them are having the greatest difficulties in making a living or finding anywhere to settle. It seems to bear hardest on a number of young and promising workers whose names would probably not be familiar to you. Many of them are married with children, and naturally have no capital on which to draw. In such cases the payment of their passages to America and a sum sufficient to live on for six or twelve months might just save the situation. If there is anything you can do towards raising such a fund I should be very glad to advise in the administration of it. Perhaps we could form a small committee for the purpose, though actually the best informed people, I believe, are the officers of the Association, Anna Freud, van Ophuijsen and myself, who are keeping a list of various movements and what is happening generally."

Having just hinted at the problem, Jones was now explicitly asking for money;[1] and in the above passages we see the beginnings of the emigration operation.

But let us spend a few more words on the American situation and what this meant for the German refugee. As I mentioned earlier (see chapter two, note 2), the immigration of psychoanalysts to the United States began during one of the worst periods in the short history of American psychoanalysis. This, in turn, affected both its administrative and its educational operations and had a strong bearing on the internal politics of the New York Psychoanalytic Society and the newer local groups in Washington, Chicago, and so on (Hale, 1978, 1995; Kurzweil, 1995). Doubtless, it also influenced its relationship with the IPA.[2]

One must also remember the enormous difficulties American psychoanalysis faced in being acknowledged by the American Psychiatric Association, which arose from the problem of lay analysis, which the APA would not recognize—to the point where some American lay analysts received their training in Vienna explicitly in order to circumvent this problem, even though they would then have had to return to the United States to work! I have hinted at these difficulties earlier on in this book, when I mentioned some of the problems encountered by those very first immigrants who had arrived in the United States from Berlin and Vienna some time before the Nazi persecution of the Jews had begun (see again chapter two, note 2). Consider, for example, the difficulties experienced by a man like Hanns Sachs, or the difficulties initially encountered by medical doctors such as Rado, Alexander, and others. Moreover, the American separationist tendencies with regard to the IPV had caused immense irritation to Jones and the British at the time the Americans created the *Psychoanalytic Quarterly*, which then began to compete with Jones's *International Journal of Psycho-Analysis*, greatly infuriating Jones. [See Jones to Freud, 21 June 1932 (Brecht et al., 1993, pp. 704–705); Freud to Jones, 17 June 1932 (p. 703); Jones to Freud, 13 June 1933 (pp. 700–701). See also Jones to A. Freud, 7 March 1934, and the correspondence between Jones and Brill; e.g. Brill to Jones, 3 February 1933, etc.]

I think one ought to insist on the disagreements and the dissensions among the American ranks on the complex issue surrounding lay analysis, as this was to become a major problem for the immigrant analysts (see chapter six). In a very important letter from Brill to Jones dated 6 May 1933, part of which I have already quoted when I related some of the problems encountered by the first immigrants to the United States (see chapter two, note 2), Brill gave an account of the terrible tensions inside the New York Psychoanalytic Society and told of his attempt to solve the problems with the American Psychiatric Association by trying to affiliate American psychoanalysis to the APA, and for psychoanalysis to become one of its sections. This, Brill wrote, would have solved the problems connected to lay analysts, "whose training by the New York Psychoanalytic Society", he said, "had been considered a violation of the Medical Practice Act, of the State of New York by the State Board of Regents under which jurisdiction the New York psychoanalyst MDs are". They had to promise "not to train lay people for the practice of medicine" (Brill to Jones, 12 May 1933).

There is also a letter on these same issues from Anna Freud to Jones, dated 23 August 1933, in which she expressed her anxieties about the fate of lay analysis in America (see also Jones to Eitingon, 24 June 1933). On his part, Jones dived in head-first to solve the problem, as he himself said to Anna Freud, in an effort "to find out [from Brill, obviously] particulars about other States in the union where the law is not so strict" (Jones to A. Freud, 19 September 1933). All these problems, therefore, were further exacerbated by the fact that analysts were now leaving Germany and heading for the United States. Anna, her father, Jones, Eitingon, Brill, van Ophuijsen, and others had to watch the situation very carefully and had to do everything in their power to keep the waters as calm as possible in New York, Washington, Baltimore, Philadelphia, Chicago, and even in San Francisco, where there was no proper psychoanalytic society. Indeed, whilst Jones and his colleagues were doing their utmost to arrange emigration to the United States, for the Berliners first and for the Viennese analysts subsequently, psychoanalysis in America was going through such a critical period that it was in danger of collapsing altogether.

Yet in spite of the difficulties experienced in New York in particular, and in Chicago too, where Alexander and Horney had begun to work (Brill to Jones, 17 November 1933), and notwithstanding the fact that the situation had deteriorated even further by the autumn of 1933 (Brill to Jones, 4 October 1933), or that the problems would last for years—roughly from 1931 to 1940 (Eisold, 1998, p. 875; Hale, 1995)—and were so serious that Jones would refer to the situation as "a psychoanalytical American civil war" (Jones to Brill, 21 November 1933), he and Brill continued to exchange letters on the refugee situation and to discuss the details of those German Jewish analysts who were applying to go to the United States. Yet what the letters Brill and Jones wrote to each other during those months also bear witness to is one of the saddest and most difficult aspects of the emigration problem—the dilemma of deciding what to do with the more difficult and the more troublesome emigrants. The fear that these individuals would further damage the established psychoanalytic societies in America becomes very clear at this point. These letters also unequivocally demonstrate Jones's, Brill's, and others' discriminative tactics in deciding which country would suit these "Sorgenkinder" best.

Indeed, as I have already said in chapter two, note 2, there was the danger that certain refugee analysts, if allowed to go to the United States, would join those factions of the New York Society that were at war with each other. For instance, the New York Society's ageing local founders were in conflict with the younger generations who had trained in Vienna, Berlin, and Budapest during the late 1920s and early 1930s. (Consider, for example, the hostilities involving Brill, Lewin, G. Zilboorg, Rado—as always—Kubie, and so forth: Eisold,

1998; Hale, 1995). Furthermore, Jones and his colleagues were concerned that the refugees might organize themselves into sub-groups, convinced as they were of possessing credentials far superior to those of their indigenous counterparts. Earlier, we saw how a similar situation had developed in Holland—and this, as we will see shortly, was to a certain extent but a prelude to what would take place in America and in Great Britain from 1938 onwards, with the second wave of refugees from Vienna, Budapest, Prague, and so on.

Let us begin with the problem of the lay analyst. Consider, for the moment, Brill's comments in a letter to Jones dated 12 May 1933 regarding the situation of lay analysis in New York and in the United States generally. The tone of this letter is quite far from the optimism he had expressed in a letter to Eitingon not even a year earlier. Brill's statements make even gloomier reading if one relates them to the situation in which so many of the lay analysts from Berlin, Vienna, and Budapest were to find themselves on their arrival to the United States (see Reik, in Brecht et al., 1993, p. 73; see also E. Federn, 1990; Sterba, 1982; Wallerstein, 1998):

> "As a result of the economic depression the medical fraternity has wakened to the competition of psychologists, lay psychoanalysts, etc. etc. and I was told that they are going to stop such practice whenever it conflicts with the Medical Practice Act. Now according to this Act psychoanalysis is a medical practice."

Then, after having explained the rules for lay analysts, he added,

> "I am just as anxious to allow suitable lay persons to enter in our field but I do not believe that we can afford to jeopardize our own position by defying our Medical Practice Act. . . ."[3]

In a letter of 11 August 1933, having discussed at length Nunberg's position and the difficulties he would have to face in New York, Brill gives Jones information on the German immigrant situation, adding: *"So far we have no newcomers to New York. . . . The other analysts who have written to me apparently find it hard to get here. I believe that I could get some money for such a Fund as you suggest"* [he was referring to the fund Jones had proposed be set up]. But note Brill's comments to him on 17 November 1933:

> "Robert Fliess is settling in New York City. *As he prefers to go into research on internal medicine he will not be much of a problem for us. At least that is my hope* [emphasis added]. A fellow by the name of

Homburger (a member of the Vienna group) who wants to settle either in New York or in Boston came to see me. He is supposed to be a good child analyst. He did not impress me much!!" [As the reader might easily guess, this was none other than Eric Erikson!!!]

But now consider the problem posed by those immigrants who were deemed to be excessively difficult or troublesome, apart from what I will specifically discuss concerning two of those *"Sorgenkinder"*—W. Reich and E. Jacobsohn. I think the following letter, from Jones to Brill, dated 2 December 1933, pinpoints just how awkward some of these other *"Sorgenkinder"* could often be considered to be!—and we have already seen what had happened with Reik in the previous months!

"I wish we could do something about Reik, who is on his beam ends. *He wants to come to England but we all object to it because of his rather unscrupulous methods in practice.* On the other hand he could do really valuable work in literary research and I wish very much there were a way of finding him a job, where he could do this, e.g. a research post, assistant librarianship or the like, perhaps at some Hebrew Universities. If you can think of anything in this line it would be doing a service. At the moment Freud is supporting him and his family out of his meagre earnings and this is too bad, for he has to support a good many other people as well. Are you having any luck in getting up a fund for these victims of Hitler? We could make some very good use of it over here in Europe."[4] [emphasis added]

Another problematic case was Simmel's (see Anna Freud's comments, chapter two).

"He was arrested a fortnight ago but luckily got out of prison after a few days. He has some sort of offer to go to Los Angeles but would like the opportunity to learn some English first. He has two wifes [*sic*] and a number of children. If there were any way of supporting him for a few months or of paying his expenses in America, it would be extremely welcome."

Consider also Brill's reply in this instance, bearing in mind the confused state of psychoanalysis, its fragile institutional life in some areas of America, other pressures, and, last but not least, Brill's cautious and suspicious demeanour. It is almost as if one were watching a game of table-tennis, made up of very complex rules, in which the *"Sorgenkinder"* were forced to participate, but which they did not always succeed in winning (Brill to Jones, 15 December 1933):

"We have the same objections to Reik as you have. If he were an MD I would be very glad to have him come, but he is very unpopular with the crowd here, and we are having our troubles with lay analysts so there is no use of taking on more. I shall, however, see what we can do to help him. I talked a number of times of raising a Fund, but nothing has been done because I myself did not do the whole thing, which I suppose I shall have to do. . . . Concerning Simmel, you probably know more than I do."

He then stressed that he knew that Simmel had received 1,000 dollars to support him. He also told Jones that David Brunswick, "a lay analyst in Los Angeles", had written to support Simmel on paper headed "Psychoanalytic Institute of Los Angeles", but, Brill added:

"The fact is that this is the first time I ever heard of it. I do not think there is anyone in Los Angeles whom we could recognize. . . . All I could get was that there are two, beside himself [David Brunswick], some woman and Libin, whom I would not admit to any place on a bet. I wrote to him that I would be very glad to get Simmel here by sending him an invitation from our Institute but I could not assume the responsibility of saying that his Institute is recognized and established when it really is not. Incidentally [and note the detail, which shows the antagonism that was felt by those immigrants who were already established in the United States towards the new arrivals] Rado and others tell me that Simmel always hated [the] English language *and that they do not see how he will ever learn English.*" [emphasis added]

After further comments from which it was clear that he would have preferred Simmel to go to Los Angeles, Brill then added: "I do not think that the whole venture in Los Angeles is worth anything although if Simmel were an adjustable person and spoke the language he could probably make his way there very soon. But I have no confidence in the situation as it is at the present time." (On the problems created by Simmel and Rado, see also chapter two, note 2)

Simmel's complex situation was the subject of some further correspondence, as Brill, in the end, had invited him to come to New

York—a decision that caused endless problems. It is in following these events that we are able to gain further knowledge of the problems the newcomers were capable of creating on their arrival in the United States. On 21 March 1934, in reply to a letter from Jones, who had asked for news of Simmel, "such a good fellow", who was "eating up his savings in Brussels while waiting month after month for an America Visum", which meant "coming back on Freud for money" (Jones to Brill, 7 March 1934), Brill informed his colleague that he would probably be able to collect $2,500 in New York. He then added the following lines, and the reader will note from them that, for at least the third time, Brill was going over the economic predicament of those analysts who were practising in New York and their concerns for the future, because of the new arrivals and the to-ing and fro-ing between one city and another of those refugees who had come some months earlier:

> "It is a very small sum which one can do anything [*sic*]. I was therefore thinking of sending that money to you and letting you use it in any way you see fit. We cannot possibly use that sum to bring over people like Dr. Happel, whom Eitingon recommends very highly to me. Incidentally, she has no idea what the situation here is when she tells Eitingon that all she wants is to settle down in a nice, quiet community and do *Lehranalysen*. The situation in New York is not very favourable for new analysts. Nunberg, I believe, is already here or will be here soon. On account of the situation in Chicago Horney is very anxious to come to New York and settle here. I advised her against it because women analysts find it difficult to get patients, and she could have an excellent practice in Chicago regardless of the Institute. [Indeed, Brill had informed Jones of the problems in Chicago on several occasions.] . . . I would not be surprised a bit if she does not take my advice and comes here. I can tell you from my own knowledge that a great many of our members hardly earn a livelihood."

Brill then asked Jones for some suggestions on the distribution of the $2,500. But note how he ended his letter:

> "The so called 'younger people' have not the slightest interest in anything outside New York and the older crowd could do much more, *but for some reason or other they do not wish to*. Remember that we also asked the Bostonians and the Chicago crowd to help,

thinking that Sachs and Alexander who understand the European situation would be able to do something. So far we have gotten nothing from them." [emphasis added]

Brill concludes his letter to Jones with a list of those who sat on the fund-raising committee: Brill himself, Sachs, Alexander, Rado, D. Feigenbaum, Ph. Lehrman, B. Lewin.

In a previous letter (Jones to Brill, 20 June 1933—see above) in which Jones tried to persuade Brill not to resign from the presidency of the New York Society, Jones had stated that "Experience seems to show that analytical Societies need a firm ruling hand. I can't imagine why they should, but it certainly looks like it!" He had then stressed how important this was, in New York particularly, *"both because there is bound to be a good deal of shifting from Europe to America* and because New York must be the fulcrum of the rest of the States" (emphasis added).

Brill's letter, quoted above, shows just how true Jones's predictions were, and how difficult it was to change human nature even in that situation, especially in the context of the fear and the need to protect one's interests at all costs, circumstances notwithstanding— and the circumstances would, with the passing of time, become even more dramatic and compelling.

Further insight into the tensions and problems on both sides of the Atlantic, and the way in which they interfered with the complexities surrounding the organizing of the emigration operation, is given by Brill—whom Freud, Jones, Eitingon, A. Freud, Oberndorf, and others, all considered to be a nice, generous person, who was perhaps a little naive at times! (See, e.g., Oberndorf to Jones, 6 October 1933: "Brill by nature . . . is very much inclined to be generous and help where he can.") Brill's humorous but disenchanted comments contained in a letter to Jones dated 5 January 1934 reflect his dismay at what was happening in New York and elsewhere, and how vain had been his attempts to save a situation in which people were literally at war with one another. There was Zilboorg, for instance, considered by many to be quite mad; there was Lewin, of course; there were Rado, Horney, Alexander, Nunberg; and more émigré analysts were arriving. In his letter, Brill comments:

"I often ask myself whether psychoanalysis really gives cognition enough to help in the controlling of emotions. My observation, particularly of the Berlin School, does not seem to show this. It would seem to me that they are all on a pregenital level, oral-anal, sadistic."

Some while later, on 11 December 1935, Brill wrote to Jones to explain the reasons for his having decided no longer to take an active part in the vicissitudes of the New York Society. This was principally due to Rado's and others' behaviour and to the fact that they had begun to antagonize some of their European colleagues and fellow refugees. Brill's objections, however, were also being directed both at Jones and at the Viennese establishment, in that their interference had made it impossible for him to have any control over the situation:

"Instead of referring matters to me and following my suggestions when I am supposed to be an authority you people in Europe listen to every Tom, Dick and Harry and allow yourselves to be influenced by them. I would have never had any difficulty in managing the local groups if there had not been all kinds of subterranean and other influences from Vienna and other places to individual members who then came and gave it out as authoritative. Now I am going to withdraw from my active work but I feel that for the future of the psychoanalytic movement there should be rules and regulations which should be implicitly enforced *regardless of whether it will be considered tyrannical or not*." [emphasis added]

But if the above provides the reader with an approximate idea of the difficulties faced by Jones and his colleagues with regard to the émigré situation in the United States during the early 1930s, one must not forget just how difficult the situation was in Europe at that time. It was even difficult to maintain communications with Berlin and Vienna, as letters were being intercepted in Germany and, as a result, had to be sent via Switzerland. In fact, one could only enter Germany and Austria via Switzerland (see Anna Freud to Jones, 19 May 1934). Consider the problems that were encountered in 1934, in organizing the Psychoanalytic Congress in Lucerne; and the situation would become even more fraught in 1936, when it was decided to hold the Congress in Marienbad. Jews from Vienna were by that time forbidden from passing through Germany, and an alternative venue had to be found, bearing in mind that Sigmund Freud was finding it increasingly difficult to move from Vienna and that Anna would have found it impossible to leave him, even for a few days. In a very moving

Rundbrief, dated 22 January 1936, in talking of the Congress that was to take place that year, Anna stressed that she would no longer be able to leave her father's side as he was too ill and totally dependent on her: *"Meine Abvesenheit ist für ihn eine Entbehrung"* [My absence for him is a deprivation]. *"Es ist unmöglich dass ich wegfahre. . . ."* [It is impossible for me to go away. . . .]

That at times there might have been a difference of emphasis in Jones's *"Sorge"* when compared with that of Anna or the Viennese is inevitable. This, after all, is also quite plain from the letters Jones and van Ophuijsen wrote to each other when they first began to discuss the emigration issue, and from which I quoted earlier. In Anna's letters, this difference is evidenced by her anguished and at times familiar tone (although one could hazard that the way in which she wrote reflected her "femininity", so to speak). More importantly, the mood of her letters would appear to be symptomatic of her being a member of the Freud family, particularly when one considers the close relationship between Anna and her father. In this respect, it is interesting to note just how often the term "family" crops up in Anna's letters—as, for example, in her letter to Jones dated 4 March 1934, written at a time when Simmel had found himself stranded and without the financial means to meet his emigration expenses. Help would come from funds collected in Vienna, or, as Anna put it, from "here in the family and around"—which very often meant from her father's pocket, as in the case of Simmel himself, and others too. All in all, I would hazard that the references Anna made to "the family" in her correspondence probably alludes also to the "Jewish family" in its wider sense (remember, for instance, Sigmund Freud's and Anna Freud's comments on the letters exchanged between van Ophuijsen and Westerman-Holstiyn).

It goes without saying, however, that when one attempts to interpret documents, one must not force either their sense or their meaning, and one must always consider them within the overall context in which they are situated—and the situation at the time Anna wrote her letters was extremely complex. If we focus on her correspondence with Jones, we find that there is undoubtedly a difference in emphasis and in perspective between Jones's and Anna's views—and particularly so in the instances where they discussed their psychoanalyst colleagues, where Jones's loyalty was mainly to psychoanalysis as an institution in Germany—as we have already seen when dealing with van Ophuijsen.

Once Eitingon had finally departed for Palestine (see his very contented *Rundbrief*, dated 17 January 1934, from Cap Ferrat; see also his letter to Jones, dated 23 March 1934, from Jerusalem) and Boehm had become President of the Berlin Psychoanalytic Institute,[5] Jones had no hesitation in giving the new President his full support; and his support for Boehm increased as the situation steadily worsened under the pressures of the Nazi regime. For the Nazis had begun to interfere quite resolutely, on ideological grounds, in the activities of the German Psychoanalytic Society, as some of its members were Jewish and as there was doubt as to whether or not psychoanalysis was a Jewish science, in view of the origins of its founder and of many of its major representatives (see Brecht et al., 1993; see also Cocks, 1985). Nevertheless, it has to be noted that in 1934–35 there still seemed to be some room for manoeuvre as far as the suspicions and the accusations of the Nazis were concerned. Jones's ambivalent attitude, therefore, towards the Jewish members of the Berlin Psychoanalytic Institute for what he felt to be their excessive personal anxieties, and his growing impatience with those who voiced these anxieties on their behalf, was induced by the damage he feared this mood would cause to the German Psychoanalytic Society. He was also worried that these sentiments, and the feelings being expressed about Boehm, would eventually be voiced too loudly, as can be seen in his letter to Boehm dated 24 July 1934. One can hardly imagine that either Freud or his daughter would ever have been able to write such lines, even though they were very diplomatic about Boehm, as I said earlier. One may perhaps surmise that Jones was worried that the anger, the anxieties, and the criticisms of the Jewish members of the German Psychoanalytic Society and the Berlin Institute might have encouraged Boehm to side with the Nazis. . . . Jones might therefore have been playing his political card in the most skilful way possible— although even in this case, as previously when dealing with van Ophuijsen, some of Jones's statements sound rather shocking:

> "I will ask you to keep this matter strictly confidential except to Dr. Müller Braunschweig. It is to prepare you for difficulties you may have to encounter at the [Lucerne] Congress. You are not likely to know the strength of the storm of indignation and opposition which is at the present agitating certain circles, especially among the exiles from Germany. This may easily take the form of a personal vote of censure against yourself or even a resolution to exclude the German Society from the International Association.

You will know that I myself regard those emotions and ultra-Jewish attitude very unsympathetically, and it is plain to me that you and your colleagues are being made a dumping-ground for much emotion and resentment which belongs elsewhere and has displaced in your direction. My only concern is for the good of psychoanalysis itself, and I shall defend the view, which I confidently hold, that our actions have been actuated only by the same motive."

And in the months to come, Jones would react with irritation to people such as Happel (see above) for what he thought to be their ultra-Jewish behaviour, which, in his opinion, was damaging psychoanalysis in Germany.

On the other hand Anna, who, although in complete agreement with Jones, was increasingly obliged to underline the fact that in Berlin those paying the highest price—and alone in the circumstances—were none other than the Jews themselves. A very high level of tension was in the air during those terrible months in and around August 1934, when Austria was busy being converted into a fascist state. In a letter to Anna Freud during this period, Jones complained that there was an error in the documents sent from the Viennese in regard to the Lucerne Congress being held in August 1934. Unfortunately, I have been unable to find this letter, but I am able to quote from Anna's reply to it (Anna to Jones, 20 July 1934). Although Anna makes an effort to reassure Jones, her letter also seems to reflect the pressures and the anxieties of those months:

"I do not know whether you attribute to me personally or to us here or to the Vienna group, the intention to claim psychoanalysis for our nation or our race. Whatever you mean, I feel that your remark is quite unjustified. There has never been any question of race or nationality, between us certainly. There is surely no reason for you to defend the international point of view in analysis, against us here."[6]

However, the difference in emphasis is even more clearly evident in a letter from Anna to Jones dated 18 August 1934, where she is also writing on behalf of her father when she comments on a draft copy of the speech with which Jones was to open the Lucerne Congress :

"Your opening address my father and I both thought excellent. We especially like what you said about Ferenczi and about the

combination of analytical and political activities. There is one remark to make though about what concerns the situation in Germany.

"Though essentially it is of course all true, it does not quite
coincide with the actual happenings. The facts are curiously
enough that the Government never made an attack on analysis or
restricted its activity in any way. The 25 members who left did so
because they were Jews, not because they were analysts."[7]

Forced by circumstances, in Lucerne Jones underlined, above all, the
problem of the relationship between psychoanalysis and politics,
emphasizing that they were mutually exclusive—and although he
made no mention of names, he made an obvious reference to Reich
and to the events that had taken place in Berlin generally, whilst also
vaguely touching on the fact that political interference and racial
prejudice were obstructing the work of psychoanalysis.[8] On this specific issue, nevertheless, both Sigmund and Anna Freud would have
been in complete agreement, as one can guess from the passages in
Anna's letter to Jones quoted above.

By the 1936 Marienbad Congress, Jones would find it impossible
not to make explicit mention of the fate that had befallen his Jewish
colleagues in Berlin, who had been forced to resign from the Society.
Nor could he fail to condemn the dictatorial regimes responsible.
(Meanwhile, at the meeting of the Marienbad Congress held on the
activities of the National Societies, it was officially announced that
the Berlin Psychoanalytic Institute had been integrated into the
"Deutsche Institut für Psychologische Forschung und Psychotherapie".) Nevertheless, even in his official speech at the 1938 Congress in
Paris, Jones was still not prepared to mention the Nazi regime by
name, and he went no further than to refer to

> the tremendous shock provoked by the dispersal of the Vienna
> Society . . . the mother of all psychoanalytical societies . . . the very
> birthplace of psychoanalysis . . .", and to talk of "the stupidity and
> destructiveness of Man which had never the less not succeeded on
> this occasion either, in totally destroying Psychoanalysis. [*Interna-
> tional Journal of Psycho-Analysis, 20*, 1939, pp. 122–126]

It is difficult to make any judgement on the choice of words dictated
by Jones's proverbial albeit at times very questionable realism, but it
is probable that Jones's foremost concerns may again have been to

safeguard the future of psychoanalysis as such in Austria and to protect those analysts who were still living there at the time. The former is confirmed by Sterba (1982), according to whom Jones had not approved of his having decided to leave Vienna, and when he had to ask Jones for help, the latter's reply was that he should have stayed in Vienna with Aichhorn, as he, Sterba, was not Jewish and would therefore have been able to play his part in saving psychoanalysis in Austria.

If we continue to follow the differences in perspective between Anna and Jones, we need to note how Jones artfully tried to distance himself from endorsing the behaviour of the German psychoanalyst Klara Happel, to whom Jones had been reluctant to grant direct membership of the IPA—although in his Opening Speech at the Congress held in Marienbad in 1936, Jones would officially acknowledge membership to all Berlin refugees. Some time previously, Happel had resigned in protest against the way in which non-German and non-Jewish psychoanalysts had conducted themselves with respect to their Jewish colleagues in 1933. As Jones put it in a letter to Anna dated 25 February 1935: "She is the only Jew in Germany who finds it necessary to isolate herself from her colleagues on this ground"— referring to the fact that Happel had not liked "the way in which members of the German society treated their Jewish colleagues two years before"—"And to support her officially looks rather like subscribing to a condemnation of the Germany society. I am naturally loath to do this unless there is a serious reason for it. Especially so since I suspect that her grounds are distinctly subjective. . . ."

And one cannot fail to understand the reasons for Anna having held a quite different view on the matter, as can be seen in her reply to Jones dated 13 March 1935:

"Now about Frau Happel. If she thinks still that she cannot go back in the German group, I think we should grant her the direct membership. I would say that every Jewish analyst, who has to live in a group, where circumstances restrict his full right as a member, would have a right to it."

That, as usual, Jones had in mind the interests of the International Association itself, and that this precluded him from becoming involved in racial discrimination at any level, is beyond doubt. Yet in a letter to Anna, written in October 1935, which spoke of the need to try to safeguard the circulation of psychoanalytic texts in Germany, he made the following comment on the decisions that were being taken by Boehm in Berlin:

"About the Jewish members I think that his [Boehm's] suggestion is the only possible one, for it would surely not be sensible to make the gesture (which would impress nobody) of dissolving the whole Society on the ground that the Government makes a foolish racial distinction."

It must also be noted that, to the last, Jones would continue in his attempts to save the situation. To this end, he also held one final meeting with Göring's nephew at which Brill, Boehm, and Müller-Braunschweig were also present. This meeting he would later describe in a letter to Anna dated 20 July 1936.[9]

In spite of these tactical moves and ambiguities, Jones nevertheless did understand the pressures Anna was under, and he continued to lend an ear to her anxieties. Of course, her worries had begun some time earlier, as can be seen in her letter to Jones on 8 November 1935, in which she denounced, in no uncertain terms, Boehm's failure to keep to his agreement to work out a compromise as and where necessary. In this letter Anna asked Jones to return to Berlin so that he could see the situation for himself because, in view of the way things were turning out, it could well mean that Jewish members would be definitively excluded from the Society (as indeed turned out to be the case). She also told him that the Jewish members were being pursued by the police and that they were therefore "in a most difficult and even dangerous position".

In another letter to Jones, written a few days later (13 November), Anna again wrote along similar lines:

"I had a telephone call last night from the Jewish members in Berlin. They naturally are very excited and feel very uncertain. Evidently their 'paradise' in the last half year, has not been quite as ideal as Boehm described it."

This letter, like many of the others exchanged during this period, must be seen in the light of the increasingly gloomy future facing the Berlin Institute at that time. Jones's worried letters to Brill dated 13 November 1935 and 29 November 1935 testify to this; in the latter he informs his colleague that he has to go to Berlin because there is the danger that the German Society "may dissolve or secede from the

IPA". In the weeks that followed, Edith Jacobsohn was arrested (see chapter five), and at the beginning of December 1935 the Jewish members of the Berlin Institute were finally be obliged to resign and the Berlin Institute was absorbed into the neo-Nazi "Deutsche Institut für Psychologische Forschung und Psychotherapie" run by Göring's nephew, with Boehm as its Secretary, as already mentioned.

Judging from the documents in the Archives of the British Psycho-Analytical Society, the final collapse of the Berlin Institute[10] would seem to mark a period of relative calm—considering the circumstances—in matters concerning emigration. If one examines the documents available for the years 1934 and 1935, very little seems to have taken place on this front: apart from the letters Brill wrote to Jones on the situation in the United States and the resettlement of E. Schilder, van Ophuijsen, and others, there is hardly any documentation on the emigration of German or other analysts for these years. Nothing else very serious happened during this period, and certainly nothing comparable to the anxieties and the problems experienced by Jones and his friends during the first months of 1933. There were, of course, sporadic problems, such as the question of Dr Staub, whom Jones did not like and about whom he wrote to Eitingon on 21 March 1935, as well as the difficulties caused by Reich, whom Brill did not want in America, as he wrote to Jones on 7 June 1934: "what you write about Reich I knew in a way and I told Wechsler about it, and the Jews have so much trouble already with radicals that we would not want him here." To Reich and all the problems connected with him and symbolized by his views and activities, I return in chapter seven of this book, but we turn to Jacobsohn in the next chapter.

CHAPTER FIVE

The final blow

Edith Jacobsohn
and the expulsion of Jewish analysts
from the Berlin Psychoanalytic Institute

At the end of 1935, the arrest of Edith Jacobsohn—who was at that time a militant left-winger belonging to a group of politically involved analysts led by Otto Fenichel[1]—by the secret police in Berlin would seem to have thrown the situation into turmoil once again. Writing to Brill, Jones assured him that he would do "everything possible to help in the situation, but we have to *be extremely careful because of the Society*"—his usual stance, as we have seen in other instances. Jones then added:

> "It looks by the way as if the German Society will soon be forced to expel all of its Jewish members. The situation for Jews in Germany is a great deal worse than any of the newspaper reports admit. It is really terrible. If you have any funds that could be used to help the German Jewish analysts I could make good use of it."

In response, Brill tried to do something immediately, and on 11 December 1935 he wrote to Jones, saying: "By this time you will have received the $1,000 and I hope you will be able to do something for Edith Jacobsohn. Like you I feel very much discouraged about the German Society, but what can we do?"

Jones had originally opposed the resignation of the Jews from the Berlin Institute, because he had feared that it would have confirmed the Nazis' belief that psychoanalysis had a Jewish ideology at its core, as I have already mentioned. Because of the enormous tensions that had arisen inside the Berlin Institute, Boehm had invited Jones to Berlin. Jones chaired the famous meeting held at the Berlin Institute (Brecht et al., 1993; Lockot, 1985, 1994), the result of which was the voluntary resignation of its Jewish members. This course of action had been suggested by Jones himself, according to the long report written by Boehm on these events (Brecht et al., 1993, pp. 128–140; Cocks, 1985; Lockot, 1985, 1994).[2]

On 25 November 1935, Anna wrote to Jones with her comments on a letter that Boehm had written to Jones, which Jones had forwarded on to her. In his letter, Boehm had described the tensions inside the Institute on the issue of its Jewish members, and he had also pointed out that the Berlin Institute had become excessively politicized, and that this would have aroused the suspicions of the Nazis. Notwithstanding her doubts about Boehm, in her letter to Jones of 25 November, Anna had replied: "*Sachlich fürchte ich hat er recht*" [From a practical point of view, he is right, I fear]. She then informed Jones that Fenichel was exceedingly angry because he was of the impression that Jones was overly sympathetic to what Fenichel considered to be Boehm's personal anxieties. Fenichel wanted Jones to pass through Vienna so that he could show him some important documents and declarations from some their colleagues in Berlin on Boehm. Anna thought that Jones would have been too tired to stop over.[3]

In this context, Jones wrote to Anna on 2 December, giving an account of the terrible situation of the Jews and the other analysts in Berlin, adding that they were under constant threat and that this had affected the whole Institute. He also told Anna of how he had been unsuccessful in his efforts to have these analysts remain inside the Berlin Institute, but that he had managed to preserve the German Psychoanalytic Association inside the IPA. He also gave Anna an account of Boehm's "faults as a person and as a leader, although there was nobody who could replace him!" He assured her that Boehm was not anti-Semitic, but he added that Müller-Braunschweig "definitively was anti-Semitic" and was "toying with the idea of combining a philosophy of psychoanalysis with a quasi theological view of *Nazisocialismus*". "I suppose the Jews will now emigrate", Jones concluded. In this letter he also told Anna of the very positive impression

E. Rosenfeld had made on him, and he informed her that he felt R. Benedek to be insincere.

In Anna's and Eitingon's replies to Jones's report of his visit to Berlin one is able to observe that both Anna and Eitingon were rather more distressed than was Jones by the predicament of their Jewish colleagues and friends at the time, and they were also much more explicit and anxious in their concerns for the future of their Jewish colleagues, as obviously they both identified very deeply with their plight. In her letter to Jones of 9 December 1935, after having commented on Müller-Braunschweig's ideas, which sounded to her pretty much National Socialist, and after having praised E. Rosenfeld's capacity to cope, Anna then anxiously asked Jones:

"Eines vor allem konnte ich nicht herauslesen. Haben die jüdischen Mitglieder auch jetzt noch weiter das Recht, die Sitzungen mitzumachen und sich zu beteiligen oder ist der jetzt notwendige Auszug ein Tatsächlicher."

[There is one thing I could not understand very clearly. Can the Jewish members even now have the right to participate in the meetings of the Society, or to play their part in it, or is emigration now a *fait accompli.*]

On 18 December, Eitingon wrote to Jones, saying that he agreed with his judgement of Müller-Braunschweig: *"Er wird bestimmt sehr leicht bereit sein sich auch mit der Nazi Weltanschauung zu identifizieren."* [He will be sure to identify himself very easily with the Nazi *Weltanschauung*] . . . because he was an opportunist. Boehm was better but . . . incapable of facing the difficult situation. Eitingon then asked Jones anxiously, as Anna Freud had also done: *"Was wird nun das Schicksal der ausgetretenen jüdischen Mitglieder sein?"* [What will now be the fate of those Jewish Analysts who have left the Institute?]

Having asked for news of E. Rosenfeld, Eitingon mention Sala Kempner, one of his oldest friends, and said that he was worried because she did not know where to go. He then commented on Therese Benedek, saying that she was a difficult woman, although a good analyst.

Jones wrote to Brill in his usual style on the 24 December 1936, thanking him for the money he had provided, adding,

"Edith Jacobsohn is unfortunately still in prison, *Untersuchungshaft* [pending trial]. The Jewish members of the Berlin Society have had to secede. Several of them are going to try to stay in Germany but many of them are looking for places elsewhere. I saw two of them in London yesterday. Alexander is securing a position at the Chicago Institute for Therese Benedek so that is one. I hear that Klara Happel is also going to America but do not know where."

And so the second wave of German refugees had begun, along with their search for a new home, in Britain, in the United States, or in whatever part of the globe it was possible to put down new roots.

Some time later Anna wrote to tell Jones that Boehm had paid her a visit. She had spoken with him for four hours, and Boehm had tried to explain what had happened, and the situation in Berlin and in Germany as a whole. He had also come to say goodbye. It is interesting that although Anna was seeking Jones's opinion of this meeting, her judgement of Boehm was not totally negative. She thought that his plans to preserve psychoanalysis in those circumstances, under a false name and working with other psychotherapists in the Institute run by Göring, was rather uncertain:

"Ich glaube er schwankt in sich selber ob er damit der Analyse eine Dienst leistet oder nur den dort lebenden Analitiker. Er selber ist so sehr Analytiker dass er sich wohl auch bei einer veränderten Existenz nicht mehr ändern wird."

[I think he himself is uncertain whether he is doing a service to Analysis itself or only to the local analysts. He is so analytic in his thinking that even acting under a different name and being different will not mean that he will change again.]

Having pointed out that Boehm was afraid of Müller-Braunschweig, that she thought he would not succeed in persuading the other psychotherapists to consider analysis seriously, and that he would be the only one to ask for direct membership to the IPA, Anna concluded by stressing that Boehm had spoken in a very dignified way. . . .

But probably the most revealing comments on the Berlin Institute's new home—and, therefore, on German psychoanalysis—are contained in a letter Anna wrote to Jones a few months later, touching on a variety of issues, including Boehm and the new Institute. Having told Jones that Boehm had paid another visit and that, on her father's invitation, he had spoken to the Board of Directors of the Vienna Society, she pointed out to Jones that Boehm was very unsure as to whether he would succeed in his plans. However, everything was now official, and psychoanalysis no longer had to fear from outsiders, the "*Leiter*" (or the "Leader", as she called Göring) of the new Institute notwithstanding.

In fact, the new Institute appeared to be without any proper leadership, at least as far as ideas were concerned, and Göring had made a very aggressive first speech. She then added: "Anyway Boehm will start his training course and see how far he can go without being disturbed. My father altogether '*hat ihn sehr ermutigt*', has supported him very much." "Boehm", Anna said, "fears his own weakness and probably that of his colleagues. But perhaps he will cope."

Yet if one looks at the situation as a whole, Jones and his friends—with the exception of van Ophuijsen, Eitingon, and others who were more exposed to Boehm's and his colleagues' conduct—were rather over-optimistic about Boehm, particularly at the beginning. One might also say that Jones's conduct was somewhat confusing, if one considers his overall views on the future of Germany and Austria, his comments to Brill on 20 May 1933 (see chapter two), and his stance until it was all too obvious that the situation had really taken a turn for the worse. It would appear that Jones had a certain amount of support from Freud and his followers in his endeavours to defend German psychoanalysis as an institution,[4] and it must be taken for granted that he would have discussed the whole issue both with Sigmund Freud and with Anna during his visit to Vienna in May 1935,[5] and on other occasions too. Nevertheless, to my mind, Jones's need to view the persecution of Jewish analysts as being separate from the institutional problems of psychoanalysis, so as to preserve his vision of psychoanalysis as being a science and therefore neutral, is indicative of just how limiting it is, not to mention dangerous, for one to want to harbour such convictions. After all, even Jones and the Freud family would have agreed that the way in which psychoanalysis and its institutions survived in Germany, particularly in the period from 1936 until the end of the Second World War, had analogies with what Benda, as early as 1927, had written in his famous book, *La trahison des clercs*. Jones's questionable attitude, and the dangerous tactics he would employ at times in the name of political realism, are reminiscent of certain aspects of the policy of appeasement adopted by Neville Chamberlain in his dealings with Hitler. Nevertheless, in my view, to infer from Jones's contradictory statements that he was anti-Semitic or that he openly and wholeheartedly supported the Nazi regime as such, would go against all historical evidence.

The events that followed are well known. Notwithstanding the exceptional difficulties in obtaining work permits and in finding work in Great Britain, at the 1936 Marienbad Congress Jones was able to announce that Britain had offered asylum to 15 or 16 analysts from Berlin. A similar number of psychoanalysts had arrived from Berlin during the first wave of departures in 1933, which meant that there were now 26 German analysts living in Great Britain.

During the following very tense year, Jones, Anna, and their friends obviously continued in their efforts to help the psychoanalysts who had arrived from Austria and Germany. In a letter from Jones to Eitingon dated 24 February 1937 we learn that even S. Bernfeld and his wife had finally arrived in London, and that they were looking for help (Steiner, in preparation). "Bernfeld is spending now two or three months in London while waiting to overcome the difficulties of obtaining a visa to go to America", wrote Jones to Eitingon. Bernfeld eventually managed to emigrate to the United States.

But it is not until February–March 1938 that we find Jones once again back in the midst of the action and expressing his "*Sorge*" for his "*Sorgenkinder*". This time, however, as he himself would admit in his opening speech at the Paris Congress on 1 August 1938, the tragic events that were then unfolding had not taken either him or the others by surprise. Given the situation they had experienced in Berlin, Jones and his colleagues were now better equipped to deal with this new wave of émigrés, all desperately seeking somewhere to take refuge.

All during 1937 contact was kept with Vienna and visits were exchanged between Vienna and London to iron out the complex theoretical differences between the more orthodox Freudians and those psychoanalysts in London who had been influenced by the work of Melanie Klein. Although these meetings did not bring any solutions, during them Jones had the opportunity of getting to know some of the psychoanalysts he would be helping shortly thereafter—E. and G. Bibring, M. Balint, E. Kris,[6] and R. and J. Wälder are just a few of the people he met who were outside Freud's and his daughter's immediate circle of hand-picked candidates. This was, to some extent, a general inspection of sorts; they were all individually assessed by Jones, as can be seen from his letters to Anna in this period—and, in a few cases at least, Jones would use this information as soon as he was required to intervene and make a decision about various people.

During the early months of 1937, a period when apprehensions had begun to subside—although there was still the feeling of everything having been put on hold[7]—both Anna and Sigmund Freud wrote Jones some of their most revealing and interesting letters. Anna Freud's first letter to Jones of this period, dated 9 February 1937, is a very diplomatic one; one may want to interpret this as an attempt on Anna's part—not that unconsciously, perhaps—to be as gentle and as friendly as she could be towards Klein. She may possibly have had in mind the fact that she could well have to emigrate to Britain in the not too distant future, and that they would then have to work in the same city—but I do not wish to surmise here, nor force the text of this letter. It is interesting to note, though, that she wrote of her new experiment with the Jackson Nursery, which she and Dorothy Burlingham had just opened (Young-Bruehl, 1988). She informed Jones that she had just opened what in this letter she called the *Kinderheim* and that it had 12 children, the youngest of whom was six months old, and the oldest two and a half years old, she stressed how much she would learn, now that she had the opportunity to observe quietly in detail all aspects of development, including the distortions that could lead to disturbances. Anna then added:

> *"Federn teilt mir gerade mit dass Frau Klein im Frühjahr nach Wien kommen wird. Ich hoffe, sie wird sich auch für das neue Heim interessieren und freu mich jedenfalls, es ihr zeigen zu können."*

> [(P.) Federn told me that Frau Klein will come to Vienna in the spring. I hope she will be interested in the new *Kinderheim*. In any case I would be happy to show it to her.]

On 2 March 1937, Freud informs Jones of his researches and writings on Moses. Indeed, his book, entitled *Moses ein Aegypter*—a fragment of a larger work, which had occupied him for three years—was going to be published in *Imago*. Freud then continues with a very gloomy picture of the situation in Austria. Here, probably for the first time, we can sense the tragedy that was soon to unfold, and which would force Freud and his family to emigrate. The pessimism expressed here is even more significant if one compares it with some of his letters to Jones and others on the political situation in Austria and on the situation of the Jews in earlier years:

> "Our political situation seems to become more and more gloomy. The invasions of the Nazi can probably not be checked; the consequences are disastrous for analysis as well. The only hope remaining is that one will not live to see it oneself. The situation is similar

to that in 1683, when the Turks were outside Vienna. At that time military reinforcements came over the Kahlenberg, today nothing like that is to be expected. And English man has already discovered that they have to defend their border on the Rhine. He should have said: outside Vienna. If our city falls, then the Prussian barbarians will swamp Europe. Unfortunately the power that has hitherto protected us, Mussolini, now seems to be giving Germany a free hand. I should like to live in England like Ernst, and travel to Rome like you."

For Jones, this may have been the first clear indication that Freud wished to escape from what he called the "Prussian barbarians" and end his days in Britain.

CHAPTER SIX

To die in freedom

The history of the exodus from Vienna is already well documented (Gay, 1988; Jones, 1957; Mühlleitner & Reichmayr,
1995), and the letters exchanged between Anna Freud and
Ernest Jones and others do not add anything that we do not already
know about Jones's contacts with the Home Office, the Foreign Office,
the Austrian Embassy in London, and the Embassies of many other
countries, in his effort to obtain resident permits for Freud, his family,
and his close collaborators.[1] We also know of the help that was given
the Freuds by Marie Bonaparte and others. The letters also tell us that
Jones travelled to Vienna at the last possible moment to help Freud
and his family. Anna's letters also speak about Freud's illness and his
worsening state of health (see Anna to Jones, 25 January 1938)—
something about which Jones (1957) and others also wrote. Yet what
Anna Freud and Ernest Jones and others wrote to each other during
the months between February and the end of May and the beginning
of June 1938, when Freud and nearly all his relatives and colleagues
managed to leave Vienna, allows us to catch and feel more directly
the internal, private moments and vicissitudes of this tragic event. It
is as if we could experience the anxieties, the personal crises, the
political manoeuvres and even manipulations, and even be able to

witness some aspects of the human generosity of Anna, Jones, and their friends—that capacity to use the hidden resources of one's own character which, when it exists, seems to emerge and to be mobilized only in certain crucial circumstances of one's life.

Furthermore, the documents I will use will allow us to understand better some of the details of this "new diaspora", which, at times, will appear to be extremely painful and even humiliating, as far as the emigration both to England but also to the United States and other countries was concerned. Indeed, it is only in a dramatic letter from Anna to Jones dated 20 February 1938 that one is able to read of the panic reigning in Vienna as a result of the sudden change in the political situation there. Anna was reassuring in her assessment of the situation, nonetheless:

"Wir machen die Panik nicht mit. Es ist zu früh, man kann die Folgen des Geschehenen noch nicht voll beurteilen."

[We are not in agreement with the panic of the others. It is still too early to judge exactly what is taking place.]

However, it should be borne in mind that this letter was written from the clinic where Anna had accompanied Freud, where he was about to undergo one of the more painful of his many operations—yet another, after the one in January 1938. At times one has the distinct impression that certain of her appraisals of the political situation might have been overly influenced by her need to avoid feeling so much anguish all in one go. Consider, for instance, the sad, worried tones of her letter to Jones dated 25 January 1938, almost a month before the letter above. In this earlier letter she wrote about her father's operation, and after having told Jones how much her father and the family had suffered during the two days they had spent in the Sanatorium where he had been operated, she added that the situation was not improving and that, according to the diagnosis, "Es ist nicht ausgeschlossen, dass die Operation nicht radikal genug war und dass man vielleicht nächste Woche noch eine Nachoperation machen wird" [It is not excluded that the operation has not been radical enough and that probably next week another operation will be performed]. (See also Molnar, 1992.)[2]

Incidentally, in this same letter, dated 25 January 1938, Anna talks of the exchange of lectures being organized between Vienna and London—Bibring, Kris, and Klein had been expected to participate, but "*Frau Klein*" had now cancelled her lecture because of ill health. She then gives her opinion of Paul Federn's work, about which Jones had asked her in a previous letter, dated 17 January 1938:

> "*Die Frage von Federns Arbeiten ist eine sehr schwierige. Zu meiner Bescheinigung muss ich sagen dass es uns allen mit dem Verständniss nicht anders geht als Du es beschreibst. Für Federn is es eine schwere Krankung besonders dass mein Vater sich so ablehnend verhält.*"

> [The question concerning Federn's work is a very difficult one to be answered properly. We all have the same feeling concerning the possibility of understanding him as you describe in your letter, I must say. Federn feels very disturbed that my father behaves in such a passive way towards his work.]

Anna claimed that she had tried several times to understand "*was er meint*" [what he means], but that she had not succeeded. The same had happened to Princess Bonaparte. Nevertheless, she added, Federn was "a good observer in clinical matters. It was obvious that he did not succeed in expressing what he meant."

Why have I quoted these statements?—the reader may well ask. Earlier in this book, I spoke of Federn's loyalty to Freud (see chapter two, note 2), and also of the difficulties the immigrants experienced with their colleagues in the various Institutions to which they were eventually admitted, the internal battles between analysts, and so on—not to mention all the socio-political and economic problems they were forced to contend with in their host countries. Furthermore, we have to bear in mind that, no matter where the refugee analysts were from—Austria, Germany, Holland, Hungary, or any other country for that matter—the way in which they were chosen very much depended on the personal sympathies or the antipathies of the decision-takers. Moreover, these likes, and dislikes, and so forth would, on the whole, determine an émigré analyst's final place of refuge, as it would his personal and professional future developments—and it is therefore probable that Jones had made enquiries of Federn as he was rather uncertain about him and might have had in mind that the latter might express a wish to emigrate to Britain.

The sudden change in the socio-political situation following Austria's *Anschluss* with Germany on 13 February 1938 was to shake Anna violently out of her understandable uncertainty about the existential and professional fate of psychoanalysis in Austria and—as can be seen from her letters—strengthen even further the passionate and intensely moving "*Sorge*" she felt for her family, her relatives, and her colleagues.

The tone of Anna's letters alters suddenly—or, to be more precise, she now seems to write with an intensity that had not always been obvious a few years earlier, at the time the emigration of analysts from Berlin was first being discussed. This becomes even more evident when one compares the feelings she expresses in these letters with Jones's apparent sense of detachment. Prudent, understanding, and profoundly concerned was how we often saw her at the time a solution was being sought for the Berliners. But now that the Viennese analysts, and, more importantly, her own family, were being directly threatened, Anna cuts an anguished and pathetic figure. This becomes even clearer if we consider Anna's "*Sorge*" (and Jones's too) in the context of all the cultural, administrative, and political prejudices, tensions, and arguments that were plaguing the international movement of psychoanalysis during that period—and the problem of where one was to send the refugees was one of the main issues.

The choices for where to send the refugees were rather restricted during those terrible months. France, the Netherlands, and Switzerland were still available in Europe, but the situation even in those countries was becoming more and more difficult. And then, of course, there was Great Britain . . . ! But there were serious problems and restrictions even in London.

What about the United States and other countries overseas, not to mention South America? Particularly as far as the United States was concerned, things did not look very easy there either for the potential refugees.

Let us first look at how Jones attempted to solve these problems. It has to be said, however, that to isolate his endeavours from Anna's is only a necessary expedient to provide the reader with a clearer idea of events, for many of the decisions he made and many of the problems he had to face, particularly in relation to the United States, were identical to those Anna had to contend with in her capacity as Secretary of the ITC (International Training Committee) of the IPA.

In order to provide the reader with as complete a picture as possible and better to understand the more or less hidden intentions and reasons behind Jones's efforts and decisions to help not only Freud and his family, but the Viennese and other Central European psychoanalysts, as evident in his correspondence with Anna, I will also have to focus in particular on a certain number of letters and documents of American psychoanalysts to him, to Anna, and to others which narrate the events then taking place within American psychoanalysis.

Indeed, as in 1933–35 (see chapter four), because of its size the United States initially seemed to Jones and to Anna Freud the country most likely to accept the refugees. It had enormous potential for economic development, and thus—notwithstanding the fact that it was still feeling, like other countries throughout the world, the after-effects of the Great Depression—it seemed to offer the refugees the most opportunities. However, as I mentioned earlier, the state of American psychoanalysis was in permanent chaos, both in terms of its relationship with the IPA and as far as its internal problems were concerned. The recognized psychoanalytic societies in the United States were few and far between, and quite a number of them were in conflict one with the other!

A few years had passed since the early difficulties encountered by Jones, Anna, and others in trying to help the Berlin refugees, but now, when due to the impending war the situation in the Nazi-occupied countries was much more serious than it had been back in 1933 and when even Vienna had to be evacuated by the Jewish psychoanalysts (and very soon the same would happen in Budapest, Prague, etc.), as if they were confronted with a tragic *déjà vu*, this new wave of emigrants and their helpers had to face a number of extremely complicated issues which seemed to be repeating themselves!

The whole strategy of the migration of the Viennese and other Central European psychoanalysts, as well as Jones's and the others' efforts to help them, has to be understood, therefore, while bearing in mind this complex scenario.

There is no doubt that Jones, in asking immediately for new funds, as he had done in the early 1930s, and in putting pressure on the Americans to raise their entry quotas for both medically but also *non-medically* qualified analysts, had obviously in mind the particular situation of the British Psycho-Analytical Society, which he was trying to protect again, and which had already been "germanized" by the arrival of many members of the Berlin Psychoanalytic Society, in addition to having to face the more general institutional and financial difficulties related to the immigration rules of Great Britain during those years as far as the Jews were concerned. Again, something that we have already seen during the early 1930s. . . . But, as I will try to show in a while, the immigration rules even of the United States were not so generous. Here again we have to think of what had already happened with the first wave of emigrants from Berlin. As will emerge from the documents I cite, there were, furthermore, some specific problems raised by the emigration of Viennese analysts— particularly *lay analysts*—to the United States. One does not need to recall Freud's hypotheses concerning the repetition compulsion to understand how difficult the situation was.

But in order to make things clearer, let us for the moment concentrate more specifically on all the issues I have mentioned concerning the United States and the situation, therefore, with which Jones, Anna Freud, and others had to contend in this respect. Having said this, I must also add that it is, of course, impossible to give an account of all that had gone on in the United States as far as psychoanalysis was concerned in the years between 1933 and 1937–38. Apart from the general literature that I have quoted, the reader must again recall what I have already mentioned about Rado's behaviour and all the problems related to it, which can give at least a partial idea of the situation of psychoanalysis in America during the 1930s and the difficulties related also to the first wave of migrants from Berlin. (See chapter two, note 2, and chapter five, note 5, as well as, more generally, chapter four.)

As the emigration of refugees from Austria, Hungary, Holland, and France during the late 1930s took place more or less at the same time as the events I want to touch upon here, I think it is necessary that we go back two years, to an event that was particularly significant, in as much as it served to muddy the already cloudy waters: the Marienbad Congress of 1936. Important matters were discussed at this Congress, including the fate of the IPA's educational and administrative systems. The deliberations on these particular issues were not at all well received by the American psychoanalytic bodies, who were already pressing for independence from the IPA. This caused their members to revolt and to threaten to break away from the IPA. The Americans objected to the fact that the Europeans had a right to exert control over the internal affairs of their Societies, and particularly that training standards were being dictated to them by the IPA. This was not, of course, a promising sign, and it showed little of the enthusiasm or the willingness with which it was hoped the

United States would receive these new refugees from Vienna, Buda-
pest, and Germany, as well as from France, where many from
Germany had taken temporary refuge during the 1930s, and from
Britain, where others had gone in the hope of obtaining a visa to the
United States.

Again, it is from Brill's letters that one is able truly to appreciate
the situation. By this time, Brill had virtually retired, and, as he
claimed in a letter to Jones written in March 1938, he had not "attended any of the New York Society meetings for about two years".
But in his usual generous and caring way he expressed his concern for
what was taking place in Austria, saying, "The situation in Austria
has naturally been on my mind, and like you I hope that things are
not as bad as they seem. The Professor has repeatedly told me that
he would never leave Vienna unless the Nazis got there." Brill then
began to provide Jones with an account of the situation as it stood in
America. I have already used parts of this letter, when I spoke of Rado
and his attempt to break away from the IPA and develop his own
views—which would eventually lead him to abandon the New York
Psychoanalytic Society and establish the Columbia Center for Psychoanalysis (see chapter two, note 2). But it is in the fol-lowing comments
that Brill very ably manages to convey the sense of what was going on
in New York, and in the United States generally:[3]

> "I naturally heard of a lot of the discussions which resulted in the
> letters that you received from Daniels. Again I am glad that I was
> not there because it was related to me that on one occasion
> Zilboorg got up and referred to all the Europeans as S.O.B.'s [sons
> of bitches]. I told my informers that Lewin [the President of the
> New York Society] and the Society should be ashamed of them-
> selves for allowing such things. It was then reported to me that
> there was considerable palaver about it, but officially I do not
> suppose anything was done."

Who was Daniels, and what was Brill referring to? In order to understand his comments, I have to remind the reader that at the 1934
Lucerne Congress, Jones (1957, p. 376), faced with the problem of
the German refugees and under pressure from van Ophuijsen and
Eitingon in particular, had decided to accept a proposal put forward
by the latter whereby the Central Executive would grant "direct"
membership of the IPA to those analysts who were forced to leave

their country for political reasons,[4] including those Austrian and Hungarian analysts who were now seeking refuge elsewhere. To quote from Jones's own words:

> "Without membership they had no privileges of subscribing to the Official Organs and attending the scientific meetings of any other Society not to speak of the moral isolation of having no contact with their colleagues. With a somewhat heavy heart I felt obliged to act on this and so issued membership on the lines of the "Nansen passport" the League of Nations was just issuing to refugees who had been deprived of their passports and so were stateless, to a number of analysts, including some lay analysts who were emigrating to America. This was resented there as foreign interference with American institutions, and at the following congress in Paris in 1938 we were faced with a most formidable document from America. This announced that the American Psychoanalytic Association, which comprises all the branches there, would be willing to "consider affiliation" to the International Associations on three conditions: that the International Training Commission, which they maintained was a superfluous institution that interfered with internal affairs in America, be abolished; that the "free floating membership" be withdrawn from analysts settling in America; and that the International Association should meet for specific purposes only and be deprived of all its administrative functions." [Jones, 1957, p. 322]

But in order to have a better understanding of the situation, one must consider the reasons why the New York Psychoanalytic Society rebelled so violently against the IPA. I believe that their reaction reflected, in part, the general unease that was increasingly being felt within the American psychoanalytic establishment itself. Earlier, I spoke of the political manoeuvring during 1934–35 of Rado—who had been the Secretary of the ITC for a number of years—and of his friends, in relation to the role they believed the ITC should have played (see again, chapter two, note 2). And the extent of the crisis in the relationship between the old and the new continents at the time is shown in an extract from a letter Anna wrote to Jones on 27 February 1936:

> *"Ich weiss nicht, wie ernst du die Frage nimmst, dass wir einen amerikanischen Zentral Präsidenten bekommen könnten. Der Gedanke scheint*

mir völlig unausdenkbar. Die europäische Analyse, hat schliesslich ein Recht auf ihre eigene Entwicklung und darf nicht zu einem Anhangel der amerikanischen Bewegung werden."

[I don't know how seriously you take the matter regarding the fact that we might get an American President of the IPA. I find this completely unthinkable. European psychoanalysis has the right to autonomous development and it must not become an appendage of the American psychoanalytic movement.]

Anna's statement is all the more significant when one considers what took place shortly afterwards, once the many Viennese who had succeeded in emigrating to America had found their feet and established themselves there! Something very specific had happened at Marienbad in 1936.

At one point the New York Psychoanalytic Society accused Eitingon, E. Glover, Anna Freud (indirectly, of course), and even Jones, as President of the IPA—the whole European establishment, in other words—of having misrepresented, at the Marienbad Congress, their views on the ITC. At the previous Congress held in Lucerne in 1934, they had wanted the ITC to be more or less dissolved, and, through Rado, they had asked to have more of an autonomous role with regard to Committee decisions. What had now particularly infuriated them was the Marienbad report, published in 1937.[5]

In a long and angry letter to Jones dated 17 June 1937, G. E. Daniels, the then Secretary of the New York Psychoanalytic Association, wrote to say that the report had attributed to Rado views that had, in reality, been those of the New York Society. Incidentally, this letter also gives a full account of the views held by the New York Psychoanalytic Association on the ITC, going back to 1934. Daniels pointed out that Rado had not been present at the Marienbad Congress, and the only person to have been authorized to represent the views of the New York Society, and which Eitingon had rather heavily criticized, had been Oberndorf. The New York Society had asked for "unrestricted local autonomy in all matters of administration and education" in respect of the International Training Committee. Moreover, in their view, the ITC had ignored the Society's proposals, which had initially been put forward in 1934—and now the ITC had the audacity to criticize the New York Society and not approve the request for decentralization it had first made in 1934!

Because their requests had been ignored in 1935–36, the New York Psychoanalytic Society had changed its views and at the Marienbad Congress had set out a proposal in which they asked:

"to transform the International Training Committee into a formal Scientific Training Conference, into an assembly of teachers of psychoanalysis; that is, into a body stripped of all governing attributes such an executive council, provisions for representation and proportional voting. Not a single word was said on the merits of this proposal at the Marienbad meeting."

Daniels furiously concluded:

"The reports misrepresent, mis-state and damage the position of both the New York Society as a whole and of Dr Rado personally. Therefore the New York Society respectfully request that this letter of correction be published in the Bulletin of the IPA and the objectionable passages be stricken from the records."

For Jones, Eitingon, Glover (who had succeeded Anna Freud as Secretary of the IPA), and Anna, this letter was a bolt out of the blue. It is obviously impossible to report in detail the correspondence that Daniels' letter generated between Oberndorf, N. Lewis, Lewin, J. H. Coriat, Daniels, and others, and Jones, Anna Freud, Eitingon, Glover, and others.[6] It is quite clear from their letters that the so-called Europeans were dismayed by it and uncertain as to the course of action they should take. But they had also become rather suspicious, as this letter dated 9 June 1937 from Jones to Eitingon will testify:

"Dear Max . . . I wonder how much of the troubles comes from the separatist tendency and how much from this being exploited by Rado's familiar *volte face* from his previous Mussolini attitude of running the ITC himself."

On that same day (9 June 1937), Anna Freud had claimed something similar in a letter to Jones, and Jones had also written to Daniels and had tried to be as tactful as possible in his reply.

Nevertheless, discussions on this particular issue between the Europeans and the Americans would last for months and at one point risked ending in deadlock, for in spite of the conciliatory proposals put forward by Jones, Eitingon, and Anna Freud, the New York Society not only considered these to be too vague, but also demanded a full apology.[7] In March 1938, Jones, Glover, Anna Freud, Eitingon, and Bibring finally agreed to publish a correction to the Marienbad Report on discussions concerning the ITC. It was also agreed to publish Daniels' famous accusatory letter to Jones.[8] But the reader ought to bear in mind that these were also the very months in which the situation in Austria took a turn for the worse! Notwithstanding all the problems with which Jones and his colleagues had to contend after the *Anschluss*, they were now forced to spend days and months trying to calm the Americans down. Throughout the negotiations, the Europeans—Jones in particular—continued to be rather baffled by the objections raised by their American colleagues, and it is quite clear that they still saw Rado's disturbing hand behind the difficulties created by the New York group, notwithstanding the latter's statements to the contrary. These views were in fact repeated some months later in a letter Jones wrote to Eitingon on 11 November 1938, in which he stressed that Rado was "still revengefully thirstingly looking for blood and had whipped up his flock of sheep".

In reading the correspondence, one finds that at one point Anna had become so exasperated with the Americans—and with Rado in particular—that she was even prepared to agree to their going their own way (see Anna Freud to Jones, 9 January 1938). Jones, however, was much more circumspect, and whilst he tried to avoid using too much pressure, he attempted to dispel the view held by quite a number of Americans (not all of whom were New Yorkers) that the IPA had been authoritarian in their handling of the issues in question (see Jones to A. Freud, 11 January 1938; Jones to Eitingon, 11 January 1938; and particularly Jones to Coriat, 19 January 1938).

But the attitude Jones took in this particular matter was motivated by other reasons—and here again, be it for good or for bad, one is able to observe just how considerable was Jones's political acumen. Consider his comments in a letter to Eitingon just a few months earlier, on 11 November 1937, where one will also observe that he had anticipated the tragic situation that was soon to develop in Vienna. At one point in this letter Jones stated:

> "On the other hand the all important point is that we know the Americans in general to be so loosely attached to us, and with so many forces at work tending to separate them from us, that it would take a very slight casus belli to effect the disaster. At least personally I should regard it as a disaster, now that the emigration has carried the Schwerpunkt of Analysis across the Atlantic. The latest political news from Austria gives

*me for the first time trepidation about the future of our work there, so that
I regard it to be all important to hold together all existing bonds in our
International Association."* [emphasis added]

Now, if the events I have attempted to reconstruct thus far with
regard to the Marienbad episode will help to clarify the statements
Jones made at the 1938 Paris Congress on the way the Americans had
behaved (as reported in Jones's 1953–57 biography of Freud, quoted
above), one ought also to consider the first departures from Austria
and elsewhere in the light of the delicate negotiations that were
being conducted during that same period between the American Psychoanalytic Association and the IPA. As I have already mentioned
in chapter four, the 1933 emigration of analysts from Germany had
taken place in not too dissimilar circumstances. However, the present
crisis was much more serious, in that one was now faced with the
emigration, *en masse*, of lay analysts from the whole of Central Europe. To make matters worse, this seriously threatened the precarious
equilibrium that Brill and his colleagues had managed to establish
with the powerful American Psychiatric Association. These factors all
had a bearing on the proposals tabled by Jones at the Paris Congress—by which time emigration from Austria had begun, and Freud
and his family had already reached London.

For the sake of historical accuracy, one has to say that the New
York Association was not the only institute to whom Jones appealed
for help. Early in 1938, on 23 March to be precise, Jones wrote to
Alexander in Chicago to ask for financial assistance. On 8 April 1938
Alexander replied, saying that the American Psychoanalytic Association[9] had already formed "an emergency relief Committee", chaired
by Kubie in New York, and that the Association was collecting funds
in New York and elsewhere. The fund was being administrated by Dr
B. Lewin in New York. In the same letter Alexander informed Jones
of the opportunities prospective immigrants would have in America.
The chances were "quite favourable" if the new refugees were prepared to settle "in the large towns of the middle west and south which
as yet have no psychoanalysts. There is a definitive need for psychoanalysis in such cities as Cleveland, Ohio, Kansas City, Missouri, San
Antonio, Texas and New Orleans, Louisiana. . . . *Of course New York,
Boston and Chicago are pretty much crowded already"* (emphasis added).
"San Francisco", Alexander continued, "has proven to be quite difficult territory. As you may know Dr Otto Fenichel is just about to go to

Los Angeles" (see Fenichel's *Rundbriefe*, Mühlleitner & Reichmayr, 1998, Vol. II; Jacoby, 1983). Just think back to Jones's correspondence with his colleagues in the United States, particularly with Brill, during 1933–34 and later during the years he had helped refugee analysts to emigrate from Germany, and what Jones must have felt in reading Alexander's letter! The latter was, incidentally, making statements very similar to those Jones had made to Brill in a letter dated 23 September 1933 (see chapter four). One wonders, therefore, whether, in this case, Jones could have had one of these experiences of *déjà vu* I mentioned earlier!

Alexander concluded his letter by stressing that the Europeans should be made aware of the situation and that American physicians were "becoming rapidly psychoanalytically conscious". There was work in the western part of the United States in particular, in Chicago, linked to Topeka, and even in Canada, because Alexander and his colleagues in Chicago were constantly receiving requests for consultations and analytical help from Montreal, Toronto, and Winnipeg. It is important to note that Alexander referred to American physicians—and we will see the sorts of problems that Alexander, as the new President of the American Psychoanalytic Association, would both raise and have to deal with, once lay analysts began to arrive from Central Europe! No one could possibly have envisaged the countless problems awaiting these immigrants, nor could one have foreseen the political difficulties that were to be encountered by certain of those immigrants—by Reich, Bernfeld, Fenichel, and the old group of left-wing analysts (Jacoby, 1983), who would also have to contend with the fear of Communist and other left-wing ideologies, matters these and other letters do not tell us of. And America would turn out to be anything but the promised land that Alexander's statements might have encouraged one to imagine!

Bearing in mind the complex American context, let us now focus on Vienna and the events as they took place during the same months of 1938. From time to time I will refer back to the situation in the United States, their struggle with the IPA, and the problems posed by the new and old emigrants. I will also attempt to give an account of what was happening in Great Britain at the time, at least as far as Jones's and Anna Freud's attempts to save the Viennese and other psychoanalysts were concerned. By March 1938, after much painful uncertainty, Anna, her father, family, and all the other Viennese analysts realized that Austro-Fascism had ended and that their lives were now at risk. They thus began to look for a way out of Austria. As I noted earlier, when I commented on the changed tone of her letters to Jones from February 1938 onwards, Anna was very concerned, and she began anxiously to bombard Jones with the names of analysts and candidates who needed to be helped. In some instances, wanting to be of as much help as possible, she would also ask him to intervene on behalf of these persons' relatives, in the hope that they would all be able to leave together (see Anna to Jones, 5 May 1938). She would also take up the case of certain friends, not all of whom were psychoanalysts. One such friend, who was very close to the Freud family, was A. Zinner, the urologist, to whom Anna referred as *"den ersten Urologen von Wien"*, "the leading urologist in Vienna" (Anna to Jones, 26 April 1938). She asked Jones to assist with as many cases as came her way, in a dramatic effort to have at least some of them put forward for consideration. The emotional tone of her letters comes through very clearly if one pays attention to her use of the question mark, to the way she would use the conditional in such phrases as "If it would be possible . . ."—"he could maybe . . ."—"Should he . . ."—"he could be very useful . . .", etc. "Do you remember our colleague Dr. Eidelberg . . .", reads Anna's letter to Jones dated 22 April 1938; and she then proceeds to tell Jones of L. Eidelberg's difficulties and of his young wife's illness, before adding, "If it would be possible he would like to remain in the English Provinces, in Oxford he has good friends. If that would not be possible", Anna continued, "he could maybe get out from England with an affidavit for America. Should he ask his friends to invite him as a guest to England?" On 4 May 1938 she again wrote to Jones, this time about a young man called Dr W. Hollitscher: "He is a very studious type, gifted and of exceptional abilities: he could be very useful working at the Bibliographical Centre in London. . . ." She also worried for those persons who had obtained an exit visa for Great Britain, but who were perhaps waiting for affidavits to be sent on to the United States—and, here again, Anna would write to Jones for his assistance. There were other cases for which Anna would have wanted Jones's help, but for which she did not have the courage to pressurize him. Eitingon seemed to have promised something from Palestine, but now this option turned out not to be possible. . . . What, for instance, could one do for Else Heipern and her husband? *"Ich traum mich nicht die Else Heipern als Analytikerin für die Englische Provinz zu empfehlen"* [I do not dream of recommending Else Heipern as a psychoanalyst who could work in the English Provinces], Anna added almost shyly, in broaching the subject in her letter of 26 April 1938. . . . But could Jones speak with Frau Abraham, Abraham's widow, who was already in England . . . she knew the Heiperns . . . perhaps something could be done. . . .

In this letter Anna also emphasizes how hopeful she had felt when she had received the copy Jones had sent her of Alexander's letter of 8 April 1938 (see above), which told of the opportunities available in America to Austrian and other analysts. She had told all those who wanted to go to America to write to Kubie[10] and to send a copy of their letters to Jones. There were young colleagues and older candidates, all neurologists and psychiatrists, who would perhaps be able to find posts in American hospitals, and, she added: "The lay analysts, particularly the young ones have already managed to get private affidavits and with the help of previous patients and of friends they will go to America and in one way or another *schon irgendwie ihren Weg finden* [find their own way]". However, as always, there were problems; Anna hinted at the odd behaviour in Boston of Helene Deutsch, whom she did not trust, and who was creating problems for the Wälders and trying to dissuade them from going to Boston. . . . One must say that at times poor Anna was perhaps overly optimistic about the Americans!

Let us again stray from the study of the correspondence between Anna Freud and Jones during those tragic days in Vienna and London and take a brief look at the problems affecting psychoanalysis in the United States at that time. This will enable the reader to gain a better idea of the tensions, the ill-feelings, and so on then existing between the American and the European establishments and the repercussions that these had on the emigration issue. Although two years had gone by, the disputes that had arisen following the Marienbad Congress had still not been fully digested by the Americans. Indeed, on 30 April 1938, and therefore in the same month that Anna wrote the above letter to Jones, Kubie—the very same Kubie who had organized the American Committee to help the refugees—wrote to Jones to express again his concern about the famous Report on the Marienbad Congress (!!), and the tensions that this was still creating. At that time Kubie was not aware of Jones's and his colleagues' decision to publish an apology, and in his letter he expressed the view that Jones should have intervened to pacify the Americans—the New York group in particular—as they were still very dissatisfied with the way the IPA had dealt with the misunderstandings at Marienbad! But the extract that follows would seem to pinpoint the problem:

> "It is not, however, primarily in order to clear us that I am suggesting this to you but rather because I think that at this time such a move is important *to make the incoming immigrants to America feel happier and more at home here.* They have been fed so much misinformation and so many malicious lies about us (by Nunberg and others) that it is hard to imagine what horrible fantasies about America in general and Rado in particular they must bring to those shores." [emphasis added]

This seems to confirm the fears Jones had expressed in his letter to Eitingon dated 11 November 1937. Kubie then went on to explain the reasons for his concern: the problem was all to do with Homburger, who had accused Rado of damaging his reputation at Yale. It had been Nunberg who had told all this to Homburger—and so much other distorted information about the Americans and Rado had been sent by Homburger and Nunberg to Vienna. Then Kubie added:

> "We do not want the incoming analysts to form around Nunberg a hostile group, *largely lay* with him as its nucleus." [emphasis added]

Kubie added that he thought it important that Jones issued a statement clarifying the IPA/American issue, and, as was his usual practice, he complained about his colleagues—in this instance about Eitingon and about Oberndorf, an "Untrustworthy and conscienceless man".

Another case of *déjà vu*, one might be inclined to think. Indeed, Kubie's statement bears out an issue I raised much earlier—that is, the fear of the U.S. analysts (the indigenous groups in particular) of refugee immigrants creating closed groups around one or more of their more prominent European émigré colleagues, thus further complicating the already chaotic political situation of U.S. psychoanalysis. Moreover, there was the added fear that the arrival of lay analysts would create even more problems! Anna was obviously fully aware of all this, as Jones had sent her copies of these letters.[11]

The situation was therefore rapidly deteriorating even further. Unfortunately, I cannot quote here all of the correspondence between Jones and the Americans, nor the letters the Americans wrote to one another. However, I think it should be pointed out that it was during the most delicate period of the Austrian exodus, when Jones, Marie Bonaparte, Anna, and others were doing all they could to save Freud and the other Viennese analysts, that the New York Psychoanalytic Society, by now very embittered with the IPA, unanimously decided "to appoint no representative to the forthcoming International Congress". (Jones was informed of this decision in a letter, dated 16 May 1938, from A. Stern, Chairman of the Educational Committee of the New York Society.)

This did not mean that single members would not be allowed to attend the Paris Congress, but unless the Society had given them written authorization to do so, they were not permitted to speak at any of the IPA meetings on behalf of the official Committee of the New York Society (Daniels to Jones, 18 May 1938). Jones was unable to persuade either the New York analysts or the other U.S. members to change their minds. As a result of this decision, apologies were received from the United States, saying that the Paris Congress clashed with other congresses in the United States, that the financial situation prevented them from attending, and so on. Moreover, in a letter to Jones on 24 May 1938, Kubie clearly reiterated that the New Yorkers were not alone in thinking that "the prestige of the International would be greatly enhanced and its value increased if it became entirely and solely a scientific organization"! . . . and many people had a definite feeling "that any form of international control in scientific matters is basically unscientific and unsound in principle."[12]

However, the matters discussed at the Marienbad Congress were no longer the only issues to so disconcert the Americans. To all intents and purposes, these now appeared to have been ironed out. In fact, in his letter to Jones dated 24 May 1938, Kubie acknowledged that the statements published in the *International Journal of Psycho-Analysis* had resolved matters quite satisfactorily, adding that, had he received the journal earlier, he would not even have written his letter dated 30 April.

The disputes were, however, not to end here. If we read the letter Jones send to Alexander on 21 June 1938, in which he asked Alexander to help him to understand the situation in New York, there is no doubt that a very worrying and serious issue lay behind the New York uprising—one that also reflected the anxieties of the whole of the American psychoanalytic establishment. What really concerned them was the threat posed by the arrival of refugee analysts from Austria, and the fact that their professional status would have created serious problems for those American societies prepared to host them. Jones had granted all refugees to the United States full and direct membership of the IPA. Kubie, in turn, had written to him to say that this would have caused resentment on the part of the U.S. psychoanalytic establishment. Jones, however, reiterated that he considered full and direct membership to be "fully justified", particularly if one considered the standing of some of the members of the Vienna Society, and that, following the sudden dissolution of their Society and its subsequent amalgamation with the German institution, they had found themselves totally unprotected. Yet, in explaining his point to Alexander, Jones also added:

> "Of course the crux of the trouble will arise over the question of lay analysts (could they indeed be practising even in America under the cover of the IPA?) and I must confess I cannot see any satisfactory solution, even temporarily, so long as so much intolerance reigns."

Therefore, as Alexander had also hinted, lay analysis had again become a primary and crucial issue. And if one looks with hindsight at all those discussions, queries, and litigations, and at those that were still to follow, concerning the personal and professional life of the refugee medical but particularly non-medical analysts in the United States, one can clearly see that the issues at stake during those months and years would play a very important role in shaping the future history and development of American psychoanalysis, *vis-à-vis* that in Europe and South America and, in particular, in Great Britain, where, in spite of Jones's tactical games and reservations towards non-medical psychoanalysts, the situation would be handled rather differently, both because of the presence of many non-medical analysts in the British Psycho-Analytical Society since its beginning, and then because of the influence of Melanie Klein and Anna Freud. As far as American psychoanalysis was concerned, a solution to these problems would only be found more than 40 years later, in the late 1980s, with the acceptance by the IPA of many of the non-medical U.S. societies of psychoanalysis, where the non-medical European refugees have played a very important role (Kirsner, 2000; Wallerstein 1998). The outlook for some of the refugees was undoubtedly pretty depressing, particularly when one considered the difficulties that had been experienced in the United States and in other countries by those lay analysts who had emigrated from Berlin during the 1930s!

I come back to the situation in the United States in a short while. Let us for the moment return to the letters exchanged between Anna and Jones during April and May 1938, and continue to follow closely their efforts to save as many of the Viennese as was possible. In this respect, one needs to bear in mind that, on 30 March 1938, "the mother of all psychoanalytical societies", as Jones had called the Viennese Society in his opening speech at the 15th International Psycho-Analytical Congress, held in Paris, on 1 August 1938, had been "dissolved"[13] and was now under the control of the German Society and headed by Müller-Braunschweig.[14]

I have already spoken of Anna's "*Sorge*" for every colleague, for every student and friend, and I have also commented that, more often than not, her "*Sorge*" was also extended to the relatives of her colleagues, friends, and so on. More should now be said about Anna's frantic and moving attempts to do everything she possibly could for all of them. At Jones's suggestion, she had sent him a list of training analysts, members, and students—and were it possible for me to quote from all the letters she wrote to Jones from the end of April 1938 onwards, there would be no doubt as to just how difficult it was for her to find an appropriate solution for them all. The number of questions they put to her—often very naive but at the same time very important to them—was overwhelming at times. However, her load notwithstanding, Anna was not oblivious to the pressures that were also being placed on Jones, as she acknowledged in a letter dated 3 April 1938:

> "*Wenn ich vor Deiner Seite die Sache aussehe so beunruhigt mich das Mass von Verantwortung, Unruhe und Veränderung das Du damit auf Dich nimmst. . . . Die Behörden auf der einen Seite, deine eigenen Mitgliedern, unsere Mitarbeitern, lauter schwierige Menschen die unter einen Hut zu bringen sind, dazu die finanzielle Seite der Dinge.*"
>
> [If I look at the whole situation from your point of view it disturbs me, the amount of responses, unrest, and changes that you have to deal with. . . . The authorities on one side, on the other your colleagues and my co-workers, sincere difficult people who need to be cared for, beside the financial aspect of the whole matter.][15]

But, as I said, it becomes increasingly clear from Anna's letters that these people were all anxiously pressing her and that she, in turn, wanted to take care of them. Could Jones ascertain whether "our professionals would find further difficulties in Dover" and "in order to avoid that, should they still do something here"? "At times here it seems that the procedure to speed up things can do some progress, but then this is an illusion and everything gets stopped", Anna wrote on 4 April 1938.[16] A few weeks later the situation began to look brighter, and Anna informed Jones on 20 April 1938 that the British Consulate had acknowledged receipt of information sent to them by her and others. Nevertheless, it is only by reading her letters of 3 and 4 May 1938 that one is able fully to appreciate just how many people she wrote about and how she had a word for each one of them, in the hope that they would all be helped, that they would all be found a home, be it in Palestine, in South Africa, or elsewhere—for Anna was fully aware of the difficulties Jones was encountering in hosting the Viennese candidates in Britain (Anna to Jones, 3 May 1938).

This, however, did not prevent her from continuing to appeal to Jones for help. Indeed, in this same letter Anna also wrote to ask him whether he was able to do something for L. Frank, who had worked with C. Bühler and was "an extremely good test psychologist". Frank would have a good chance with "The Child Guidance Council, Institute of Medical Psychology where from, a certain Mrs Dr. Calver had come to work with her here in Vienna. . . . It would be a pity that she could not become an analyst . . . could she be accepted as a candidate?" Concerning Dr C. Kronengold, about whom Jones had asked Anna for information: "*er ist ein netter stiller Mensch*" [he was "a nice, quiet, individual"], and she went on to detail his positive characteristics. And what about E. Stengel? "He is very motivated to come to England and I think it would be a good idea for him. . . ." She again wrote to Jones on 4 May 1938 with regard to, among others, Dr Pappenheim: "I have spoken with her and she is asking me whether once in Bristol could she practise later on as a doctor? . . . Her mother has become severely melancholic whether as a reaction due to the separation or whether she would have become like that in any case, it is difficult to say".

She again wrote to Jones a few days later, on 9 May 1938, to inform him that Eidelberg seemed to have solved his problems and that M. Steiner now appeared to have the opportunity of going to England: "*Er ist ja wirklich ein armer Kerl, der sonst hier völlig hilflos wäre*" [he is really a poor chap, who would have been completely without help here]. In giving Jones this good news, she also took the opportunity to recommend two other Viennese analysts, Dr O. Isakower and Frau Dr. E. Gutmann.[17] They had just married, "*und sind dadurch aus zwei*

Problemen zu einem geworden" [and therefore two problems had now become one]. *Sie ist sehr still und zurüchgezogen, aber eine der schärftsen und kritischsten Analytikerinnen"* [she is very quiet and withdrawn, but one of the most brilliant and critical analytic minds]. Frau Gutmann was also a doctor. "If you could send them to the Provinces", Anna added, "the situation will not become worse but better." She then asked Jones whether he had a city in mind—Liverpool, for example.[18] I could go on quoting. However, when one reads all these names, one is also obliged to wonder just how advantageous it was for some of these refugees to be recommended as a special friend of Freud's—as in the case of Maxim Steiner, for example! One may also want to ask oneself how seriously Jones took account of these connections when it came to deciding on where these individuals should settle.

For many months, Jones and the British Psycho-Analytical Society were inundated with lists of names and personal details—in which Jones had the full backing of the members of the British Psycho-Analytical Society, notwithstanding the anxieties Melanie Klein had expressed to him in a letter in late spring 1941 (King & Steiner, 1992, p. 228). At the same time, all manner of decisions had to be taken and arrangements made, including monies to be collected, funds to be allocated, and so on. As I have already hinted at (see chapter two), one should not forget that the Jews who came to Great Britain to settle were bound by certain conditions (Ash, 1991; London, 2000; Sherman, 1973, 1994), and probably as a result of the large number of refugees entering the country, these had become even more stringent than during the late 1930s. According to Ash (1991, p. 112): "The Home Office routinely consulted Jones in his handling of work and residence permit applications by Freudian analysts." (See also Sherman, 1973, 1994; Wasserstein, 1999, p. 13.) At that time, immigrants to Great Britain were not permitted to be a burden on the state and therefore had to be in a position to provide for themselves. As with the previous emigration wave, a parallel can be drawn between the mass emigration of Jews from Austria and Germany in 1938 and the emigration of refugee analysts. Furthermore, for a variety of reasons, of those psychoanalysts and candidates who were hoping to emigrate or who had already reached their destinations, several were experiencing financial hardship, and their reluctance to approach Jones directly with their problems made their situation even more difficult. In certain instances, this required Anna's diplomatic and sagacious

intervention—as in Stengel's case, for example. Showing great consideration for the latter's predicament, Anna wrote to Jones on 14
May 1938, saying,

> *"Er weisst nicht ob du weisst, dass er tatsächlich absolut mittellos ist,
> und auch nicht wie die Anderen die Möglichgkeit hat für die erste Zeit
> von Verwandten etwas auszuleihen."*

> [He does not know whether you know that he is without any
> support; furthermore he cannot rely on the help of relatives in the
> immediate future as others can.]

Nor had the Freuds themselves been able to avoid encountering
financial difficulties, for the Verlag monies had been confiscated and
they were forced to find other means of paying for their permits to
leave Austria. In Anna's letter to Jones of 20 May 1938, she apologized
for its format but said that she was writing it whilst waiting at the
Bank in Vienna, where she was trying to sort out some of their financial problems. She then added that the uncertainties were still very
great. At the same time, however, she again took the opportunity to
give Jones details of the situation others were in, Stengel particularly,
and the Hollitschers . . . but that M. Steiner was now ready to leave.
Her following comments will give the reader an idea of the kind of
tensions and problems that were being suffered. Having thanked
Jones for his reassurance that she would be able to work in London,
Anna added with great modesty but with typical down-to-earth realism:

> *"Ich habe nur ein bischen Angst, was geschehen wird wenn die Span-
> nung in der ich jetzt lebe vorüber sein wird. Ich möchte so gerne etwas
> daraus gelernt haben und nicht vielleicht irgendeine Reaktion darauf
> bekommen."*

> [I fear only what is going to happen when the tension in which I
> am living now will cease. I would really like to have learnt some-
> thing from all this and not perhaps to develop a sort of Reaction]

(Anna was quite obviously referring to the negative reaction she
might have to these difficult experiences.) Indeed, one could pass
many an hour going over all the names and the minutiae of the lives
mentioned in these letters. Apart from Jones's unwavering efficiency,
and his deeply felt need to attend to the problems of all, what strikes
one most on reading these letters is Anna's force of character and the

way she looked on Great Britain as some sort of fond and kindly mother, who would gather all the Viennese *"Sorgenkinder"* into her arms—including those who were just passing through, waiting to emigrate to the United States. As time went by, though, and as the tensions with the United States increased, despite or together with her optimism toward America Anna began to view America as a distant and hostile country. But, as we know, her opinions in this regard were to change somewhat!!

Anna Freud's negative feelings for America at that time can be seen in a letter dated "Mai Sonntag 1938", in which she mentions Kubie and criticizes his behaviour; furthermore, two particularly interesting letters on the situation in the United States and on Kubie's conduct ought to be quoted. In the first of these, dated 14 May 1938, Anna informs Jones of the efforts of Dr W. Langer, an American analysand, who had gone back to the United States to attempt to clarify the refugee situation with Kubie:

> *"Kubie hat ihm auch eine Menge Brauchbarer allgemeiner Nachtrichten schriftlich und mündlich für prospektive Einwanderer mitgegeben. Aber kein Wort, ob er die Möglichkeit hat Affidavits zu verschaffen . . . und kein Wort über einzelnen Personen."*

[Kubie gave him a whole lot of useful general information, in writing and orally, for potential immigrants. But no word about the possibility he has of producing affidavits, and no word on specific persons who could emigrate there.][19]

Incidentally, having brought Jones up to date, as she always did, on the situation with many of her colleagues and on their prospects of finding a refuge abroad, Anna ended this letter with a sad note:

> *"Wenn die Auswanderung länger dauert, werden hier in finanzieller Not sein: Frau Dr. Mahler, Frau Dr. Herz, Frau Dr. Grünspan, Frau Dr. Erdheim, Friedjung. Im Augenblick haben alle noch etwas zu leben."*

[If the emigration is going to last any longer, Frau Dr. (M.) Mahler, Frau Dr. Herz, Frau Dr. Grünspan, Frau Dr. Erdheim, Friedjung will be in financial trouble. For the moment they have still something they can live on.]

There is no doubt that Anna was asking for financial help on their behalf!

Anna was kept fully informed of the situation in the United States, and her second letter to Jones, dated 28 May 1938, is probably even more explicit. However, it also brings to light the terrible uncertainties and anxieties so many hopeful emigrants were being forced to experience. It is obvious that Kubie and the others were very careful about making any promises or allowing people into the United States. In commenting on Kubie's statements on the state of affairs between the IPA, the American societies, and the refugees, Anna is very unequivocal in telling Jones that, in her view:

> *"Aber hinter diesem Vorschlag von Kubie steckt natürlich die ganze Schwierigkeit des Verhältnisses der amerikanischen zur europäischen Vereinigung die sich auf diesem Congress hoffentlich klären wird. Es scheint mir dass es schon jetzt in Amerika eine Nebenvereinigung gibt und dass auch ohne die jetzige Immigration diese Nebenvereinigung im ständigen Wachsen ist."*

> [Yet behind Kubie's proposals lies the whole difficulty of the relationship between the American and the European Societies, which hopefully will be clarified during the coming Congress (referring to the Paris Congress). It seems to me that in America there is already in existence a parallel Society even without today's Immigration, and that this parallel Society is growing quite fast.]

In this letter Anna also mentions the fact that Sachs had left Boston, that Simmel had been excluded from Chicago, and that the Wälders were experiencing difficulties, as none of the American societies was prepared to accept them. (The latter experienced the same problems in England, too—see chapter eight.) This was all evidence to Anna of just how powerful and independent the Americans were becoming.

She then indicated that there was another matter that worried her: people were waiting for Kubie to reply to them—mainly young doctors, neurologists, psychiatrists; all people who knew the state of affairs with the medical profession in America, and who were not making false claims to Kubie:

> *"Es sind aber auch alles Leute, die wirtschaftlich nicht lange aushalten können und schon jetzt ohne Verdienst sind. Sie können sich meistens über ein paar Wochen noch hinüberhelfen."*

> [But they are all people who cannot maintain themselves economically for long and they are already now without a salary. They can help themselves over for only a couple of weeks at most.]

Anna then mentions the lengthy rules involved in obtaining affidavits, and the difficulties in dealing with the consulates:

"Es wäre also gut wenn Kubie das was er machen kann, möglichst bald macht. Ich weiss nicht, ob er das von drüben aus versteht."

[It would also be good if what Kubie can do he would do it as soon as possible. I do not know whether he understands from over there what is happening here.]

A letter from Alexander to Jones, dated 26 July 1938, would seem to confirm the complaints Anna had made some months earlier in the letters referred to above. Alexander asks Jones to reflect on Kubie's and the Relief Committee's efforts, adding:

"Your letter sounds reproachful. If you could tell me more defini- tively what I could and should do in speeding up relief activities, I would be most eager to follow your suggestions in spite of *my vacation* which is anyhow approaching its termination."

As we know, *"drüben"* ["over there"]—that is, in America—the situa- tion was rather messy, although their sympathy was genuine, as was their wish to help. Unfortunately, matters took a turn for the worse following the 1938 Paris Congress, as many American analysts pan- icked at the prospect of so many European refugees entering the States (Langer & Gifford, 1978; Lorand, 1969; Stepansky, 1988, p. 102). Yet one has to say that a careful reading of the letters—many of them four to five pages in length—exchanged between the IPA and the American society in 1938 and 1939 shows that both Kubie and Alex- ander were doing all they could to find a solution to the refugee problem. On the other hand, if one considers the deep-seated feelings of resentment and the problems and the pressures that were brought to bear on the people still living in Vienna in April–July 1938, one can understand that they may not have been in a position fully to appre- ciate all the efforts that were being made to assist them, and that they might have had a somewhat different perspective on the matter.[20]

It was also because it was precisely during the months of June and July 1938 that the problems of the continental lay analysts coming to the United States emerged with astonishing clarity as related in the correspondence between Jones, Kubie, and Alexander that I quote in note 20 of this chapter. There are also the extremely significant statements by Alexander concerning the necessary *"fortunate and un- avoidable" medicalization of psychoanalysis in the United States, as a prac- tice due to the progress in psychosomatic medicine, and so on,* and note also what Kubie wrote to Alexander concerning the danger that unaccepted lay analysts coming from Europe could create their own groups, increasing the number of non-medically trained psychoanalysts not controlled by the APA. *Contained here are some of the main trends of the future development and conflicts of American, and not only American, psychoanalysis: for instance, the issues related to its scientific and medical credibility when left in the hands of lay analysts, and so on, as I have already hinted at above.*

However, before I conclude my comments on Anna's "*Sorge*" during those months, I would suggest that certain of her letters reveal many other aspects of her personality. I do not mean those small, yet so very interesting fragments where we see her anticipating the moment of her arrival in London by poring over a map of the city (Anna to Jones, 3 April 1938), or where she informs Jones that, notwithstanding her father being so much weaker and "*unruhig*" [restless] (Anna to Jones, 30 May 1938), she would take him out for walks, old and fragile as he was, in order to get him used to being on his feet again, in readiness for the journey to London (Anna to Jones, 20 and 28 May 1938—these same letters contain other details of Anna's feelings). These snippets speak for themselves and give us a glimpse of how Anna and her father passed that terrible spring in Vienna, with swastikas daubed on every wall and Anna and her father walking along those streets, observing and commenting on what they saw.[21]

In this regard, there are also various letters during those same months from Freud to M. Bernays, who had already left Austria, and others, in which he speaks of his daughter. However, some of his most moving comments about Anna are to be found in a letter to Jones on 13 May 1938. Having informed Jones that his physical condition is poor, and that this has prevented him from writing, he adds:

> "Sometimes one even tells oneself '*Le jeu ne vaut pas plus la chandelle*' and although one is right one must not admit that one is right. The advantage that emigrating will bring Anna is worth all our petty sacrifices. For us old people 73 (Martha), 77 (Minna), 83 (myself) emigrating would not have been worthwhile. Anna is untiringly active, not only for us but for countless others as well."

"I hope", Freud added, very diplomatically, probably thinking of Melanie Klein in London, "that she will also be able to do much for analysis in England, but she will not obtrude herself."

It may perhaps also be worth quoting an extract from a letter from Freud to his son Ernst, who had already arrived in England and was trying to find a proper home for the whole family in London. In this letter, dated 12 May 1938, Freud uses practically the same words to describe Anna. In stressing that it is mainly on Anna's account that emigrating makes any sense—because for him, his wife, and her sister *"zwischen 73 and 82 hätte die ganze Unternehmung keinen Sinn gehabt"* [for us between 73 and 82 the whole enterprise would not have any sense anymore]—Freud adds:

> *"Zwei Aussichten erhalten sich in diesen trüben Zeiten. Euch alle beisammen zu sehen und to die in freedom* [the phrase was written in English]. *Ich vergleiche mich manchmal mit dem alten Jacob den seine Kinder auch im hohen Alter nach Aegypten mitgenommen haben wie uns Th. Mann im nächsten Roman schildern wird."*
>
> [Two possibilities subsist in these troubled times. To see you all together again and *to die in freedom*. I sometimes compare myself to old Jacob who was taken to Egypt by his children when he was already very old, as Th. Mann will describe in his next novel.] [emphasis added]

But to go back to the feelings and the thoughts Anna expressed in her letters to Jones, it would seem that at times one is able to detect a sign of rebellion, or even of envy for the good fortune of others, such as after she had just succeeded in finding a place of exile in Honolulu for two paedagogists from the *Kinderheim* she had opened in 1937, which the Nazis had forced her to close down when they arrived in Vienna a year later. On this occasion, Anna confesses to Jones that:

> *"Wenn ich nicht in der Weise gebunden wäre, in der ich bin, hätte ich Lust es mit einer ganz neuen Welt zu versuchen. . . ."*
>
> [If I were not tied down by my commitments as I am, I would like the adventure of trying to make do in a totally new world. . . .]

One further letter also merits attention. In this, Anna writes to Jones to tell him which of the analysts had already left and which were on the point of leaving:

> *"Heute früh sind Kris und die Bibrings abgereist, morgen fahren die Wälders, Hoffers und Hartmann haben ihre Passe schon in Ordnung und warten nur noch."*

[This morning Kris and the Bibrings left. Tomorrow the Wälders will leave too. The Hoffers and the Hartmanns already have their passports and are just waiting to leave.]

Having told him that things were looking better, she pauses to comment for a moment on the difficulties she is encountering in her attempt to help those friends who are suffering from anxiety or depression—some of the older ones, such as Federn, E. Hitschmann, and M. Steiner, in particular, who were being forced to leave their country without any great prospects in front of them.[22] Then, almost as if she wanted to give a sense of the difficulties she was being forced to come to terms with whilst also being obliged to contend with all the tensions around her, she exclaims:

"Und während ich es nicht schwer habe, den jungen Leuten aus ihren Stimmungen zu helfen nützt es bei den anderen nichts; sie beneiden mich höchstens dass ich noch nicht so alt bin, und mehr Aussichten habe als sie. Was macht man da? Es ist sehr traurig es mit anzusehen."

[Though it comes easy to me to help the younger ones, I don't manage to do so with the older ones. What they most envy me is the fact that I am still not quite so old and that I still have many more prospects than they do. What is to be done in such cases? It is heart-rending to have to witness.]

The above letter is undated but would have to be from sometime around the middle of May 1938.

Finally, of the many letters I could choose, I would like to quote from Anna's letter dated 25 May 1938, which perhaps she thought would have been her last from Vienna. Her comments are rather bitter, but lucid as always, and they give us some idea of the nightmarish atmosphere that must have been hanging over the city in those final days. Having informed Jones that Max Schur, Freud's doctor, has suddenly been taken ill, which meant that he would no longer be able to accompany her father to England, and that she was hoping that Dr Stross would be able to travel with them instead, Anna then gives a very detailed report on Stengel, O. Isakower, and G. Pisk, on F. Grünspan, who was probably going to go to Palestine, and on Hartmann, who for the moment was still in Paris. The persons for whom Anna feared most were E. Pappenheim and her mother, who still had nowhere to go; they were also experiencing financial difficulties, but Anna was no longer able to help them with this. She then adds the following comment, which sums up the situation perfectly:

> *"Manchmal ist das Ganze wirklich so, dass man auch nicht erstaunt wäre wenn es hundert Jahre so weiter geht. Wir sind nicht mehr ganz hier und noch gar nicht dort. So ist es sonst nur in den Hemmungs Traumen, in denen zwei Tendenzen gegeneinander wirken und man immer wieder am gleichen Ort steht. Aber der Vergleich ist eher optimistisch, denn die erledigen sich ja am Ende, immer durch das Aufwachen."*

[From time to time everything that is here taking place is such that one would not be surprised if it were all to continue as it is for another hundred years. We are no longer completely here, and yet, nor are we completely there with you. It is a situation which you can only come across in dreams of inhibition, where two contrasting tendencies are in conflict and in the end one always finds one is back at the same point as before. But the comparison is rather optimistic, for this dream conflict always resolves itself in the end, through awakening.][23]

However, a few days later her mood appeared to have changed, and she seemed more hopeful. In her letter to Jones of 29 May 1938, Anna insisted, on her father's behalf, too, that Jones took his Whitsun holidays and tried to forget all their problems—and thinking ahead, she wrote saying:

> *"Wenn es etwas gibt was ich in der ersten Zeit tun oder nicht tun soll, dann bitte lasse es mir schriftlich zurück. Darf ich z.B. mit den Leuten die ich von hier habe gleich zu analisieren beginnen oder muss ich auf eine officielle Arbeitserlaubnis warten?"*

[If there is something that I can or cannot do immediately after my arrival, please leave it behind for me in writing. For instance, could I start analysing the people who are coming from here with me, or should I wait for an official work permit?]

It must be said that the nightmare she had hinted at in her previous letter lasted neither the one hundred years Anna had prophesied nor the one thousand years Hitler had had in mind. As for the rescue of her *"Sorgenkinder"* and her family, with Jones's help she managed to save most of them, except for a number of Freud's relatives—his old sisters—who were to die in concentration camps. Some of the last letters she wrote to Jones in the months following her arrival in London testify to Anna's "*Sorge*" for those persons left behind in Vienna. On 1 January 1939, in one of the last letters to him concerning the emigration of her colleagues, she pleads with him to help her to find accommodation for the Hungarian psychoanalyst Kata Levy and her children (cf. Anna's letter to Jones, 24 August 1938), again returning to the same theme and enquiring of Jones: "What can be done about it?"

But at this point one may ask oneself whether anything was done for those analysts who were still in Central Europe during those terrible months, or whether anything more could have been done for them. Consider the vicissitudes of the Hungarian analysts, for instance: is there something in London that would help us to understand what happened to them? I would say that even in this instance it is possible to reconstruct, in part at least, the policies that were adopted by Jones and the way he tried to help his Hungarian colleagues reach places of safety.[24] Indeed, the Archives of the British Psycho-Analytical Society contain a certain amount of correspondence that, although fragmented, enables us to piece together the various episodes of this part of the "story". The correspondence, in this case concerning some of the minor figures, gives a sense of the feverish anxiety and the tribulations suffered by those forced to emigrate, and what it meant for them to have been lucky enough to have landed on the other side of the globe, in countries such as Ceylon, Australia, New Zealand, South Africa. They also tell of the grief and the sadness of having to lose contact with the Old Continent, of being forced to leave relatives and friends behind, in the knowledge that they would never meet them again, whilst at the same time having to cope with a new culture, a new language, and so on.

Let us begin by taking G. Róheim's predicament as an example. Róheim cannot, of course, be considered a minor figure, but because of the situation in Budapest, and in Hungary generally, he had to wait some time before arrangements could be made for him to leave. Róheim felt that the situation in Hungary was going from bad to worse—though, as we shall see in a short while, Hollos, President of the Hungarian Society, was of a different view, for a while at least. Consider the emotional tone of his words, and what can be read between extremely polite lines with which he replies to J. Rickman, who has informed him that the evacuation from Vienna of Freud and his family was to take priority.[25] Of the many letters written during those years, Róheim's is one of the most touching. It also perfectly expresses the isolation that was felt by so many Continental analysts:

"My dear John,

"Of course Vienna comes first, I knew that, it is quite obvious. The point is that everybody is trying to get away from here before something happens, and it may be too late and we shall be in the same plight. Maybe this is only a group psychosis but one never knows. Now there is just one thing you can do for me. Please let me have a fictive invitation to give lectures at the Institute of Psycho-Analysis say for a year, so that I can use this if I want an English visum suddenly.

"Are Jewish circles doing anything for the Vienna people? By which I mean will they, if we are in the same situation, do anything for us? As Dr. Eder is dead I suppose the only Jewish analyst whom you could ask about this would be Dr. Franklin.

"Thanks at any rate, and I quite understand about the Vienna people. With the kindest regards to you both. Yours ever, Géza."

Yet there is a postscript—an even more anxious attempt to communicate with Rickman. One has the impression that, after he had ended his letter, all of Róheim's anxieties and fears returned suddenly, and he was no longer able to disguise them. It is as if the letter were composed of two texts, the second revealing that Róheim's defences were breaking down. It was in fact written by his wife, Ilmka Róheim, whose handwriting was much smaller than the one in the main text! And it is as if, as well as being herself, she were also another part of him!

"Dear John,

"The things look too bad [sic] and very little hope [sic]. God knows what brings the next future [sic]. We are all very sad about the Wienna people [note that here Róheim's wife uses the letter "W" instead of the letter "V"] and know very little about them. Please if you can do something try it [but was she referring only to the Viennese?]. I am not quite well. Best regards both of you [sic] from Ilmka."[26]

But there is further evidence of just how complex, difficult, even tragic were the lives of these Central European analysts, who could do nothing but wait, in the hope that someone would come to their rescue. I. Hollos' letter to Kubie, for instance, was also sent to Jones, who had to be kept informed of Hollos' efforts to emigrate to the United States with his Hungarian colleagues. This letter was written on 9 January 1939, by which time the Hungarians had lost almost all hope[27]—for how many of them would be able to leave, and where would they be able to go?

"Dear Dr. Kubie", wrote Hollos from Budapest, with the request that Kubie send his reply to H. Meng in Basel, as post arriving from America would arouse the suspicions of the Hungarian authorities,

> "During the Paris meeting in August 1938 [Hollos was referring to the IPA's last International Congress] I communicated to our colleagues that our Hungarian members are [sic] decided to stay under every possible circumstances in their country and so continue their work there as far as that would be possible."

But now the Hungarians needed the help and the support of their European and American colleagues "Though our recent situation is not yet so difficult, but its turn to the worst can be expected in a very short time [sic]", Hollos wrote. He had written to Jones along these same lines, but Jones had told him to write to Kubie—and we know the various reasons why Jones should have suggested this to him. In his letter to Kubie, Hollos mentions having received a very detailed and encouraging letter from Jones, but he then adds:

> "I feel it as my duty towards our members to let also you know the present condition and our circumstance and *beg you* [emphasis added] to get in touch with the competent members and in agreement with them to consider our difficult position."

Hollos then asks Kubie for advice on how to proceed, and where he and his colleagues ought to try for help. There were 15 of them, all with a personal history, with material belongings, financial problems, and anxieties; all waiting to go somewhere, all hoping that it would be possible for them to leave Hungary soon. But perhaps they had waited too long!

Kubie's reply was not very different from the position Jones would take with the Hungarian analysts M. and A. Balint, or with those analysts from Austria and Germany who would eventually be allowed to settle in Britain. In hindsight, his reaction must be seen in the context of what was taking place in the United States at that time, particularly when one considers the problems that were being encountered as a result of so many Jews and non-Jews emigrating to the United States in such a short space of time (Breitman & Kraut, 1987; Jahoda, 1969; Jeffrey, 1989).

The 15 psychoanalysts still trapped in Budapest must have found Kubie's sombre letter rather difficult to digest, even though the news was not completely negative. In writing to Hollos on 19 January 1939, Kubie explained that although he and his colleagues were very willing to help, there were great difficulties, as so many Hungarian Jews and refugees had applied for visas to the United States, and the quota had already been reached. It would not be possible to add another 15 people to a list that had been "over applied for a matter of ten or more years". There was no hope of entering the United States as a permanent immigrant on a regular quota. For that, it was too late. However, with his colleagues, they would try to do all that was possible. He then suggested a number of alternatives: it might be possible for one to obtain a visitor's visa, but this was only valid for six months, although there was the possibility that it may be extended once or twice. A second alternative would be for them to invite the analyst, asking the authorities for a non-quota visa. For this, however, the applicant would need to have had at least two years' experience as a teacher "in a school which is recognised as a teaching organization in Hungary". But, Kubie added, proof of this would have to be submitted to the American immigration authorities, including certificates from the Hungarian colleagues. A third option would be to come over on a provisional basis, in transit to another country, where the applicant would wait his turn to come back to America on a quota visa, as a proper immigrant. But in order to do this, the Hungarian analyst would need someone in the United States to guarantee that he would not become an economic liability to the U.S. system—in other words, "affidavit of support". Many American analysts were prepared to sign affidavits, but even this would take time, Kubie concluded, whilst asking for a list of names, for their curriculum vitae, and so on. The letter was signed by Kubie on behalf of the Emergency Committee on Relief and Immigration.

But consider Hollos' worried—not to say desperate—appeal to Jones, after he had learnt that the non-quota teacher's visas, on which he had placed all his hopes, were not as easily obtainable from the American consulate in Hungary as he had first thought. At this point the Hungarians found themselves totally on their own, as the support of their friends was clearly limited in that they were unable to intervene, as Jones had been able to do in Freud's case. It is here that the vicissitudes of these Hungarian analysts seem to mirror the desperate circumstances in which so many Jewish refugees also found themselves in these final hours, hopelessly wandering, all over Europe, from one Consulate to the other.

Writing from Budapest on 26 April 1939, Hollos informs Jones of the situation and the practicalities of Kubie's recommendations. And, of course, Jones was well aware of the contents of Kubie's letter. The situation was not very easy, Hollos told Jones; there were now "*29 Aspiranten aus deren Curriculi [sic] nach dem lezte Briefe Kubie's, höchtens 8–10 placiert werden könnten*". The numbers had now increased to 29 "aspirants", as Hollos called them, and of these, only 8 or 10 would have any chance of being allowed into America, if one read their curriculum vitae and if Kubie's information was correct. But things were not that simple, even for those teachers with all the right qualifications:

> "*Nun ist das Consulat heute nicht geneigt unsere Institut anzuerkennen. Doch könnte die Anerkennung des Konsulates [sic] erwirkt werden, wenn die I.U.K als moralische Korporation den Ausbildungs und Lehrkarakter des ungarischen Institutes und die Lehranalytiker als richtige Teachers bestättigen würde, umsomehr da viele auch im Auslande arbeitende und anerkannte Analytiker ihre Ausbildung in Budapest gewannen.*"

> [Now the (American) Consulate is not prepared to acknowledge our Institute. It would be possible for them to acknowledge it if the Institute of Psycho-Analysis of the United Kingdom would act as a moral supporter of the achievements and the teaching nature of the Hungarian Institute of Psychoanalysis and would guarantee that the Hungarian training analysts were true teachers. This also because many of the analysts who today work and have a name abroad trained in Budapest.]

Hollos then asked Jones whether it would still have been possible for some of his colleagues to be sent to England. He would even try to speak with the Princess Marie Bonaparte. . . .

But if these documents tell the official story of the Hungarian Society's difficult diaspora, there are also a few letters in the Archives that tell of some of the problems experienced by these analysts at a much more personal level. More often than not, as mentioned in chapter two, it is in reading the testimonies of relatively unimportant people that the historian is best able to feel the "pulse" of a situation, where he can truly appreciate the trials and the tribulations of the ordinary person and his friends. After all, not even at that time was psychoanalysis made up solely of the history and the personal vicissitudes of its cultural heroes!

Take, for example, the letters exchanged towards the end of 1938 between the Hungarian analyst E. Gyömröi-Glück and Ernest Jones.[28] Gyömröi and her husband were desperately trying to leave Hungary. Consider the difficult situation they were in, and the shame they must have felt in having to ask Jones for a loan of £100! Furthermore, this request for money was accompanied by some Byzantine instructions on where the money was to be sent, so that they would be sure of being able to cash it! In this letter, dated 20 December 1938, Gyömröi also informs Jones that she and her husband had obtained, from the British Consulate in Budapest, a *"colonial visum"*—a visa to emigrate to one of the British colonies! She had originally thought of going to the United States, but considering the difficulties she would have had with Kubie, she had decided she would try for Ceylon. But was there any possibility of her being able to come to London, she asks Jones![29] In another, sent from Budapest and dated 26 December 1938, Gyömröi again attempts to explain the difficulties of the situation, stating pathetically: *"Wir brauchen Ihre Hilfe so sehr dass wir uns one Sie gar nicht rühren können. . . ."* [We need your help so much that without you we cannot move. . . .] She ends her letter by telling Jones that she and her husband had borrowed some money,

> *"und wir haben zwei Tickets für den Dampfer der am 8 II von Triest abfährt bestellt. Hoffentlich ist noch Platz da und hoffentlich können wir bis dahin mit den hiesigen Behörden alles erledigen so dass wir die Reise nicht verschieben müssen."*

> [and we have ordered two tickets for the steamboat which will leave Trieste on 8 II 1939. Hopefully there is still place on that boat and hopefully we will be able to settle everything with the local authorities until then so that travel will not be delayed.]

One can only imagine what it must have been like for Jones having to deal with a number of emigrants in this situation, having to listen to their requests, follow all their personal setbacks, misfortunes, etc.—all from the safe haven of London. But what Gyömröi's letters do manage to communicate so vividly, apart from the anxious and at times demanding overtones of her words, are the adversities and the sadness that she experienced. I think it is not difficult to understand and to identify with the desperation in Gyömröi's statements when one considers the ordeals she and her friends had to go through. On her way to Ceylon, she wrote to Jones from Port Said, on the letterheaded paper of the Lloyd Triestino, the Italian owners of the ship she was sailing on. Having apologized again to Jones for all the problems she had caused in asking him for the £100 loan, and having explained how difficult it had been to write letters from Budapest in the terrible situation everyone was in, Gyömröi adds: "*Sie können sich nicht vorstellen was für uns jetzt das wiedergewonnene Gefühl menschlicher Freiheit bedeutet*" [You cannot imagine what it means for us the feeling of having won back human freedom]. She then tells Jones that she would be letting him know about her work in Ceylon, and whether there would be any opportunities there for other colleagues.

It is in the description she gives, after her safe arrival in Ceylon, of her attempts to settle down and work that we can capture further glimpses of the complexities surrounding the personal and professional lives of those individuals who, by force of circumstance, were obliged to emigrate. Gyömröi's story is a typical example. In a letter to Jones dated 15 March 1939,[30] Gyömröi tells him that she has begun her work as an analyst. Unfortunately, her first consultation was with a paranoic young man. Could Jones help her to find someone in England to whom she could send this patient? His mother was very keen to help him, but Gyömröi felt the case was beyond her capabilities. Not even when she still lived on the Continent and worked as a lay analyst had she ever taken on a psychotic patient. There was also the problem, Gyömröi adds, that she did not want to compromise her new practice with cases that had such an unfavourable prognosis "*da ich glaube dass wenig sichtbare Erfolge zur Popularisierung der Analyse sehr beitragen wurden*" [because I think that unnoticeable results would not greatly contribute to the popularization of psychoanalysis]. But was it only the popularization of psychoanalysis in Ceylon that Gyömröi had in mind? Or was it her own survival too? Far from her country, cut off from the support she would have had from her colleagues and from the Hungarian Institute of Psychoanalysis, and working as a lay analyst must have been quite difficult and even dangerous at times. As she said in her letter to Jones, she was still uncertain about her prospects, and the future for other colleagues was quite uncertain too. What she could say for sure was that medically trained psychoanalysts would not have any possibility of developing their practice, "*Aber vielleicht is später etwas für Laie möglich*" [But perhaps later on there would be some possibilities for lay people]![31] But, in order to complete the picture of Gyömröi's difficulties and hopes in Ceylon, I think it also worth while to mention briefly her letters to Rickman. One dated 8 May 1939 echoes what she had written to Jones: "we have rather a hard time here dear Dr Rickman . . . the beginning of a new life is never easy, but here it seems to be particularly difficult and I have days when I nearly lose my faith"— although in the same letter she also stressed, of course, how happy she felt for having been able to escape from Hungary. The second letter, dated 23 July 1939, is much more detailed—in it, Gyömröi informs Rickman about the terrible illness of her husband and the difficulties she had in building a practice in order to survive, because she had been manipulated also by some local doctors, who had promised to help her: "My life is a *grand guignol*. . . . I do not know how I will be able to stay here when I am left alone" (she meant once her husband had died). "Where could I go from here? How could I come to England?" She was asking in a desperate mood, although she fully realized what she would have to face in England: "I am less afraid of war as of this isolation here. My only dream is to go to England or where I could go . . . ? I will never get patients here. They are consulting me and then they try the shaman once again."

A similar account of the difficult fortunes of the forced migration of psychoanalysis—as one might call it—is found in the correspondence between Jones and another Hungarian analyst, one even less known than Gyömröi—Dr P. Schonberger. In reading Dr Schonberger's letters to Jones, we are able to see, or at least to imagine, what would have been the problems faced by those who had found it impossible to emigrate to Britain, and the fate that would have been reserved for them, notwithstanding the help they would have received from Jones. As I said earlier, when circumstances prevented an analyst from coming to Britain, Jones would suggest other countries where it would be easier for them to acquire entry visas and to settle. The indirect consequences of this was that psychoanalysis was introduced into countries such as Australia and New Zealand. However, one must not forget the suspicions that psychoanalysis would have encountered in these countries, nor the restrictions that would have been placed on its practice, to say nothing of the envy that it would have aroused in the medical professions at a local level and within the psychotherapeutic establishment of the BMA itself.

Several of Schonberger's letters to Jones provide an account of his travails in this respect. On 23 January 1939, he seems to be full of hope, telling Jones that he has been in contact with a Dr F. Winn, a local Australian doctor, who was prepared to help him emigrate to Australia. According to Dr Winn, there appeared to be good opportunities for eight graduate doctors from foreign universities to practise in Australia, and there would be no need for them to go through the last three years of the Australian medical course:

> "Dr Winn is prepared to do all that is in his power, he will argue that a psychoanalyst's practice does not compete financially with that of any other type; and that regarding the amount of neurotics in Australia the psychoanalyst's are extremely unlikely to fail in making a living."

Entering Australia as a physician and in this way would have allowed Schonberger to begin practising psychoanalysis there.

If the contents of the letter were not about such a serious matter, one might be inclined to think that it had been dictated by an eccentric Englishman with a rather ironical sense of humour!

Everything seemed to be fine, and those doctors who, like Dr Schonberger, had originally intended to go to New Zealand, could now hope to emigrate to Australia instead, notwithstanding the fact that there were "common difficulties with which we meet in introducing our methods; people are unable to distinguish between qualified and unqualified analysts on the one hand, and lay analysts are regarded as quacks, on the other". Schonberger asks Jones to intervene and to help him obtain an entry visa to Australia as a physician.

Matters seemed to be proceeding smoothly, and others, having heard of this possibility, were trying to follow Schonberger's example. Even Sterberg, Schonberger said, if he were not to be accepted by the United States, had plans to go to Australia. One has to imagine the unpredictable circumstances in which these analysts were living during that period, and just how desperate they were to try whatever avenues were suggested, or whatever looked like a viable proposition. In a letter dated February 1939, Schonberger even tells Jones that "Mrs Levy [Kata Levy, whom Anna Freud mentioned to Jones in a letter I referred to above] asked if a non-psychoanalytical physician, whose name she did not mention, could be included into the proposed group". "Not knowing your opinion in this matter", Schonberger added, "I advised her to write you directly". One must, of course, read between the lines and imagine the position Jones was in and the pressures that would have been put on him, to say nothing of the guilt he would have felt if he were to have ignored the help required of him by another potential victim of the Nazis.

However, in a very complicated letter dated 13 May 1939, Schonberger informs Jones that "Dr Winn admitted that he was 'misinformed by the secretary of the B.M.A. concerning the 8 graduates' who would have been allowed to practise immediately in Australia"—in other words, Schonberger had had his application for "a permit to enter Australia" refused. Although there were many people in Australia interested in the development of psychoanalysis, they were not prepared to fight the decisions of the BMA. One can imagine how Dr Schonberger and his friends must have felt on receiving this news. They now had to find a different means of obtaining their permits and visas. "I can't help repeating what a pity it is, that a plan supported with so great efforts by you and Dr. Winn", concluded Schonberger, "so well founded both as to doing pioneer work for psychoanalysis in Australia and as to securing me a living for the time of the medical course, should fail".

The following sentence, I believe, speaks for itself and needs no further comment. There can be no better words to convey the solitude and the dignified awareness of someone like Schonberger of the difficulties he was up against:

> "I should like to express my thanks for all that you have done so far and I wish I could count on your kind help also in the rather improbable case when owing to a sort of *Deus ex machina*, I could leave this country."

I think it is obvious from the excerpts I quote above that this is but one of many similar cases one could read of, that tell of how those Hungarian, German, and Austrian professionals managed to escape and to survive. An exhaustive story of the emigration of psychoanalysis and its diaspora has yet to be written; it would certainly constitute a very important chapter in the intellectual and socio-political history of the twentieth century.

CHAPTER SEVEN

Special *"Kinder"* and special *"Sorge"*

Wilhelm Reich, Edith Jacobsohn,
and political neutrality in psychoanalysis

Perhaps it is now time to move on to consider what can be
further unearthed from my brief comments and from my
analysis of the term *"Sorgenkinder"* and "special *Sorgenkinder"*,
as in the case of Reik, Simmel, and others (see chapter four). I have
already put forward the hypothesis that, in a certain sense, Jones
might well have considered Freud and his family his *"Sorgenkinder"*,
so to speak (see chapter one). Jones's political and strategic master-
plan, of moving Freud and his daughter to London, would have
matured, at least as far as one can gather from his letters to Anna,
during the early months of 1938, though his letters do not reveal
much, apart from Freud's attitude towards the prospect of having to
emigrate.

Freud's decision to leave was left to the last possible moment.
From the time the Nazis first began to persecute the Jews, Freud had
been fully aware of what went on in Germany; and he also knew
about the concentration camps, as can be clearly inferred from his
correspondence with Zweig, despite his and Anna's optimism in the
early 1930s as far as Austria was concerned. So one might even have
the impression that there was a deliberately contrived disregard for

danger on Freud's part. (Dr Stross was also of a similar opinion when I discussed this possibility with her—she also wittily remarked that it could also be considered an instance of "*Wiener Schlamperei*"!) What his letters also reveal is Freud's detachment with regard to his own possible tragic death. There may have been several reasons for this; it is probable that both his age and his illness contributed to his attitude with regard to what was happening around him at the time (King & Steiner, 1992, pp. 228–229). But when the time came, Freud faced the departure from Vienna with extreme calm, as can be gathered from Anna's chronicle of events in her letters to Jones.

To return to the kind of "*Sorge*" that Jones and the British Psycho-Analytical Society may have felt towards Freud, his daughter, and their circle of friends, one needs to turn to the correspondence contained in the Archives. They were all individuals of a certain standing, and their arrival would inevitably have added to the worries of all concerned, but on reading the letters one finds a substantial amount of previously unearthed information that merits being looked at in greater detail.[1] For example, these documents confirm that certain problems cannot simply be conceived as having been the result of a rescue operation put into place to help fleeing analysts, as I have already mentioned in chapter six. It was also a shrewd and very carefully considered plan of action, in that it not only found the emigrants a place of refuge, but it did so by evaluating each individual according to his professional competence, his personal idiosyncrasies, and, when necessary, according to political and ideological criteria that, if not discriminatory, were decidedly "selective". Both in the short and in the long term, this process was to have a profound effect on psychoanalysis in general.

The above confirms a point I made very early on regarding the researcher's need to bear in mind the "monument-cum-document" aspect of such letters, and not least the need for him to continuously interpreted and re-interpret them. It also confirms the specificity of psychoanalytical history and is evidence that the unconscious is always present, via those various "filiations" of which I spoke earlier.

I would like now, therefore, to illustrate briefly the importance and the implications of these rules for selection, which were applied not only in the case of Freud and his family and friends, as we know, but in all cases, and which were based at times on political and ideological criteria, together with more personal and often unconscious reasons. Although these criteria were obviously related to the conditions of those years and to the particular socio-political context of the emigration, just think of the problems left-wing immigrants experienced everywhere. The problems were multiplied in situations beyond that of psychoanalysis, and they extended even to the characteristics of particular personalities. But these problems can be studied in order to try to make sense of—or at least point out the existence of—certain recurrent problems in psychoanalysis, in the context of its further developments in various countries and in different cultural and socio-political situations.

In addition to the case of Freud and his family and friends, on which I touch in chapter eight, two specific episodes provide an idea of the situation at the time, although the reader will also have to bear in mind that they are but the tip of the iceberg, so to speak.

As I mentioned above, the Archives of the British Psycho-Analytical Society contain some very interesting letters concerning Wilhelm Reich exchanged between Anna Freud and Ernest Jones—letters that would merit a very lengthy analysis, given the issues they raise. This correspondence discusses one major problem: what was one to do with Reich? By March–April 1933, Reich had begun to move to and fro between Berlin and Vienna. He later went to Denmark, from where he was expelled, and then moved to Scandinavia. All during this time he had the following and the support—at a distance, at least—of colleagues such as Fenichel and Bernfeld, among others.[2]

Bearing in mind that Anna would have been writing with her father at her side, in her letter to Jones dated 27 April 1933 she states quite categorically that Reich is too much of a danger for psychoanalysis, not just for his ideas, but also because, given the historical circumstances of the moment, psychoanalysis in Germany and in Austria was already in a very precarious situation. One must also remember that Vienna had been inundated by psychoanalysts fleeing Berlin, and it was obvious that the Viennese establishment was extremely concerned about Reich's and his colleagues' ideological commitments and activities. M. Langer (1989, p. 80) gives a rather disturbing portrait of the way in which the Viennese psychoanalytical establishment, worried about some of the Berlin refugees they were hosting, held back from political commitment of any kind after 1934, in view of the ever-increasing pressures imposed by Austro-Fascism.[3] But the fact that Reich strongly opposed the Nazis did not seem to matter. Indeed, these are Anna's comments to Jones on the situation:

"Was dass in heutigen Zeiten für die analytische Vereinigung bedeuten kann, weisst jeder. Wir sind hier alle jederzeit bereit uns für die Analyse zu exponieren, aber keineswegs fur Reich's Ideen, die keiner von uns teilt. Der Ausspruch meines Vaters darüber ist: wenn die Psychoanalyse verboten wird, so soll sie als Psa. verboten werden, aber nicht als das Gemisch von Politik und Analyse dass Reich vertritt. . . . 'Mein Vater' kann nicht erwarten, Reich als Mitglied loszuwerden. Ihn beleidigt die Vergewaltigung der Analyse ins Politische, wo sie nicht hingehört."

[What all this[4] could mean for the psychoanalytic community, everybody already knows. Here we are all prepared to take risks for psychoanalysis, but not for Reich's ideas, with which nobody is in agreement. My father's opinion on this matter is: If psychoanalysis is to be prohibited, it should be prohibited because of what it is, and not for the mixture of politics and psychoanalysis which Reich represents. My father can't wait to get rid of him inasmuch as he attaches himself to psychoanalysis; what my father finds offensive in Reich is the fact that he has forced psychoanalysis to become political; psychoanalysis has no part in politics.][5]

In this same letter of 27 April, Anna asks Jones for his opinion on the matter. And Jones's reply is not long in coming. At first extremely cautious, to the point of separating Reich's political interests from his abilities as an analyst, which Jones did not underrate, Jones writes back to Anna on 2 May 1933:

"Before forming an opinion about the Reich problem, I should like to be better informed about the objections to him. My own knowledge is that he is a very clever analyst, but somewhat wild and unreliable in his theoretical judgements. That the Berlin group have objected to him mixing up psychoanalysis and communism, I can well understand. But is there anything further? I understand that he has been up to now an accredited *Lehranalyst* in Berlin. If so, I think he would have the right of going to another place to found a *Lehr Institut* and I do not see how Eitingon or anybody else could forbid him."

However, a few days later Jones was to recommend Reich's expulsion from the Berlin group,[6] stressing that one should take advantage of the fact that the Berlin Institute wanted to rid itself of those Jewish analysts still remaining and, with greater reason, of the Communists as well[7] (see Jones to A. Freud, 2 May 1933; Jones to P. Federn, 29 November 1933; and Jones to A. Freud, 2 December 1933). A few months later, after Jones had met Reich in London, Jones would appear to have changed his mind yet again, notwithstanding the fact that he had written to the Danish Government requesting that they obstruct Reich's activities in that country (see Jones to A. Freud, 7 November 1933).

I have on several occasions referred to Jones's concept of psychoanalysis, with which Freud and his daughter were in full accord. For Jones, psychoanalysis was to be considered a pure science, its field of research being the study of psychic truth and nothing more. As such, in Jones's view psychoanalysis was not open to any political influence or contamination. This approach was a typical product of the cultural context in which psychoanalysis first took root at the end of the last century. However, as President of the International Psycho-Analytical Association, Jones was to go further, and he would adopt this traditional stance for the purposes of political expediency. Just remember again, for instance, his speeches at the Marienbad and Paris IPA congresses (see chapter five).

But to return to Jones's meeting in London with Reich, Jones interviewed him with the assistance of Klein and Riviere, among others—and all the people present at the interview would have had some previous involvement with the Berlin Institute. I would say, however, that this meeting did not change his views as such—it merely prompted him to speculate as to whether one had the authority to prevent a psychoanalyst from exercising his right to become involved in politics. In his letter to Anna Freud of 9 December 1933, he expresses himself in this regard:

> "We felt that it would be a serious thing to take up the position that no analyst could be allowed to play an active part in social life and movements, whatever they may be, and we felt that such a question should be decided by the Society of the particular analyst."[8]

In fact, Jones even claimed to have been favourably impressed by Reich at a personal level, although he had found his theories to be rather naive (Jones to A. Freud, 9 and 15 December 1933). Anna would also appear to have been partly in agreement with Jones's assessment of Reich's character, although she emphasized that he was unstable and that things could well have ended badly for him—all of which she had deduced from having had Reich's wife, Anna, in analysis with her (see Anna Freud to Jones, 1 January 1934).

This correspondence would, indeed, merit a much more in-depth analysis, particularly as Reich's case brings some extremely complex problems to light. At the basis of their condemnation of Reich was the fact that he was intent on interpreting psychoanalysis from a specific ideological perspective, which reflected his Marxist beliefs and his endorsement of the Russian Revolution. This, in turn, would imply that Sigmund Freud, Anna, and Ernest Jones were themselves politically active, for their influence in the International Psycho-Analytical Association was such that they were in a position to decide, on the basis of the political convictions of those individuals under review, who should and who should not belong to the Association. At times this fact would seem to have registered with Jones, at least when in the company of his friends. Perhaps when considering this matter one ought also to bear in mind just how complex were the problems faced by analysts living in Berlin at the time and by those who had emigrated to London from there, and all the internal tensions and discussions that ensued as a result of their having to depend on Vienna, including the pressures they would have been under had they attempted to develop their own ideas, as in Klein's case, for example.

Furthermore, as I noted earlier, Jones had the added problem of having to defend the IPA. To make matters worse, the Nazis tended to confuse the International Psycho-Analytical Association with Communist International,[9] as we have seen from the letters exchanged between Jones and van Ophuijsen in 1933 and 1934. A typical example would be the strategies Jones had to adopt when, in 1936, he tried, unsuccessfully, to have Edith Jacobsohn released from prison. (Jacobsohn eventually managed to escape from a guarded sanatorium in Prague in 1938, and from there she emigrated to the United States— Brecht, 1987; Brecht et al., 1993.) In his efforts, Jones had to take the utmost care not to involve the International Association as such—a fact borne out by his letters concerning Jacobsohn to Brill, to Anna Freud, and to Federn, Fenichel, and others.

But let us take a closer look at Jacobsohn, as her case is the second of the three I mentioned a few pages earlier. The Archives of the British Psycho-Analytical Society contain a number of letters on Edith Jacobsohn, and her case is a typical example of the difficulties that psychoanalysis, as a science and as a purely non-political entity, was to encounter in certain situations. In a letter to Anna dated 31 October 1935, Jones described the circumstances that had led to Jacobsohn's arrest, and he told of what was happening to some of her patients and pupils, such as Frau R. Benedek and Frau L. Liebeck Kirschner. It is quite clear that whilst Jones wanted to help Jacobsohn, *he was also reluctant to use the International Psycho-Analytical Society to do so*, as he was afraid of the reactions of his German colleagues. The state of affairs with the Berlin Institute and the German Society was extremely difficult, as we know (see chapters four and five), and the situation with the Jewish analysts living there very precarious. Boehm and Müller-Braunschweig were putting pressure on Jones, as can be inferred from letters written by Jones to Fenichel, dated 11 November 1935, and to Anna Freud, on 14 November 1935, where Jones openly states that Boehm was worried he would use the IPA to put pressure on the German Government, thus jeopardizing the situation of psychoanalysis in Germany.[10] This letter also mentions the state of terror reigning in Germany at the time, and the enormous amount of money being demanded by lawyers to defend Jacobsohn, who was a Jew. The situation is further discussed in other letters between Jones, Fenichel, Federn, Spitz, Anna Freud,[11] and Brill. In two letters to Brill, dated 13 November and 24 December 1935 respectively, Jones gave an account of events and also set out his position in the matter. The first letter reads:

> "Presumably you have not yet heard of the arrest of Edith Jacobsohn by the secret police in Berlin. They first arrested some of her patients and murdered one of them, and we have been very much afraid of her being tortured to give information. We are of course doing everything possible to help in the situation but we have to be extremely careful because of the Society. It looks by the way as if the German Society will soon be forced to expel all its Jewish members. The situation for Jews in Germany is a great deal worse than any of the newspaper reports admit. It is really terrible. If you have any funds that could be used to help the German Jewish analysts I could make good use of it!"

In the second letter, in thanking Brill for the money he had sent, Jones writes:

> "It was exceedingly generous of you and I can tell you that the money will be specially welcomed. Edith Jacobsohn is unfortu-

nately still in prison, *Untersuchungshaft*, and we cannot help suspecting that her lawyer is in with the other side and is arranging to keep her in longer than necessary so as to increase his already exorbitant fees."

As can be gathered from a letter to Fenichel on 12 April 1936, Jones would eventually meet Jacobsohn's lawyer in Berlin. He would find Dr E. Kussman ruthless and manic. In another letter, dated 26 September 1936, Jones wrote to Prof. Namier, the famous historian, to ask him whether he would arrange for him to be introduced to Lord Lothian, in order that he might put pressure on Ribbentrop, the new German Ambassador to Britain, for Jacobsohn to be released.

There is no doubt that the problems experienced with Reich and the failed attempt to have Jacobsohn released both confirm just how complex and tortuous were the rescue and the emigration processes. Another factor that comes to light is the extent to which the political and personal ideologies of those persons who were desperately in need of assistance would often clash with the tenets of those who were attempting to save their lives, and how these differences would exacerbate and hamper what was already an extremely difficult situation. It also demonstrates how personal loyalties and commitments had to give way to what could be called the *"Realpolitik"* of the time, and how people were at times obliged to make painful compromises. Jones may have wavered and may have contradicted himself where Reich was concerned, but one could say that his case was, on the whole, pretty straightforward.

As far as Jacobsohn's arrest is concerned, however, it is obvious that this would have caused him to struggle with many conflicting feelings, although naturally Jones did everything he could to secure her freedom, to the point where even Fenichel—who, generally speaking, was not a great supporter either of Jones or of the Austrian establishment—acknowledged his efforts.

Both incidents touched upon the complex problem of the scientific, ethical, and social status of psychoanalysis as such. Could psychoanalysis really be dissociated from political and social ideologies? Could it really be considered as neutral as Freud and Jones thought it ought to be? Or was it not, perhaps, a question of considering what kind of political and social ideologies were implicit in psychoanalysis? As is quite evident from the documentation and the *Rundbriefe* written at the time and as certain of today's scholars will confirm

(Brecht, 1987; Lockot, 1994; Mühlleitner & Reichmayr, 1998), there were quite substantial differences, at least from 1934 onwards, between Reich's views and his political commitments and the *"Neu Beginnen"* group—a sort of *avant-garde* group at the left of the German Social Democratic Party—of which Jacobsohn was a member. It therefore follows that Reich and Jacobsohn, and Fenichel's *"Rundbriefe* Group" to which Jacobsohn later belonged, would each have had a rather different conception of the relationship between psychoanalysis and Marxism, between psychoanalysis and the Communist Party, and between psychoanalysis and the Russian Revolution. There is no doubt that all this might today appear rather naive, but one must put these beliefs in the context of the times and consider the humanistic and progressive stimuli they contained (see also Mühlleitner & Reichmayr's editorial comments to Fenichel's *Rundbriefe*, 1998, Vol. II, pp. 1949–1955). A detailed discussion of these matters would entail having to reconsider the role that was played by left-wing ideologies during the 1920s and 1930s and their influence on many analysts and on at least two generations of intellectuals living in the Weimar Republic! Not all left-wing psychoanalysts supported Stalinist Russia, for instance. Moreover, it is far easier to judge events with the benefit of hindsight. What, I believe, matters more at this point is that it would be impossible to deny that Freud, the Viennese establishment, and Jones were themselves influenced by social and political ideologies and that these did determine the decisions and the choices they made! That they were more or less actively practising a political ideology of one kind or another emerges quite clearly from all the material in this book.

That matters were as complex as I have suggested is borne out by the fact that Freud and his circle had to abandon Berlin and Vienna for reasons that went well beyond the unpredictable political situation, and their departure also came to be identified with other factors. Their exile came to be seen as the symbolic condemnation of the Nazi totalitarian values that had precluded psychoanalysis from existing as an institution and as a science, because it believed in the basic principles that guide human relationships, because it respected the patient as an individual, and because it fostered tolerance both in its clinical practice and in general. Could one deny that these reasons, choices, principles, and so forth do not in themselves have wider socio-political implications? Broadly speaking, these values form part of the liberal, radical, democratic values that modern Europe and

America have inherited from the Enlightenment of the second half of the eighteenth century, and without which neither the cultural nor the scientific aspects of psychoanalysis would have been conceived. And these principles were, and continue to be, fundamental to the institutional life of psychoanalysis and to psychoanalysis as a social science.

That the problem did not end with the conclusion of Reich's case or with Jacobsohn's escape from prison is quite evident from the fact that politics have continued to influence all of the efforts that are made in psychoanalysis to construct a history of our discipline and to understand why and how psychoanalysis has developed in different ways in different cultures and under different socio-political regimes. Consider, for example, what happened to those German and Austrian left-wing analysts who emigrated to the United States and to South America (Coser, 1984; Friedman, 1990; Harris & Brook, 1991; Jacoby, 1983; Langer, 1989), and the concerns expressed for present-day psychoanalysis in general. Of no lesser importance are the problems with which psychoanalysis has had to contend, and continues to contend, in Eastern Europe. Incidentally, in certain parts of Latin America, such as in Argentina, in Brazil, and, until recently, in Chile, dictatorship or military rule has tended to be the norm rather than the exception (Bessermann, 1997), and this, too, had and continues to have profound implications for psychoanalysis.

A study of the documents, whilst bearing in mind the particular needs of psychoanalysis, its system, and its methods of research, shows that it was obviously impossible for it to endorse an ideology that, being dictatorial, in essence negated both the development of the individual and the autonomy of any institutional or social structure. From this we may conclude that the neutral stance that psychoanalysts as clinicians must adopt ought not to imply silence in the face of social and political situations where the very values of psychoanalysis are threatened. *Silence and neutrality in such situations are tantamount to collusion and neutralization.*

CHAPTER EIGHT

Jones, Anna, the Viennese *"Sorgenkinder"*, and "the English way of life"

There is one final episode I wish to bring to the reader's attention, as to a certain extent it is related to Reich's case, and to Jacobsohn's, at least in the sense that it too chronicles the particular way the emigration problem was dealt with. It also narrates the inevitable repercussions of the refugee issue, at an individual and an administrative level, both on the institutions associated with psychoanalysis and on the cultural and social make-up of those psychoanalytic societies that had agreed to accept refugee immigrants. As we have seen, certain of the criteria that were used by these societies in administering the immigration problem (such as restrictions on the number of immigrants, and so forth) were dictated by external circumstances, and, as I have already stressed in chapter one, there is no doubt that one will find analogies between the rules that were applied in such instances and the policies that were often adopted at a more general level. Indeed, the criteria by which a refugee would be accepted, rejected, or displaced—be they determined by unconscious or conscious reasons or even based on the more or less explicit use of psychopathological diagnoses—together with the selection criteria based on political and ideological reasons, would tend to overlap and become confused with the more typical political, social, and cultural methods of discrimination. When all was said and done, psychoanalysts did not always conduct themselves so very differently from politicians. I have already talked of the way the Americans handled the refugee problem. Nevertheless, the letters between Anna Freud and Ernest Jones and the other documents deposited in the Archives of the British Psycho-Analytical Society are particularly useful in that they allow us to focus quite closely on the policies Jones adopted to solve the dilemma of how best to deal with those refugees who wanted to settle in Great Britain in the case of the Viennese, in addition to what I have already noted in the case of psychoanalysts coming from Berlin. These methods are quite revealing at times, as they again underline just how overdetermined was the notion of psychoanalytic neutrality when one found oneself faced with such extensive problems; they also serve to highlight just how inevitably limited the traditional British notion of "tolerance" was on occasion.

Rickman's *faux pas* is a case in point. As we well know, the first part of 1938 was an exceptionally difficult period for the Viennese, who were, among other things, all desperate to leave.[1] It was in this climate, exceedingly tense and fraught with anxiety, that Rickman visited Vienna in May–June 1938 and met with Anna Freud. In his conversations with her, he made various comments that Anna understood as meaning that the Viennese would encounter many serious problems should they decide to come to London. One must bear in mind, in this context, the many long, bitter disagreements between Melanie Klein and Anna Freud dating back more than ten years (Grosskurth, 1986; Steiner, 1985; Young-Bruehl, 1988), and only in 1937 had the visits exchanged between London and Vienna succeeded in calming matters down (see Jones to Anna Freud, 20 April 1938; Jones to Anna, 25 April 1938; Jones to Anna, 25 April 1938; Anna to Jones, 26 April 1938; Anna to Jones, 28 April 1938).[2]

All of Jones's diplomatic capacities were again required to calm the turmoil caused by Rickman's remarks. Jones told Anna that Rickman had been in a highly emotional state at the time, and he was very harsh indeed about Rickman in some of his comments. At the time, Rickman was in analysis with Melanie Klein, and Jones did not fail to underline this. He also insisted that Rickman had not gone to Vienna on official business, and that his statements were totally unfounded (see Jones to Anna, 25 April 1938; see also Klein to Jones, 1941, in King & Steiner, 1992, p. 228). However, at around the same time that this unfortunate episode took place, Jones and Anna were also exchanging letters on issues concerning Melanie Klein, as mentioned above. In one of these letters Jones was very open in some of his affirmations, and he quite clearly explained to her that: "Dreams have to compromise with reality if they are to be fulfilled, and then neither of us is omnipotent." And speaking of himself, he added:

> "as regards my personal omnipotence, I cannot ignore entirely the attitude of my British colleagues, otherwise I should lose all power of effecting my aim of bringing about the greatest amount of harmony between us and the newcomers and of making the future lives of the latter as successful and happy as possible." [Jones to Anna, 20 April 1938]

Indeed, it would be omnipotent on my part, too, if I were to claim that, in view of Jones's foregoing declarations and his subsequent activities, he would have been able to avert all the arguments that were to take place in the years to come and to culminate in the Controversial Discussions. At the end of the day, the British Psycho-Analytical Society did, in fact, manage to survive the head-on collision between Anna Freud and Melanie Klein, notwithstanding the fact that the controversies continued from 1941 through to 1945 (King & Steiner, 1992; Steiner, 1985, 2000).

These conflicts were probably inevitable, even if it is a relatively easy matter to discuss them in retrospect and with the benefit of having been able to examine the particulars that emerge from these documents in their cultural and socio-political context. But there is no doubt that the impact on the British Psycho-Analytical Society of the Viennese was felt as potentially rather shocking by Jones and his friends, judging by what I have already quoted.

As far as this issue is concerned, the letters exchanged between Jones and Anna Freud have still more to reveal, as they also provide us with information on the characteristics of the British Psycho-Analytical Society, its cultural environment, and the way it would react to these events. Indeed, the arrival of Freud and his circle posed enormously difficult problems, all of which had to be dealt with. *But as can be clearly deciphered from the letters, Jones and his colleagues had to monitor the emigration issue in such a way as to leave intact the identity and the characteristics of their own particular conception of psychoanalysis. The need to protect the British Psycho-Analytical Society was of paramount importance* (see also chapter six).

Although I am unable to agree unreservedly with Anderson's views (1968), touched upon earlier, I have to say that we have here a perfect example of the way in which certain indigenous members and certain institutions of a particular culture are able to remain fully in control of their principles. Consequently, whilst these individuals were not indifferent to what was happening around them and they would not have neglected to offer help to those who required it of them, they would do so only on a case-by-case basis and only within certain parameters. I do not wish to be misunderstood, however. Even though they might have done everything in their power to prevent an "undesirable" psychoanalyst from settling in Britain, there is not one letter in which Jones and his colleagues do not openly express their willingness to help rescue a fellow in need, in the hope that he would then be able to continue his career with dignity. Not even in Sterba's case was assistance denied to him in the end, in spite of Jones's deep irritation because, although not being a Jew, Sterba and his family had left Vienna, instead of staying "together with August Aichhorn as a memory of psychoanalysis or a better time"— as Jones wrote to Sterba (1982, p. 163; but see also chapter four). Jones was extremely reticent when Sterba asked him for help, but he offered Sterba his support to emigrate to South Africa (Sterba, 1982, p. 164; see also Jones to A. Freud, 6 May 1938). In the end, however, due to the difficult situation in South Africa, Sterba and his family managed, with great relief, to emigrate to the United States.

Even when faced with the dilemma of having to decide what to do with Reich, who would have wanted to settle either in Paris or in London, Jones did not wash his hands of the matter; he was committed enough to seek some sort of a solution, eventually recommending that Reich should go to the United States or to Russia. As we have seen, this was the way of things for many other psychoanalysts.

Nevertheless, apart from the objective difficulties associated with the economic crisis and the obstacles to finding work in Britain, one of Jones's and his associates' concerns was to ensure that an individual who wanted to emigrate to Britain was capable of integrating into British society. I do not believe that one needs to be endowed with any particular gift of interpretation to understand the following assertions, already made in reference to the Berliners and concerning the situation that had arisen as a result of quite a number of them having emigrated. In a letter to Anna dated 2 July 1934, Jones says:

"It is in all events plain that the old Berlin Society has transferred its interminable personal quarrels to other countries, which after Abraham's death were no longer to be concealed."

In a letter he wrote to Eitingon on the same matters, on 3 July of that same year, Jones is even more forthright: perhaps I may be forgiven for underlining the frankness with which he approaches the issue:

"The story from America is certainly very dismal and we must do our best to support Brill in his desperate endeavour to lead a peaceful life, in which one can work. The quarrelsome Central Europeans seem to have retained their home habits in other countries and are doing their best to infect these with them. I hope we shall have better luck in England than in America, *which was the reason why I made a very careful selection*." [emphasis added]

It is quite obvious that subjective factors, such as Jones's personal like or dislike of an individual, inevitably played a part in the selection process. After all, every analyst, notwithstanding his analysis, is nothing but flesh and blood. The interviews, and at times the selection processes themselves, were conducted along the same lines as those for candidates applying for training. (And indeed, when analysts who had already begun their training in Vienna were interviewed, the criteria were applied even more strictly.) It was inevitable that the procedure initially adopted with the German refugees would be continued years later when the Viennese emigrants began to seek refuge—not least because, as had been the case already for the analysts coming from Berlin, the economic situation in Britain at the time was such that there were very meagre prospects of finding work for these analysts, and even less so for those who happened to be lay analysts (see Jones to Anna, 29 April 1938).

But let us see how Jones operated *vis-à-vis* Anna and the Viennese and some of the Hungarians, bearing in mind his views on psychoanalysis. The people mentioned in the correspondence are many, and to have to evaluate the relative merits of each individual could not have been an easy matter for him; nor could it have been very pleasant to have to reject those individuals who were thought unsuitable. In fact, one can at times detect signs in the letters of the painful embarrassment that such circumstances must have caused, and the caution with which any major altercations were avoided. Anna was clearly extremely sensitive on those issues, although she had to accept what Jones was telling her. This is shown in the following extract, from a letter Anna wrote to Jones in May 1938 (undated):

> *"Zur Frage der Placierung der Immigranten wollte ich Dich noch einmal bitten, niemanden der Wiener Immigranten (besonders nicht Bibrings oder Hoffers) wissen zu lassen dass wir über diese Frage in Korrespondenz sind. Du weisst wie schwierig die persönlichen Verhältnisse in eine Vereinigung gewöhnlich sind, wieviel sich da von Übertragungen, Freundschaften, Konkurrenze etc. durcheindander kreutzen. Die Entscheidigungen jetzt muss man nach sächlich nicht persönlichen Motiven treffen. Es ist dabei sehr viel leichter für mich und auch für die Leute selbst, wenn sie nicht wissen, dass ich auch etwas im negativer oder in positiven Sinn damit zu tun habe."*

> [With regard to the problem of where to place the immigrants, I must ask you once more not to mention anything of all this to any of the Viennese (especially to the Bibrings and the Hoffers), that we are in correspondence concerning this matter. You yourself know how difficult personal relations generally are in a society and how transferences, mutual friendships and rivalries etc. crisscross with such confusion. At the moment decisions must be taken on a practical basis and not for personal reasons. For this reason it would be much easier, both for myself and for the people concerned, if they were not aware that I too am taking part, both in a positive and a negative sense, in these decisions.]

In this correspondence, the professional status and the personal qualities of many of those whom it was decided not to accept for settlement in England were discussed. We read about the Wälders, L. Rubinstein, Lampl-de Groot, along with many other candidates. Perhaps one should also consider Jones's comments on Rubinstein: "very aggressive. . . . I wish he could go to South Africa or America"[3] (Jones to Anna, 29 April 1938), and on 6 May, Jones reiterated: "We have advised Rubinstein *to go to America* [emphasis added]. His unmannerliness has made an increasing impression and it would not be so noticeable there." I do not think that this last statement by Jones deserves further comment! America seemed really to work as a sort of dumping place and England a place of higher civilization and culture. But see also what he writes in the same letter: "We have discarded Dr. D. Ezriel because of a letter from Kronengold about his schizoid personality and advised him to take up some other branch of medicine. . . . This morning I saw M. Morgenstern [whom Anna had highly recommended to Jones], who makes a good impression."

In this context, it is of some value also to consider the official documents of the British Psycho-Analytical Society of this same period—that is, April 1938. Jones dealt with the documents in the above-mentioned letter to Anna, dated 29 April 1938, where he made various references to a General Meeting, a Council Meeting, and two Committee Meetings, all held by the British Psycho-Analytical Society to discuss the decisions that had to be taken in preparation for the arrival of the immigrants to Britain.[4] And I must insist on emphasizing that all those who expressed a wish to settle in Britain would receive the assistance of Jones's contacts at the Home Office to obtain permission to enter the country, and when they did arrive in Britain, they would be interviewed without delay.

Jones seemed to be operating at two different levels: in his capacity as President of the International Association he was responsible for the rescue of his colleagues, and as President of the British Psycho-Analytical Society he was responsible for all matters of a local nature. As I noted earlier, as President of the British Psycho-Analytical Society, Jones formally reiterated the need for all the training analysts and candidates who wished to remain in Britain to be interviewed immediately they departed from Vienna. In his letter to Anna of 29 April 1938, after having underlined that there were not enough patients for everyone in London, he returns to the problem by adding:

> "It is much harder for foreigners to get work in England than in America, where so much of the country is already foreign. Here there is a considerable prejudice against people speaking with a foreign accent."

Jones then explains that during the previous two or three years only eight analysts from Berlin had been accepted, adding one very important point:

> "coming to England is not the same as coming to London. . . . It will be hard for more than eight analysts at the most to settle in London. They will of course be your father and yourself, Dorothy [Burlingham], Hitschmann, the two Kris and either the Bibrings or the Hoffers at their choice. Five provincial towns come into consideration, though we are not yet sure of more than three. They

are Edinburgh, Glasgow, Manchester, Bristol, Oxford and Cambridge."

As one can see, Jones and the British Society had made a very thorough investigation of the work situation in hospitals and similar establishments to ascertain whether there were openings for the analysts and psychiatrists who had psychoanalytic experience. This research also gave Jones and the Society the opportunity to consider expanding psychoanalysis beyond the confines of London and to establish centres in other major cities.[5]

In this same letter, Jones also informs Anna:

"I already have permits for Dr. Schur and Dr. Stross to practise in England as soon as they passed their examination. Naturally they will both stay in London. I also have permits for Kris, Bibring, Hoffer and Hitschmann to practise analysis in England."

In the same vein, Jones tried to meet Anna halfway with regard to her own future in Britain. In his letter to her dated 20 April 1938, he says that he hopes that she would be able "to continue the work you have carried on in Vienna if possible with those who co-operated with you there". It is important to note, moreover, that Jones would have been speaking on behalf of all the members of the British Psycho-Analytical Society when he emphasized that he was in favour of younger psychoanalysts, as they might find it easier to adapt to life in Britain:

"There is naturally a preference for members who we think can work harmoniously with our Society and would have some prospect of assimilating themselves to the English ways of life. I am sure that some people would be better suited to England than to America and vice versa."

Again, Jones would have been speaking for the British Psycho-Analytical Society as a whole when he says:

"Every opinion expressed about the Lampls by those who knew them was unfavourable on personal grounds, particularly as regards him. There is also a strong feeling that it is unfair of them to wish to displace their colleagues who might be in greater need."

There was a place for them to stay in Holland, and Holland, after all, was only two or three hours' journey from England by air. Jones's opinion of the Wälders was also negative, echoing what he had already felt while listening to Wälder's discussion of a paper by Joan Riviere in Vienna during the spring of 1936 (Jones to Anna, 6 May 1936), where he characterized Wälder as a lawyer, not a psychologist, and very intellectualistic.

"It is even more strongly felt that the Wälders would neither work harmoniously with our Society nor be able to adapt themselves to England."

One has to add, nevertheless, that although Wälder's application was rejected, Jones had a certain regard for his intellectual abilities and he and Freud would help him to obtain a teaching post at the New York Institute for Social Research, then under Horkheimer's directorship (see Jones to Anna, 26 April 1938). I must reiterate that it is important to keep all these variables in mind, although one must not, of course, exaggerate their import.

As for Balint, his arrival in Britain would appear not to have pleased Jones one little bit. Jones would lose no time in accusing Rickman of having made yet another of his *faux pas*. In a letter to Anna dated 25 April 1938, after having apologized for the anxiety that Rickman's previous gaffe had caused her, he exclaims: "The first thing I heard was that he had invited the Balints to England", although in a letter to Anna of 6 May 1936 he had appreciated Balint's "open-mindedness", stressing nevertheless that he was still too much under the influence of Ferenczi's theories. Needless to say, Balint did not settle in London on his arrival but spent the war years living and working in Manchester. What exactly lay behind all the Society's pronouncements (with Jones as spokesman) that it would give special consideration to those analysts whose approach indicated that they would be able "to work harmoniously with our Society and would have some prospects of assimilating themselves to the English way of life"? And what, indeed, were the ideological assumptions of a selection process that was based on variables that were so thoroughly steeped in a very specific, time-worn tradition and cultural empiricism as was the "English way of life"?

Although many of these issues would warrant a much more indepth analysis, space unfortunately prevents me from doing so here.

However, it would be a pity not to mention that the Archives of the British Psycho-Analytical Society also contain other very touching letters about the life in England of some of the refugees more or less immediately after their arrival—just think of the moving note Anna

Freud wrote to S. Payne, for instance, when the latter was asking for biographical information on 11 October 1938: "My full name is Anna Freud, I have no others. And I hold no degrees at all." On more general matters, see, for instance, Jones's letter to Eitingon dated 19 September 1939 which discusses Freud's death, Anna's state of mind, and other matters,[6] and one on 15 July 1940 which talks about the impending war[7] and the status of "aliens" declared by the British Government for many German-speaking colleague refugees. On 17 November 1940 Jones again discusses the first months of the war, which both he and Eitingon hoped would end quickly. But it was to be "a long war . . . with many dark days still ahead . . ." even for the immigrants and the European and indigenous American members of the various psychoanalytical societies. From Jones's comments, it is clear that Eitingon had looked forward to returning to Berlin.

But of course we all know that life turned out somewhat differently for them all. And what happened in the years following this minor exodus to those individuals who eventually settled in Britain and in America with their anguished families, with their nostalgia, their books, their furniture, and their many different theories, views, and languages, is by no means a simple story, and it still remains to be written, following in detail as many individual personal and professional lives and vicissitudes as possible.

But before I conclude this book, I would like to quote from a few other letters, as they give an account of the experiences and the difficulties some of the refugees encountered in the course of their forced acculturation. Apart from the financial issues, this was, indeed, probably the most important problem the European psychoanalysts—as, indeed, all the refugees—had to face. In some of the letters I quote, in addition to those already mentioned in chapter six, it is possible to catch those difficulties, even in minor details of everyday life, which nevertheless become extremely meaningful if seen in this context. Indeed, it was due to the forced acculturation that psychoanalysis, like many other aspects of Central European culture, had to change its character and status once transplanted to Great Britain and all over the United States! I do not think that it is necessary here to quote again the more general literature on this issue that I have already cited. It goes without saying that if one wants an idea of the effects of cultural alienation and estrangement, one ought also to read Stengel's beautiful and very original essay entitled "On Learning a New Language", published by the *International Journal of Psycho-Analysis* in 1939, in which he tries to make sense, from a psychoanalytical perspective, of his personal experiences and considers the problems that one encounters when one is forced to learn a new language. (Stengel, whose native language—like that of many others—was German, had to learn English when he was no longer a young man.) The paper obviously referred to the specific problems of continental psychoanalysts as refugees, but its implications were much broader.

The first of the letters to which I want to call the reader's attention was sent to Jones by Federn, who was then living in New York. The second letter is one Freud wrote shortly before his death; this letter is addressed to Zweig.

Federn in his letter dated 7 June 1939 wrote to inform Jones of the difficulties he was having in New York in dealing with Rado's group (see chapter two, note 2), who were unwilling to recognize him as a training analyst. The situation had reached a point where Federn thought there might well have been the need to set up a new group "for teaching and promoting psychoanalysis scientifically when the New York group would continue to refuse to accept Psychoanalysts like Nunberg, me and some other Viennese members in the New York Association." And at one point Federn explained: "I refrained from fighting because I know that always it takes some time before new horses are tolerated in a stable; with men and their associations it goes the same way."

Freud's comments to Zweig on America seem to be oddly more optimistic than those of Federn, who nevertheless had hinted at the need for some time to settle there. Oddly enough, in spite of his admiration of and gratitude to England, he seems to be echoing here what he had written to Ferenczi on 2 April 1933, when he mentioned "the uncomfortable life" that refugees had to expect in settling down in England and in Switzerland. Indeed, writing from London on 5 March 1939, Freud has this to say:

> "I think you are right to have chosen America instead of England. In most respects England is better, but it is very difficult to adapt oneself here. America seems an Anti-Paradise to me, but it has so much space and so many possibilities and ultimately one does come to belong there. Einstein told a visitor recently that at first America seemed like a caricature of a country to him, but that now he feels quite at home there."[8]

That Freud was dealing with the inevitable *malaise* that is associated with "not belonging", increased in his case by age and terminal illness, is quite obvious. We have further glimpses of this feeling of estrangement in some of his other letters to Eitingon from London, where he provides some rather moving and at the same time amusing descriptions of what life was like in England for an old newcomer. The reader may already be acquainted with his famous letter to Eitingon dated 6 June 1938, where, in describing the happiness he felt now that he was free—"*das Triumphgefühl der Befreiung*" [the triumphant feeling of being liberated]—he also adds that the same feeling "*vermengt sich zu stark mit der Trauer, denn man hat das Gefängnis, aus dem man entlassen wurde immer noch sehr geliebt*" [is mixed up too strongly with sorrow, because one had, after all, still loved the prison from which one has been released quite a lot]. In this same letter he also alludes to the difficulties of being faced with what he called the "*Kleine Eigentümlichkeiten der fremden Umwelt*" [small peculiarities of the foreign environment]. But another letter to Eitingon, dated 19 November 1938, reveals Freud's feeling of detachment and cultural alienation much more openly—as he tells of his anxieties about the delay in the translation into English of his *Moses and Monotheism*, saying that Jones's wife was translating this work but she was often away on holiday. Indeed, in a sad but rather humorous mood, giving us a graphical example of those "small peculiarities" of a foreign environment, he then adds:

> "*Ich fange an zu verstehen dass diese Abwesenheiten über weekend von London, über Feiertage von England ein wesentliches Stück im Lebensplan der Engländern sind um ihre englischen Probleme zu bewältigen. Ich kann da leider nicht mittuhn.*"

> [I start to understand that those absences from London during the weekends, from England during the holidays, are a substantial part of the way the English plan to live in order to manage their own English problems. Alas, I can't join in there.]

Apart from the problems related to his age and illness, the "*malaise*" and the feelings of not belonging that Freud was expressing are part and parcel of having to adapt to a new environment, and they can be taken as a symbol of innumerable experiences of this kind of refugee during those years. But if one thinks particularly of his letter to Zweig, one cannot deny that he was also referring to the fact that all "aliens" go through a process whereby, paradoxically, they also eventually "graft on" and "hybridize", so to speak—at least to a certain point. It is obvious that this process would have been different in Great Britain and in the United States—particularly when one compares the issues discussed in Federn's letter with the statements Freud made in his.

This *malaise*, which affected all refugees to varying degrees for years and which was probably never completely overcome by most of them, coupled with the continual process of "grafting on", has profoundly influenced the history of psychoanalysis, on both the old and the new continent. Indeed, these factors have conditioned the way the unconscious has been conceived and approached, for one need only consider the many different cultures with which it has come into contact. Nor should one forget the demands that a new environment will have made on the individuals concerned, nor their personal and often traumatic vicissitudes. The feeling of alienation that comes with immigration has in this case had far-reaching repercussions, and one is still able to feel the effects of it to this day. Having said this, the gradual disappearance of that particular generation of immigrants has meant that we now appear to be sailing on much calmer waters. I have to admit, however, that I personally do not agree with the idea of a general *"embrassons nous"*, as it only creates confusion.

Some of the differences that the "new" diaspora engendered are therefore bound to remain—or, to be more precise, they are destined to be worked out slowly with the passing of time. With these observations in mind, I would now like to conclude by taking inspiration from a well-known tale, "The Princess Gone Astray", drawn from the traditions of Hebrew theology and reworked in a fantasmagorical fashion by that great narrator of tales, Nachman von Breslaw. His version of the tale owes much to Luria. In Anna Freud's unpublished letter to Ernest Jones of 6 March 1934, which I have quoted so often in this book (see chapters one and two), Anna Freud spoke of "a new kind of diaspora", referring to the first waves of refugee Jewish analysts from Berlin. In the same letter she mentioned the destruction of the temple of Jerusalem (ordered by the Roman emperor Titus in 78 A.C.). It was this event that caused the original diaspora of the Jews. Interestingly enough, according to Sterba's (1982) moving personal memories, even Freud mentioned the destruction of the temple of Jerusalem and the diaspora of the Jews to his Viennese colleagues and friends during the last meeting of the Board of the Viennese Psychoanalytic Society held on 13 March 1938 at his home. Freud also added (Sterba, 1982, p. 160) that after the destruction of the temple of Jerusalem, Rabbi Jochanan ben Sakkar asked for permission to open a school at Jabineh for the study of the Torah. Freud told his friends and colleagues that they all, metaphorically speaking, should follow the example of the Rabbi, "being after all used to persecution by their own history, tradition and some of them by personal experience" (Sterba, 1982, p. 160).[9] There is no doubt that, thinking at all this and given the way in which the Viennese, in particular, lived out their tragedy and emigrated, trying to find their own new Jabineh, in their minds *their Society of Psychoanalysis* and *their way of understanding psychoanalysis* could be identified with the temple of Jerusalem and its unique importance.

In my efforts to gather together and assemble all of these fragments, names, dates, and events, for what was inevitably to be only a partial and a limited account of this story, I found myself pondering on the tale of the Light of God (and the God of Luria) contained within the ten vessels of the ten Sefirot, as in von Breslaw's story.

In the story, at one point the vessels find that they can no longer hold within them the Light, and seven of them disintegrate, leaving the Light and the broken vases to fall in fragments over the length and breadth of the Earth, falling on the Hebrews and the Gentiles; on the animals, the plants, and the waters of the lakes and the rivers, and so forth—all of this being the symbol of a catastrophe, and at the same time almost of a necessity (similar themes can be found in Scholem's *Sabbataï Sevi*, 1973). When the vessels break, the last of the Sefirot, Sechina, the female countenance of God, goes off into exile to travel the highways and byways of the Universe.

Here one is once again dealing with a diaspora of sorts, as the sparks of light run the risk of falling prey to the darkness of the demon. The sparks of light in von Breslaw's "The Princess Gone Astray" need to be rescued. . . . The endless efforts of the Jews moving from one country to the other in those years seem to symbolize this attempt to collect . . . to rescue . . . to restore. . . .

Now, if I am allowed to use some analogies and to freely associate around von Breslaw's work, if one compares the Light of God contained in the vessels and in the Sechina with the image of Freud and his thinking and that of the Viennese Psychoanalytic Society, and if one compares the fragments of light precipitated by the breaking of the vessels mentioned by von Breslaw with the "new" diaspora occasioned by the destruction of the Viennese Psychoanalytic Society— bearing in mind that Luria's God was never to be really known and never to be found—one could even be tempted to say that the former can remind one of the true nature of the unconscious as described by Freud in *The Interpretation of Dreams* (1900a): the unconscious as never directly knowable, except in a fragmentary and derivative way.

The psychoanalytic diaspora seems to have increased this fragmentary and only derivative way in which the unconscious can be known. Although, if we think of psychoanalysis as it was before the "new diaspora", I believe it would be incorrect to maintain that one could describe it as having been a completely unified movement. Apart from the heretical tendencies that divorced themselves from the main body of psychoanalysis, consider Adler, Jung, and others too, such as Melanie Klein, who had great difficulties in trying to cross the threshold of the "Temple of Jerusalem" that was Vienna at that time.

To proceed by analogy is always a dangerous business, and I myself would be greatly perplexed if I were to be asked to accept a direct equation between psychoanalysis and religious reasoning and thought. I wish simply to adopt these analogies while acknowledging the divide between one system of thought and another, between theological thought and our own reasoning.

Yet, in the process of considering and acknowledging all this, I would like to remind the reader that even in our case one is dealing, as, indeed, one is always dealing, metaphorically speaking, with a series of fragments of light that need to be rescued from the darkness and oblivion using the light of our own reasoning.

In our particular case as historians of psychoanalysis, the problem is one of retrieving the fragments of light from a past that speaks to us of the Nazi catastrophe—a catastrophe that also had its origins in the unconscious forces of the death drive as it manifested itself historically and socially during those years of persecution, exile, and massacre. It is our task now to bring these still unheard fragments of the history and vicissitudes of our discipline to the attention of the generations to come, while constantly bearing in mind the enormous import and portent of such fragments. Because it is only via the constant rational and emotional reconsideration and reinterpretation of our documents and our memories and the acknowledgement of our personal responsibility as heirs of those fragments of light and, indeed, of that darkness that hope may be kept alive. I am not alluding to some utopian vision of the reconstruction of all the broken vessels, nor to a possible return of Sechina to the lap of God . . . nor still less to a heavenly paradise of light. Psychoanalysis, too, must come to terms with its state of perpetual exile.

Yet those of us who value the lessons of the past may—if we make a constant effort to bring back memories of our past, each of us with his or her fragments of light and reason but never forgetting the darkness that is also always within ourselves and without—perhaps also play our part in preventing the past from being repeated, in helping to ensure that there will never be another diaspora of this kind, and in making people aware of the dangers of remaining silent on issues that are crucial to us as psychoanalysts and as human beings.

APPENDIX ONE

Extracts from several letters between Ernest Jones and Anna Freud on the subject of Wilhelm Reich may help the reader to understand the difficulties and the contradictions encountered by Jones and others over the years. All the letters are from the Archives of the British Psycho-Analytical Society.

20th April 1933

Dear Anna,

Before forming an opinion about the Reich problem I should like to be better informed about the objections to him. My own knowledge is that he is a very clever analyst, but somewhat wild and unreliable in his theoretical judgements. That the Berlin group have objected to his mixing up psycho-analysis and communism I can well understand. But is there anything further?

I understand that he has been up till now an accredited *Lehranalytiker* in Berlin. If so, I think he would have the right of going to another place to found a *Lehrinstitut* there, and I do not see how Eitingon or anyone else could forbid him. The question of a subsequent recognition of such an *Institut* would depend on the reports we get about its activities and could hardly be settled *a priori* in such a case; it would be different if it were a question of someone who had never been recognised as a training analyst. What does your father say about the problem?

Ernest Jones

2nd May 1933

Dear Anna,

[. . .] I am really not well enough informed to express a definite opinion on Reich's views as a purely scientific question. I have tried to read some of his Communist discussions in Berlin, but found them so obscure and tedious that I didn't get much out of them. His phrase that psycho-analysis is *"ein Kernelement des Kulturbolschewismus"* has really no meaning to me. If it is meant as a scientific prediction that a detached observer deduces from psycho-analytical discoveries that the tendency of human nature is towards Bolshevism, I should think it probable that his scientific interests had become mixed with other tendencies in the same way as evidently happened with Mary. But in any case, although I have always been a student of political history, I have never yet been able to isolate a given political movement into a pure tendency. Having therefore no clear perception what Bolshevism means in psychological terms I cannot compare it with my psycho-analytical knowledge. It seems to me plain that every political movement is a compound of extraordinarily mixed, and often contradictory, tendencies: oppression and freedom, and so on. When Reich says that the political reaction against psycho-analysis in Germany is because of its signifying Bolshevism, I should like to know why there should be a political reaction in Russia against psycho-analysis. Were he to answer that the latter unfortunate accident is due to their misunderstanding its true nature, that leaves the same possibility for Germany.

So much for my personal attitude. Coming now to the more official one, I should without hesitation say that, according to the Statutes, the aim of the International Psycho-Analytical Association includes not only the search for specific knowledge, but also the furtherance of the *possibilities for such research*. And there is not a shade of doubt that Reich's activities, if let loose, would very seriously endanger the furtherance of this essential aim. Too put it plainly, if Reich did everything he was to do, he would be acting in such a way as to endanger the opportunity for the free pursuit of psycho-analytical knowledge in Germany, and would provoke similar hindrance in other countries as well: not to speak of the risk to his colleagues' lives which is also involved. The British Society has a Bye-law enabling a three-fourths vote of members to expel even a full member from membership. I expect the German Society has some similar power, though their rules are not accessible to me at the moment. And it would seem to me they would be acting within their rights to take advantage of such powers. You have probably heard that the few remaining members in Berlin are apparently deciding to expel all Jews from official positions in the Society. This indicates they are in such a mood they would have no hesitation over the question of Communism for the grounds I have mentioned above.

I should be very sorry if anyone made to Reich the suggestion you mentioned, namely that he should found a new Society in which the word "psycho-analysis" and Bolshevism or Communism were combined. I am sure such a thing would be a danger to psycho-analysis even if outside the IPA though we should of course do all we could to disavow it.

My own opinion is that Reich should come to a definite conclusion about which is more important to him, psycho-analysis or politics. It is simply impossible to have both equally at a moment when their interests are in diametrical opposition. It is to the *interest* of psycho-analysis to keep free of political entanglements just as its *nature* is to follow only one tendency, the search for knowledge. It can of course respect a man who feels so strongly about a political movement that he puts it before everything else, but he should at least, in justice to other people, be clear about what he is doing.

Ernest Jones

7th November 1933

Dear Anna,

I hope you will agree with my solution of sending a private letter direct to the Dutch government which Dr Reich will not see. The chances are that he has already left the country.

Ernest Jones

9th December 1933

Dear Anna,

This is all about Reich who arrived here this week. He came to discuss his position and activities with me and to obtain my opinion whether those people are right who suggest that he should no longer be a member of the IPA. Externally his situation is that he is not allowed to remain in Denmark and has gone to Malmö in Sweden, which is only one hour's sea crossing away. There his students visit him and after three months there he can spend six months in Denmark. He proposes to go on playing, what we call, this Box and Cox game until they are trained and can form a new Society. After that he said he would have to decide between London and Paris for a permanent residence, though I suggested to him that a better choice would be between Russia and America. I had only known him slightly before and have received now a more favourable impression of his personality than I had got from recent accounts of him, though I suspect that this impression would not go on indefinitely improving at still closer quarters. I spent a hectic hour with him and then arranged a four hours' discussion which took place last night with him, Dr. Payne, Mrs. Riviere, Mrs. Klein, Glover, Strachey and myself. I am to see him again this afternoon, so you will see we have gone into the matter pretty thoroughly.

Our judgement about the problems was unanimous. Reich's communism is not so much economic; it is essentially the belief that communism would give more chance of *Sexualreform*, which is the central idea of his life. He has taken some of your Father's early teachings very literally and pursued them with a certain consistency. On the view that neuroses are produced by a conflict brought about by the internalising of an external prohibition (*Überich von Elternimagines*), he turns his interest away from the complicated internal consequences of the process and bends it to dealing with what he considers the essential dynamic factor, namely the external prohibition. Thus to him *äussere Versagung*, which leads to regression, and so forth, is the all in all and this leads to the prophylaxes of neuroses becoming identified with sexual reform. He even speaks highly of his results in 30% of his cases by treating the *Aktualneurose* which is the kernel of every psychoneurosis. It all sounds very plausible but the trouble with Reich altogether is that, with all his cleverness, he is really rather naïve and simple-minded. At the same time he appears to be thoroughly honest and very much in earnest.

With most analysts one can of course detect side by side with their pro-analytic tendencies, i.e. towards exploration of the unconscious, also various anti-analytic tendencies. The proportion between the two is surely a variable and shifting one. When one says that a given person no longer ought to be regarded as an analyst one means really that the second set of tendencies predominates over the first. We find this hard to say in Reich's case, and I do not think that on this ground of theory alone he could be singled out from various other analysts one could mention sufficiently to warrant his being excluded from the International Association. One could only say that he has been insufficiently analysed, and in this connection I should like to ask you for some information about his original training.

On the other question of his external activities we felt that it would be a serious thing to take up the position that no analyst could be allowed to play an active part in social life and movements, whatever they may be, and we felt that such a question should be decided by the Society of the particular country where any conflict arose between the person's activities and the laws of the country. Obviously this would vary in different countries. What is allowed in England or France is not allowed in Italy or Germany, and so on.

The matter is complicated by Reich's activities in a new country. Here we felt, most of all Mrs. Riviere, that it was not so much the political activity that mattered as the fact that Reich, in presenting psycho-analysis to a new audience, is seriously misrepresenting it and is not qualified to be an official exponent or teacher of it. The practical conclusion I draw is that Reich should be dissuaded from work in a new country (except perhaps Russia) and be told that his *Lehranalysen* there, or any Group he might found, would not receive official recognition.

Ironically enough, just when we are discussing whether his association with communism should lead us to expel him from psycho-analysis, he was himself expelled ten days ago from the Communist Party because of his association with psycho-analysis. This does not look as though the two movements felt a specially strong affinity for each other.

> Ernest Jones

13th December 1933

Dear Anna

Nachtrag zu Reich. I saw him again after writing to you and told him I did not propose to take any steps, at least at present, towards excluding him from the International, but that on the other hand we regarded him as being imperfectly analysed and as presenting the subject of psycho-analysis in a misleading way, so that it was more than doubtful whether any members trained by him or any Group organised by him would be officially recognised. I hope you agree with this. In reply he said that this would lead to a split in the International Association, since he has so many followers behind him who are of the same way of thinking. Among them he quoted Fenichel (!) and all the members of the new Scandinavian Union (to which he proposes to belong) with the exception of Dr. Tamm whom he says he would not allow to belong to any society of his. I expressed a doubt whether the temperament necessary for critical scientific research was compatible with that of an ardent social reformer, though obviously both types are of use in the world. He said he would prefer to do nothing but research work but felt he would not be able to resist the pressure brought to bear on him to lead a great social movement in the direction of sexual reform, and this I regard as highly probable. So we shall see what we shall see.

Ernest Jones

APPENDIX TWO

I thought it would be interesting to show those parts of Jones's letters that concern Reich, as well as Reich's letters to Anna Freud, which she then forwarded on to Jones in order to help him to understand Reich's position. Appendix two by no means comprises all the correspondence on Reich, nor are the letters quoted here the only ones written by him. They are only those that I found in the Archives of the British Psycho-Analytical Society. The English translations of Reich's letters are by A. Reynolds, M.Sc.

> *Dr. W. Reich, dz. Wien I.*
> *Wipplingerstr. 14*
> *6.IV.33.*

An das Sekretariat der IPV
z. H. Frl. Anna Freud.

Sehr geehrtes Fräulein Freud!
    Ich bringe Ihnen hiermit zur Kenntnis, dass der Verhand sozialistischer Mediziner in Kopenhagen mich zur Einrichtung eines psychoanalytischen Ausbildungs- und Behandlungsinstitutes eingeladen hat.

Derzeit bemüht sich ein Komité um Durchsetzung der Gründung bei den Sanitäts-, Unterrichts- und Polizeibehörden. Ich werde das Sekretariat vom Erfolg dieser Bemühungen verständigen. Ich ersuche um Mitteilung, in welcher Form die offizielle Angliederung des zu gründenden Institutes an die IPV zu erfolgen hat.
Ihr ergebener
      gez. Reich.

                                        Dr W. Reich, dz. Vienna I.
                                            Wipplingerstr. 14
                                                  6.4.33

To the Secretariat of the IPA
For the attention of Miss Anna Freud.

Esteemed Miss Freud,

    I am writing to inform you that the Association of Socialist Doctors in Copenhagen invited me to set up an institute for psychoanalytical training and treatment. A committee has been formed which is at present endeavouring to make arrangements for the foundation of this institute with the medical, educational and police authorities. I will inform the secretariat of the result of these endeavours. I request information as to the form in which the official affiliation of this shortly-to-be-set-up institute to the IPA should be effected.
    respectfully yours
        Reich

                                        Wien I. Wipplingerstrasse 14
                                              bei Dr. Gal.
                                                10.IV.33.

An das Sekretariat der IPV
Frl. Anna Freud.

Sehr geehrtes Fräulein Freud!
    Ich erhielt heute von Dr. Eitingon einen Brief, in dem er mir mitteilt, dass er mir keinen Lehrauftrag nach Kopenhagen erteilen könne und dass die Gründung eines psa Institutes unter meiner Leitung bei der IPV auf Schwierigkeiten stossen würde. Gemeint ist offenbar die Anerkennung der Ausbildung. Begründet wird diese Massnahme mit der angeblich ablehnenden Stellung der "Oberwiegenden Mehrheit" des deutschen

Lehrausschusses zu meiner Person. Ich wende mich daher an die Leitung der IPV mit dem Ersuchen, mir mitzuteilen, ob sie diese Stellungnahme Dr. Eitingons teilt, wenn ja, welche Gründe sie dazu bewegen, mir nunmehr den Lehrauftrag zu entziehen (ich konnte bis zuletzt ausbilden und Kurse lesen) und schliesslich, ob ein Rekurs dagegen an irgendeine Stelle, z.B. Intern. Kongress möglich ist. Ich halte es für meine Pflicht, die Leitung der IPV davon zu verständigen, dass ich mich ohne eingehende Begründung dieser Stellungnahme und ohne Befragung der Mitgliedschaft nicht an persönliche Beschlüsse halten kann. Die angebliche Gegnerschaft einer überwiegenden Mehrheit des deutschen Lehrausschusses erscheint mir fraglich, sonst hätte ich davon bisher in irgendeiner Form Kenntnis erhalten müssen. Ich weiss, dass bisher keinerlei Beschluss herbeigeführt wurde und dass von den Lehrausschussmitgliedern Drs. Fenichel, Simmel, Müller-Braunschweig, Böhm bestimmt nicht gegen meine Lehrtätigkeit sind. Im Uebrigen ist das Ganze eine Angelegenheit der IPV, und ich ersuche um Mitteilung, wie ich mich den Statuten gemäss zu verhalten habe.

    Gez. Ihr ergebener

    Reich

Vienna I, Wipplingerstasse 14
c/o Dr. Gal.
10.4.33.

To the Secretariat of the IPA
Miss Anna Freud

Esteemed Miss Freud,
I received today from Dr. Eitingon a letter in which he informs me that it is not possible for him to grant me official permission to teach psychoanalysis in Copenhagen and that moves to found a psycho-analytical institute under my direction would encounter difficulties with the IPA. What is meant is obviously the matter of recognition of the training. The reason given for this measure is the allegedly negative attitude of the "great majority" of the German Training Committee to my person. Consequently, I am now directly requesting of the leadership of the IPA that you inform me as to whether you share the position expressed by Dr. Eitingon, if so, what reasons have led to your now withdrawing from me the right to teach psychoanalysis (I have been able, right up until this,

to train students and to give classes) and, finally, whether an appeal against this to any authority, such as the International Congress, for instance, is possible. I consider it my duty to advise the leadership of the IPA that unless thorough grounds are given for the position stated and unless the membership are consulted on this issue, I cannot consider myself bound by any personal decisions. The alleged opposition of a great majority of the German Training Committee seems questionable to me; if this were the case than I would surely have already been in some way aware of it. I know that so far there has been no resolution of any kind to this effect and that, of the members of the Training Committee, Drs. Fenichel, Simmel, Müller-Braunschweig and Boehm are certainly not opposed to my activity as a teacher. Besides, the whole thing is an affair of the IPA and I request information as to what is required of me by the Association's regulations.

respectfully yours
Reich

11.IV.33.

Sehr geehrtes Fräulein Freud!

Ich schrieb Ihnen gestern einen Brief, in dem ich offiziel bei der Leitung der IPV um Stellungnahme zu meiner Uebersiedlung nach Kopenhagen als Lehranalytiker ersuchte. Sie werden daher erstaunt sein, in der gleichen Angelegenheit auch ein privates Schreiben zu erhalten. Da aber die privat betriebene Politik mancher Kollegen gewisse Grenzen überschreitet und eine sachliche Ordnung der Angelegenheit erschwert, erlaube ich mir, Sie auch davon in Kenntnis zu setzen, vor allem deshalb, weil ich momentan nicht weiss, wie ich der genannten privaten Politik begegnen soll.

Zwei dänische Studenten wollten, als sie hörten, dass ich nach Kopenhagen gehe, bei mir die Ausbildung durchmachen. Sie sprachen darüber mit einigen Wiener Analytikern. Einer von diesen riet ihnen ab, weil die Ausbildung bei mir angeblich nicht anerkannt werde. Er wusste also mehr als ich darüber. Ein anderer versprach den aufgescheuchten Dänen, sich bei den hiesigen Lehranalytikern zu erkundigen und kam mit der Auskunft wieder, die Lehranalyse bei mir sei in diesem Falle nicht ratsam, weil die Dänen Marxisten seien, ich ebenfalls Marxist bin und daher "die Gefahr der Identifizierung zu gross" ware. Ich war über diese Anschauung nicht wenig erstaunt, denn bisher schien es fast selbstverständlich, dass man Theologen zu Pfister und Ethiker zu Müller-Braunschweig sowie angepasste Sozialisten zu Bernfeld schickte. Die "Gleichschaltung", um den modernsten Ausdruck zu gebrauchen, scheint also nur bei mir nicht angezeigt zu sein. Ich bin gegen derartige Methoden, die ich nicht näher kennzeichnen möchte, machtlos, fürchte sie auch nicht. Ich war bisher stets bemüht, über sie still-schweigend zur Tagesordnung überzugehen und die schwebenden sachlichen Konflikte offiziell in sachlicher Weise auszukämpfen. Da ich mich um keinen Preis der gleichen Methode des Kampfes bedienen möchte, auch keinen Skandal provozieren will, muss ich mit umso grösserer Sorge um die offizielle Stellungnahme der Leitung der IPV bemüht sein. Dann werden alle, auch die "Wohlgesinnten" wissen, woran sie sind. Sie sind in ihrer Eigenschaft als Sekretär der IPV sowohl berufen wie auch sonst sicher interessiert, hier Klarheit zu schaffen, vor allem deshalb, weil das Skandalöse der Affaire sich nicht lange geheim halten lassen wird. Denn ich kann wohl selbst schweigen, aber nicht verhindern, dass die Dänen die Angelegenheit aller Welt mitteilen. Ich kann Ihnen nur versichern, dass die Sache in Dänmark und Schweden einiges Aufsehen erregen wird— Ich bitte Sie also nochmals auf privatem Wege, hier einzugreifen und die offizielle Stellungnahme zu beschleunigen. Ich muss wissen, ob die in Kop. von mir und meinen Freunden durchgeführten Analysen von der IPV anerkannt werden oder nicht. Da eine Anzahl jüngerer Berliner Analytiker sich wahrscheinlich auch im Norden ansiedeln wird, bin ich nicht nur für diese sondern auch für diejenigen, die bei uns Analyse studieren werden, verantwortlich.

Ich weiss auch nicht, ob Sie wissen, dass Dr. Harnik mit ausdrücklicher Zustimmung Dr. Eitingons als Lehranalytiker nach Kopenhagen geht. Die psychotische Erkrankung Dr. Harniks lässt einen solchen Schritt als höchst bedenklich erscheinen. Ich erspare es mir, hier auszumalen, was es an Komplikationen, wenn nicht schlimmerem geben muss, wenn man im Norden die Psychose feststellen wird. Dass es der Entwicklung der Analyse nicht gerade förderlich sein wird, ist klar. Die Verantwortung, die Dr. Eitingon jedenfalls auf sich lud, Dr. Harnik an exponierte Stelle zu setzen, ist nicht gering.

Ihr Sehr ergebener
gez. Reich

11.4.33

Esteemed Miss Freud,

Yesterday I wrote you a letter in which I officially requested of the leadership of the IPA a statement of your position on my move to Copenhagen as a training analyst. You will be surprised, then, to now receive a private communication in respect of the same matter. Since, however, the private political manoeuvres in which many of our colleagues are engaging are now overstepping certain limits and hindering an impartial and objective settling of this matter, I am taking the liberty of informing you too of these manoeuvres, above all because I do not for the moment know what my response to this "private politics" ought to be.

Two Danish students, upon hearing that I was going to Copenhagen, decided they wanted to train under me. They spoke of this to some Viennese analysts. One of these advised them against it, because, he alleged, training under me was not recognized. He was better informed than I on this matter, then. Another promised the Danes, who were by now rather startled at all this, to make enquiries among training analysts here in Vienna and returned with the news that training analyses with me would be, in their cases, inadvisable, because the Danes were Marxists, I too am a Marxist, and consequently "the danger of identification" would be "too great". I was not a little astounded on hearing of this view of things, since until now it seemed almost to go without saying that one sent theologians to Pfister, students of ethics to Müller-Braunschweig and reformist [angepasste] socialists to Bernfeld. It seems then that it is only in my case that "Gleichschaltung",[1] to use the most modern expression, is held to be inappropriate. I am powerless against these "methods" (I should not like to give them a more exact designation) but I do not fear them. Until now it has always been my endeavour to pass over them in silence, to concern myself with the business of the day and to fight out those objective conflicts which remained unresolved in an official and objective manner. Since I refuse at any price to adopt these same methods of struggle, and also wish to avoid provoking scandal, I must be all the more concerned to elicit an official statement of position from the leadership of the IPA on this issue. Then we will all, including the "well-disposed", know where we are. In your capacity as Secretary of the IPA, it is not only your duty but certainly also in your interest to clear things up here, above all because the scandalous aspects of this affair will not long remain secret. For though I can for my part remain silent about it all, I cannot prevent the Danes telling everyone of the affair. I can only assure you that the matter will cause some stir in Denmark and Sweden.

I ask you therefore again, on a private level, to intervene here and to hasten the formulation of an official statement of position by the IPA. I must know if the analyses to be carried out in Copenhagen by me and my friends will be recognized by the IPA or not. Since a number of the younger Berlin analysts will probably also move to the North, I am responsible not only for these (my friends) but also for those who will be studying analysis with us.

I do not know either if you are aware that Dr. Harnik, with the explicit consent of Dr. Eitingon, is going to Copenhagen as a training analyst. Dr. Harnik's psychotic illness makes such a step seem highly dubious. I shall not need to paint a picture here of what complications, if not worse, will result from people's observation of the psychosis in the North. That it will not exactly promote the development of psychoanalysis is clear. The responsibility which, in any case, Dr. Eitingon is taking on himself by placing Dr. Harnik in such a position is no small one.

respectfully yours
Reich

Dr. Wilhelm Reich etc.
22.IV.33.

An das Sekretariat der IPV.

Sehr geehrtes Fräulein Freud!
Ich komme nochmals auf die gestrige Vorstandsitzung der Wiener psa. Vereinigung zurück und will zur Vermeidung von Missverständnissen die Sachlage festhalten. Der Vorstand der Vereinigung fordert von mir mit Rücksicht auf die herrschende politische Situation die Einstellung meiner politischen Arbeit and soziologisch-wissenschaftlichen publizistischen Tätikeit. Er fordert eine ausdrückliche Zusage, obgleich ich erklärte, dass meine Lebensumstände mir in der nächsten Zeit nicht gestatten werden, diese Arbeit in der bisherigen Weise fortzusetzen, was den Wünschen des Vorstands ja entgegenkommt. Ich erklärte, eine solche Zusage nicht machen zu können. Ich machte Ihnen jedoch den Vorschlag, unter einer Bedingung mit den weiteren Publikationen ein bis zwei Jahre

zu warten: wenn die IPV offiziell zu meiner Arbeit Stellung nehmen würde, damit eine Grundlage für die Entscheidung geschaffen wäre, ob sich meine Arbeit und Theorie der Sexualökonomie mit meiner Mitgliedschaft verträgt oder nicht. Ich habe das grösste Interesse daran, zwei Tatbestände aus der Welt zu schaffen: erstens die bisherige Totschweigetechnik der IPV meiner Arbeit gegenüber, zweitens die daraus hervorgehenden Versuche, mich auf inoffizielle, indirekte, stille Weise kaltzustellen. Die private Stellungnahme Dr. Eitingons zu meiner Berufung nach Kopenhagen als Lehranalytiker, von der ich Sie in Kenntnis setzte, der private Vorschlag Dr. Federns, ich sollte zum Austritt aus der IPV bewogen werden, die privaten Versuche verschiedener Analytiker, meine Kompetenz, Analytiker auszubilden, zu bestreiten, und meine rein analytische Tätigkeit zu desavouieren etc. stellen ungeeignete Versuche dar, einen Konflikt zu lösen, der nur durch offene, offizielle Stellungnahme geklärt werden kann. Ich habe gestern zu zeigen versucht, wo die Schwierigkeit liegt: die verschiedenen offiziellen Funktionäre der IPV, die gegen mich sind, können schwer nachweisen, dass ich aufgehört habe, ein legitimer Vertreter der Psychoanalyse zu sein, dass sich meine Theorien ausserhalb der zulässigen Variationsbreite befinden. Anderseits ist der Charakter meiner Arbeit unbequem geworden. So sehr ich auch die Tendenz begreife, die sich daraus ergibt, nämlich ohne Aufsehen damit fertig zu werden, kann ich im Interesse dieses historisch bedeutsamen Konflikts innerhalb der psa. Bewegung eine offizielle Stellungnahme nicht ersparen. Ich erklärte dementsprechend gestern Abend, dass ich unter keinen Umständen, bei noch so grossen Demütigungen und inoffiziellen Ungerechtigkeiten selbst aus der IPV austreten werde, nicht zuletzt auch deshalb, weil ich mich zu den wenigen wirklich legitimen Vertretern der Psa. zähle und als solcher von einer entscheidenden Anzahl von Mitgliedern der IPV angesehen werde. Es beibt, wie ich bei genauer Ueberlegung der Sachlage feststellen muss, mithin kein anderer Weg den Lösung als der, sich entweder von meiner Anschauung, dass die Psa. ein Kernelement des Kulturbolschewismus ist und als solches von der politischen Reaktion bekämpft wird, sachlich und organisatonisch abzugrenzen, oder mir jene Freiheit der Forschung und Tätigkeit im Rahmen der IPV zuzubilligen, die men anderen Richtungen ohne weiteres zu gewähren bereit ist.

Sie werden es begreiflich finden, dass ich vor weiteren Entscheidungen auch die Stellungnahme den IPV zur Ansicht von Dr. Eitingon abwarten muss, nach der mir nicht nun meine soziologische, sondern

auch rein klinisch-analytische Lehrtätigkeit in Kopenhagen untersagt werden müsste.
In den Erwartung, vom Sekretariat sehr bald Bescheid zu bekommen bin ich Ihr ergebener
            gez. Reich

                                        Dr. Wilhelm Reich etc.
                                                22.4.33
To the Secretariat of the IPA.

Esteemed Miss Freud,

I return to the matter of yesterday's meeting of the executive of the Vienna Psychoanalytical Association and would like, in order to avoid misunderstandings, to set down the facts of the situation. The executive of the Association demanded of me that, in the light of the present political situation, I should cease my political work and my activities as a sociologic-scientific journalist. It demanded an explicit undertaking to this effect, although I explained that the circumstances of my life would not allow me, in the immediate future, to continue this work in the way that I have until now, a situation that concurs with the wishes of the executive. I declared that I could not provide them with such an undertaking. I made to you [*Ihnen*] however the suggestion that I could postpone further publications for one or two years on one condition: that the IPA make an official statement of its attitude to my work, in order that a foundation be provided for a decision as to whether or not my work and my theory of "Sex-Economy" is consistent with my membership. I have the greatest interest in putting an end to two situations: firstly, the technique of "ignore-him-and-he'll-go-away" which the IPA has adopted until now with regard to my work, and, secondly, the attempts which have arisen therefrom, unofficially, indirectly and quietly to neutralize me. Dr. Eitingon's private declaration of his position on my being called to Copenhagen as a training analyst (of which I informed you), the private suggestion of Dr. Federn that I should be induced to resign from the IPA, the private attempts of various analysts to challenge my competence as a training analyst and to disavow my purely analytical activity—these represent highly inappropriate attempts to solve a conflict which can only be cleared up by an open, official statement of position. Yesterday I tried to show where the problem lay: the various officials of the IPA who are against me find it very difficult to prove that I have ceased to be a legitimate representative of psychoanalysis, that my theories overstep the permissible range of variation. On the other hand, the character of my work has become embarrassing. Much as I understand the impulse which hereby arises, that is, the impulse to get rid of me quietly, I nevertheless must, in the interest of this historically significant conflict inside the psychoanalytical movement, insist on an official statement of position. I therefore declared yesterday evening that I will under no circumstances, no matter how great the humiliations and unofficial injustices I am forced to suffer, myself resign from the IPA, not least because I count myself one of the few truly legitimate representatives of psychoanalysis and am looked upon as such by a decisive number of the members of the IPA. There consequently remains, as I must conclude after exact consideration of the facts of the matter, no path to a solution other than the following: either to take substantial and organizational steps to distance oneself from my view that psychoanalysis is an essential element of "*Kulturbolschewismus*" and that it is as such that it is attacked by reactionary political forces, or to accord to me that freedom of research and activity within the structure of the IPA that one allows to others as a matter of course.

You will find it understandable that I must await, before further decisions, also a statement of the position of the IPA on the view of Dr. Eitingon, according to which not only my sociological, but also my purely clinical-analytical teaching activities in Copenhagen, must be forbidden to me.

In the expectation of a quick decision by the secretariat,

I am respectfully yours
Reich

NOTES

CHAPTER ONE

1. "Old" indeed, if one is to base one's judgement on the correspondence between Jones and Anna Freud.
2. I consider Sherman's and London's work to be the best-informed research yet
   to be carried out on the immigration of the Jews to Great Britain.
3. Dr Stross had obviously never practised in Great Britain before.
4. The specific help given to the refugee analysts by the British Psycho-Analytical
   Society and by the American Psychoanalytic Association is detailed below.

CHAPTER TWO

1. Klein's work in London during the 1930s has been documented by Grosskurth
   in her 1986 biography of Klein (but see also Steiner, 2000c).
2. It must be borne in mind that the letters, exchanged mainly between Jones and
   Brill, and between Jones, Eitingon, Anna Freud, and others, can give us only a
   partial view of the situation; nevertheless, they still give an idea of the intri-
   cacies of the politics of immigration, where, in this as in other cases, many
   different parallels, stories, issues, and variables all have to be dealt with simul-
   taneously. Because organizing the material proved so complex, the reader will
   find that in setting out the details surrounding Rado's case, I have not been
   able to limit these to the period in which this "new diaspora" first began, but

I have had to include information relating to subsequent events, to some of which I will have to return in greater detail later on.

Indeed, the Archives of the British Psycho-Analytical Society contain a large amount of correspondence on Rado, and this, *per se*, provides us with an idea of the extent to which his personal and professional vicissitudes caused concern to Jones, the Freuds, Eitingon, Brill, and others, all of whom, in the meanwhile, were also attempting to deal with the pressing Jewish refugee problem. Rado's case is paradigmatic of the conduct of certain of those Central European immigrants who were to greatly aggravate the already serious problems that were beginning to emerge in Berlin—and which were also to be experienced in Vienna and Budapest shortly thereafter. To my mind, one of the most interesting letters is one Brill wrote to Eitingon very early on. In this letter, dated 4 August 1932, Brill gives Eitingon news of Rado (who had by that time already visited New York, had taught there with great success in 1931, and had been invited back to settle and teach in the autumn of 1932), of Alexander in Chicago, where he had founded its Institute, and of Nunberg, who was working in Baltimore, where a new Institute, named the Washington Baltimore Institute, had been founded in that same year. It is obvious from this letter that the newly created branches of the American Psychoanalytic Association were seeking European-trained analysts to improve their teaching and clinical skills. But it is also obvious that they were attempting to seek recognition from the IPV (later called the IPA) of their Associations and of the APA. It must be borne in mind that at that time the IPV was mainly in the control of the Viennese and the Europeans, and that Ernest Jones was its President. The endeavours of the APA and its branches, and their attempts to recruit European-trained analysts, have to be viewed in the light of the complex problems experienced by the APA's affiliates in New York, Chicago, and other cities, in that the American Medical Association, and the American Psychiatric Association, both extremely powerful, looked upon psychoanalysis with great suspicion. Already at that time the problem concerning lay analysis was an extremely difficult issue. These problems were hinted at in Brill's letter to Eitingon, and although Brill appeared very optimistic about the future of psychoanalysis in the United States, he did refer to the uncompromising attitude of both the American Medical Association and the Medical Practice Act in some of the States.

There is no doubt that Rado played on all those difficulties and that he tried to portray himself as being one of the most reliable and most scientifically oriented psychoanalysts, who was able to create further links with the American Psychiatric Association. At the same time, however, he was becoming increasingly embroiled in the disputes that were taking place between the founding members of the New York Society and the new generation of analysts, such as Zilboorg, B. Lewin, and others—most of whom, incidentally, had also been trained on the Continent during the 1920s. Gradually Rado began to develop his own ideas, and increasingly he began to side with Freud and the orthodox Viennese. As is well documented in the correspondence held in the Archives of the British Psycho-Analytical Society, these activities, coupled with his political objectives, made him one of the most influential figures on APA training issues. The person who, rightly or wrongly, particularly thinking of his own character and political manoeuvres, pointed out Rado's ambitions and the danger he posed—in his view at least—was Jones. Brill, generous and rather naive as he was, had written to Jones to support Rado's settlement in New York. On 24 March 1933, Jones had replied, saying: "I was glad that you are able to keep Rado and I am sure he is wise to settle. Presumably Sachs and the others will do the same." However, a few months later, on 20 June 1933 after having heard from Brill of all the problems he had had to face with the New York Society (and on which I will focus in a short while), Jones replied, saying:

"I am afraid you are greatly mistaken in Rado. He is getting older now and has been evidently more cautious in feeling his feet and exploring the situation in New York quietly. But at heart he is an intriguer quite unreliable in the last resort, and I am afraid he would in time only exploit the situation to his personal advantage and no one else." [emphasis added]

Rado's manoeuvres in regard to the New York Psychoanalytic Society, the APA, and the IPA would be endlessly discussed in the following years by Jones, Eitingon, and by Brill in particular. They would also become a topic for discussion by both Anna and Sigmund Freud. Especially interesting are Rado's attempts to take total control of the training standards of all the American Societies. (See Brill's letters to Jones of 8 and 9 December 1934; the following letters also discuss Rado's "case": Jones to Eitingon, 24 June 1933, in which Jones insisted on Rado's manipulative tendencies; A. Freud to Jones, 28 August 1933; Eitingon to Jones, 6 January 1934; Brill to Jones, 7 June 1934; Jones to Brill, 18 June 1934; Brill to Jones, 7 November 1934.)

Brill's letter to Jones of 7 November 1934 is very important insofar as these issues are concerned. In it, Brill gives Jones an account of the opposition that was being mounted by Rado and Lewin against Schilder, a Jewish analyst who had emigrated from Germany and who, they thought, did not possess the appropriate scientific credentials. Like a number of his fellow refugees, Schilder, tired of feuding with his colleagues, would later decide to create a new psychotherapeutic society with the support of local neurologists. Space prevents me from going into the details of Rado's decline within the New York Psychoanalytic Society. However, it is clear from the letters Brill sent to Jones that from 1936 onwards Rado was increasingly distancing himself from what was considered to be the orthodox teaching and interpretation of Freud (Eisold, 1998; Frosch, 1991; Kirsner, 2000; Roazen & Swerdloff, 1995; Tomlinson, 1996). For example, there is a very interesting letter from Brill to Jones, dated 29 February 1936, in which Brill informs his colleague of the "non Freudian views of Rado" (emphasis added), who at that time was attempting to forge links with the enormously powerful American Psychiatric Association. Brill had told Rado that he had nothing against new theories, but that "in the Institute and the New York Society only Freud's theories could be taught" (emphasis added). There is a further very important letter from Brill to Jones, dated 5 March 1938, in which Brill, by now semi-retired, informs Jones that he has casually met Rado, and has reiterated that he (Brill) was open-minded as far as his views on new theories were concerned. In his letter to Jones, Brill did nevertheless add that he had heard rumours that Rado "was trying to develop a psychoanalysis of his own . . ." [but that the New York Society and the Psychoanalytic Institute] had been founded expressly for Freud's psychoanalysis" (emphasis added). Although one must not forget that Brill was also an early immigrant from the early years of the twentieth century, what can be observed here is how, be it for better or for worse, the old generation would react to anyone who threatened what they believed to be the true Freud—something that, in all probability, not even Jones would have accepted! And in Brill's *unwavering stand in defence of the orthodoxy of a certain way of interpreting Freud*, we have a glimpse of the way in which the New York Society was to develop, its views being further reinforced with the arrival of new refugees.

However, it was not only Brill or the older generation of founding members of the New York Psychoanalytic Society who were worried about Rado's misinterpretation of Freud. Consider, for example, the following interesting letter from Paul Federn to Jones. It not only concerns Rado and Freud, but it also reflects the position of many of the New York refugees. In this letter, written about 18 months after Brill's of 5 March 1938, Federn, who had just arrived in New York from Vienna, describes the difficulties he and his friends had met with in New York, because the Americans had not wanted to acknowledge his status as a training analyst. Federn recounts how he had had to formally comment on Rado's papers and views during public meetings, and at one point he says: "*Yet I could not be silent in regard to Rado's attitude to psychoanalysis and to Freud*. Rado is a shrewd fellow. The applause and private communications showed me that the greater part of the young psychoanalysts enjoyed my discussion and shared my views. Rado became quickly aware of this. My aim is reached in so far that since the first discussion he has abstained of [*sic*] injuring Freud in his course and misquoting him" (emphasis added). Federn, of course, took the attitude that "*bei uns war es besser*" [at home we did it better], so typical of so many of those refugees who had to overcome the terrible "*Heimatweh*" and the forced acculturation process on which I will focus in a short while. There is no doubt, however, that Federn was also trying to find his own way in New York and with his new American colleagues, and to succeed in discrediting Rado might have brought political advantages!

Nevertheless, one should not forget that even Federn had been critical of Freud, and that he, too, had tried to develop his own views on some important theoretical issues, without always realizing exactly how his views were considered by the Freudian establishment! With Federn, therefore, we have an example of the way the refugees were in conflict not solely with the indigenous members of the American Association, but also with those who had come to America during the early 1930s, in the first emigration wave—just think of all those I have mentioned: Brill, Federn, Lewin, Rado, Schilder, and so many others. . . . Jews in conflict with other Jews. Human nature never changes, one might comment, and what this reveals is that, when circumstances of a certain kind arise, there is more than a grain of truth in the old dictum, "*homo homini lupus*".

3.   That one is here dealing with a situation that bordered on the regressive and was, at times, totally regressive is seen from the numerous letters that talk of the help that was being proffered the refugees. One particular example is found in a letter from Anna Freud to Jones, dated 4 March 1934, where she confirmed that Simmel was in Brussels, penniless, waiting to depart for Los Angeles, and that money to finance his trip was being collected "here in Vienna in the family and around". Similarly, in a letter from Jones to Eitingon, dated 24 February 1937, Jones refers to Simmel's plight in these terms:

"Simmel and Frau [F.] Deri . . . have already undergone some regression as a result of the particularly enervating influence of America."

4. Her tone would become more familiar, and whereas up until that time she would address Jones as "*Dear Dr Jones*", or "*Lieber Dr Jones*", she now began her letters by calling him "*Dear Ernest*", or "*Lieber Ernest*".

5. Incidentally, in this same letter Freud offered financial assistance to Abraham's widow and her daughter, notwithstanding his own financial worries, brought on by his children, Oliver in particular.

6. Approximately one year later, on 3 March 1934, Freud informed Eitingon of the upheaval in Vienna, emphasized just how dangerous the situation was, and told him that the family had contemplated the idea of leaving Vienna through Merano but had then decided to stay. Yet Freud was even now very optimistic, but only to state, in a much more sombre and resigned tone, that "*Ortwechsel in meinen Verhältnissen is wahrscheinlich ebenso viel Suicid also Rettungsversuch*" [To change abode in my condition is probably as suicidal as a rescue attempt]. (See also the letters of Freud to M. Bonaparte, Ferenczi, and Jones, quoted in Jones, 1957, pp. 186–194, 486.)

7. According to Brecht et al. (1993, p. 68), at Eitingon's request an immigration office was later established in London under the control of the IPA. Among other things, the Archives of the British Psycho-Analytical Society also contain details of the provisional addresses of all the refugees from Vienna and of many of those from Budapest.

CHAPTER THREE

1. On the issue of Communism and German Jewish psychoanalysts, Jones's views are stated even more clearly in a letter to van Ophuijsen dated 25 April 1933.

2. See also Jones to Eitingon, 27 May 1933; Jones to Freud, etc., and Anna Freud's moving *Rundbrief* dated 4 June 1933 on Ferenczi's funeral in Budapest.

3. Van Ophuijsen would explain all the problems related to the creation of the new Dutch Society in a *Rundbrief* dated 7 November 1933.

4. Freud had been very downhearted for some months, and in a letter to Jones dated 7 May 1933 he had expressed his impotence and his worries for the future of his children and grandchildren, which he saw as "bleak and endangered". By the summer of that same year he had become even more depressed, although he told Jones that the situation in Austria would never tip into chaos: "we too will get our fascism, party dictatorship, elimination of opposition, applied anti-Semitism. But we should retain our independence . . .", and "we will be able to stay in Austria" (Freud to Jones, 23 July 1933). In August, he again wrote to Jones, and on this occasion, in speaking of the IPA, he said: "I am almost prepared for the eventuality that our organisation will also perish in the current world crisis. Berlin is lost, Budapest devalued for the death of Ferenczi and one cannot tell in which direction they are drifting in America." In the same letter he confirmed his faith in Jones as President of the IPA (Freud to Jones, 21 August 1933).

The letter Jones wrote to Freud on 18 September 1933 is of particular interest, because in spite of his private worries, Jones was, as always, very reassuring in his letters to Freud. At the same time, however, this letter shows his cool and at times rather distant way of evaluating the situation. Jones wrote:

> "First of all please let me say that it is perhaps possible to exaggerate the blow to our work caused by recent events in Germany. *It is easy in Germany or perhaps even in Austria also to forget the rest of the world.* Deplorable as the whole affair had been particularly in its personal reverberations among our friends, *I am confident that we shall survive it as we have other blows. Nothing can lastingly set back the progress of our work.*
>
> "We shall certainly miss Eitingon very much. I see this much advantage in von Hattinberg's appointment by Hitler, namely that his calling himself a psychoanalyst will have the result that psychoanalysis will not be forbidden in Germany. There will be of course the tendency to dilute it with other material and it is there that we will have to fight." [emphasis added]

Then Jones mentions Boehm and that he had to meet with him in The Hague, adding "we have good reason to be suspicious of him". (In a letter Freud had written to Jones on 23 July 1933, he had characterized the German psychiatrist von Hattinberg, who had obtained a lecturership in Berlin, as "a fool, an aristocratic, Aryan blockhead, a bad sort, in other words in every respect the right man for the post"!)

Jones then comes back to the refugee problem. But just note his comments, which would appear to be reiterating his conviction that the best place for psychoanalysis to grow would be in Great Britain:

> "I am very distressed at the suffering caused to our colleagues in Germany, but not despairing at the blow dealt to our movement, which I am sure we shall survive. Even since Abraham's death the *niveau* of the German Society has steadily deteriorated both from emigration and from internal dissensions."

Having mentioned the troubles of the Dutch and the French, and particularly Brill's in New York—including the problems Brill's proposed retirement would cause, which he viewed as "a fatal blow to the New York Psychoanalytic Society"—Jones then adds: "The British Society continues to be one of the bright spots on the horizon, and I do not think Brill exaggerates when he says in a recent letter that it is 'the real Bulwark of the psychoanalytical movement'." And he concluded triumphantly:

> "We have checked any slight tendency to the formation of cliques [although whether this was really so is of course another matter!] and work together harmoniously. The intellectual level of the work and discussions is very gratifying and we are slowly consolidating some prestige in the profession, etc. outside."

5. But see, for instance, Freud to Eitingon, 17 April 1933, where Freud speaks of Boehm's visit to Vienna and the doubts he had about him and Müller-Braunschweig.

6. Van Ophuijsen, after the new Dutch Society was set up, would leave for the United States, where he would have problems in settling. He first went to Detroit, and then moved to New York, but his personal difficulties, and the hostility displayed towards him by Rado and others, made his new life very complicated. See Brill to Jones, 9 December 1934; Jones to Eitingon, 13 December 1934; Brill to Jones, 7 June 1936.

7. For a clearer picture of just how complex were the first few months after emigration first began, one really ought also to read the correspondence between the Freuds and van Ophuijsen, Eitingon, Brill, Bonaparte, etc.; see, for instance, an early letter from Eitingon to Freud, dated 27 April 1933, in which he informs Freud that Laforgue had visited him from Paris and had wanted to create a fund *"für Emigrationhilfe"* (a fund to help the emigrants). In this same letter, Eitingon provides Freud with information on the whereabouts of the German analysts.

8. See also Boehm's report of this meeting (in Brecht et al., 1993, pp. 118–125). In this report Boehm also describes his meeting with Federn and with Freud in Vienna and says that, at this meeting, Freud had suggested that he succeeded Eitingon when Eitingon left Berlin. See also the letter signed by Eitingon, Müller-Braunschweig, and Boehm, dated 7 April 1933 (in Brecht et al., 1993, p. 113).

CHAPTER FOUR

1. Later, immediately following the annexation of Austria in 1938, the American Association would created a proper Emergency Committee on Relief and Immigration (Jeffrey, 1989).

2. This last factor seems to be marvellously reflected in a letter Jones would write to Brill some years later, in which he mentioned quite clearly his fear that some of his interventions, as President of the IPA, to regulate the complex situation of the American membership (i.e. had they or could they belong to one or more societies?) would be considered by the Americans "as one more example of European tyranny and interference in American affairs" (Jones to Brill, 29 November 1935).

3. See also Oberndorf's comments from New York on 6 October 1933 in response to Jones's appeal for help:

    "I have been greatly affected by the situation in Germany and it seems possible that we might find room for some of these men in the United States. Perhaps the main difficulty is that New York City at present is almost the only place where psychoanalysis has been established sufficiently well to enable a foreigner to step into a livelihood in a short time. In the other cities the position of psychoanalysis is still uncertain and not accepted by the general medical profession to which in the last analysis the psychoanalyst must look for his practice. *It is also true that a foreign born Jew* is additionally handicapped in the smaller western and southern cities. In Washington where psychoanalysis stands under the weighty protectorate of White [a very powerful local psychiatrist], it cannot be practised with financial success excepting in rare instances. The same is more or less true of Philadelphia and up to now also in Boston. Whom had you in mind to send? Perhaps Brill, [A.] Stern, [B.] Glueck and I could arrange between us to help someone for the first few years."

    Of course, at this stage Oberndorf could not have imagined that this "someone for a few years" was to turn out to be a very large number of immigrants from Germany, Austria, and Hungary, nor that these refugees would have such an strong impact on American psychoanalysis.

4. Reik's complex situation and the problems it created are also described in a
    series of letters between Sigmund Freud and Jones, Jones and Eitingon, and
    Brill and van Ophuijsen. The contents of this correspondence, in which Jones,
    as always, played a major role, has a very sad and disturbing edge to it at
    times Reik emerges from it as one of the most troublesome of all the "*Sorgen-
    kinder*". Jones, of course, had tried to help him, whilst at same time doing his
    utmost to keep him from emigrating to Britain. In this he would eventually
    succeed, as Reik would later go to the United States. But if one follows the way
    in which Reik's case was discussed and dealt with, one obtains a very clear
    view of the whole rescue operation, including the procedure by which emi-
    grant candidates were selected and deemed either suitable or unsuitable. In a
    letter to Max Eitingon, dated 20 May 1933, Jones announced that many people
    had applied to come to England from Germany, and "the most pathetic appli-
    cation" had been "perhaps from Reik". At the same time, according to van
    Ophuijsen, who had written to Jones on 26 May 1933, Reik had asked his
    Dutch colleague to emigrate to Holland. In his letter van Ophuijsen expresses
    his doubts about Reik, because of his character and his "unwillingness to
    cooperate and to take the consequences thereof upon him" [*sic*]. Furthermore,
    Reik was not German . . . and, according to van Ophuijsen, there were others
    much more in need of help than Reik, who, incidentally, still had sufficient
    funds to survive without practising for two years.
        Jones replied to this letter on 29 May 1933, claiming that, in spite of the
    strong support Eitingon expressed for Reik, he did not think that Reik would
    settle in England, because he was a "lay analyst which undoubtedly makes it
    more difficult to get a permit to work here". This Jones repeated to Eitingon on
    3 June 1933, saying: "Reik could not settle even in Cambridge because there
    would be no medical cover up for him. . . ." Maybe the best thing would be for
    him to go to Rome, as Jones had already suggested to him.
        Those first letters are still very circumspect, and Jones seemed to want to
    insist on the purely factual matter of Reik being a lay analyst, that lay analysts
    had difficulty in working in Britain. But, gradually, if one follows the corre-
    spondence between Jones and his various colleagues, something much more
    radical and "*ad personam*" begins to emerge—that is, that Reik was unsuitable
    for either Britain or Holland because he was a troublemaker and a very bad
    and untrustworthy analyst. Those worries began to be expressed by some
    Dutch analysts, who were extremely concerned by the prospect of German
    analysts, Landauer and Reik included, emigrating to Holland. As I said earlier
    in this book, the reasons for this were connected to their fear of competition
    and the personal financial difficulties this might cause them.
        I have already quoted extracts from the correspondence on Reik, and earlier
    I showed that Jones supported the views of the Dutch analysts (see chapter
    three). But now Jones's views on Reik would become even more openly ex-
    pressed. Although he understood that van Ophuijsen worried for his col-
    leagues and was concerned by their hostility towards these foreign analysts,
    because, as Jones said to van Ophuijsen in a letter dated 19 July 1933, "it
    thwarted your well known eagerness to help people in distress", Jones's prime
    concern, as always, was to cool down emotions and to ensure that the situation
    was viewed as realistically and as objectively as possible. Reik was not to come
    to Britain. In a long letter to Reik dated 30 November, Jones makes this quite

clear (this notwithstanding Freud's warm interest in Reik, for Freud recognized Reik's characterological difficulties and was aware that these had been exacerbated by the tensions caused by the political situation of the day—see Freud to Jones, 26 November 1933, pp. 731–732).

Jones was very open in his reply to Freud on 1 December 1933: "Reik is in every way unsuitable for therapeutic work where his irresponsibility towards his patients and unscrupulousness towards his colleagues have so often been demonstrated" (Freud, 1993, p. 732; see also Jones to Max Eitingon, 1 December 1933, along these same lines (!), and Jones to Oberndorf, 2 December 1933).

Nevertheless, Jones did also stress the need to find Reik a research post, so that he could continue his work in applied psychoanalysis. He wrote to Reik along these lines, although he did, of course, omit his heaviest judgements on his clinical work. He also told him that, as a lay analyst who seemed not to like the way lay analysts worked in Britain—that is, under strict medical control—it would have been impossible for him to settle in England. Jones also suggested that Reik should try Palestine, should no research post be found for him in Europe or in America, and he added that Eitingon was setting up a new group in Jerusalem.

Unfortunately, it is impossible to quote from all of the correspondence on Reik deposited at the Archives of the British Psycho-Analytical Society. There is, for example, a *Rundbrief* written by van Ophuijsen and supported by Anna Freud (*Rundbrief*, 11 January 1934) in which van Ophuijsen says that if Jones, in spite of all the difficulties, was unable to accept Reik in Britain (where, incidentally, he would have been less of a danger than in Amsterdam or Rotterdam, considering the fragile situation of the Dutch groups), he would do his best to host Reik in Holland. (Also of interest are van Ophuijsen's *Rundbriefe* dated 24 December 1933 and 8 January 1934; but see also Jones to Oberndorf, 13 November 1933; Oberndorf to Jones, 21 November 1933, in which Oberndorf informed Jones that he was unable to help Reik to emigrate to America.) There are further letters and *Rundbriefe*, such as Eitingon's dated 17 January 1934, where Eitingon becomes rather angry with Jones as a result of Eitingon having misunderstood, and seen as unfair and misleading, Jones's views and the way he had behaved towards Reik. We also have Jones's reply of 23 January 1934, in which he attempts to clarify the misunderstanding, claiming he wants to help Reik but that he is unable to accept him in England. And Jones repeats his belief that Reik is unsuitable for England even in a letter to Eitingon dated 31 January 1935. Only in a much later letter, written by A. Freud to Jones and dated 3 May 1938, is it possible to read that Reik had arrived safely in America, having managed to travel there from Holland. Anna Freud's comments leave no doubt as to her and her father's views on Reik:

> *"Ich bin froh dass Reik nach Amerika geht. Obwohl er so gescheit sein könnte wenn er wollte, ist er doch für jede Vereinigung eine Belastung denn er wirkt irgendwie zersetzend statt aufbauend. Ich denke das wird die Verhältnisse in der holländischen Vereinigung sehr erleichtern."*

[I am happy that Reik has gone to America. Although he could be very wise if he wanted to, he is a burden for every psychoanalytical society because somehow he has a destructive rather than a constructive effect on it. I think that his departure will be a relief to the Dutch Society.]

5. To put Jones's attitude into its proper context, it is important to understand the situation at the IPA at that time. Opposition inside the IPA was very decidedly left-wing. Fenichel, in Oslo at that time, kept in touch with all the left-wing emigrants then living in Paris, in Prague, etc., and would later also keep in contact with those in London, in the United States, and elsewhere. In 1938 he emigrated to the United States and settled in California.

    A rather interesting view of what went on in German psychoanalysis, and particularly with psychoanalysis in Berlin, can be gleaned from the anonymous *Rundbriefe*, which, from March 1933 on, Fenichel arranged to have distributed among his friends. These *Rundbriefe* contained all sorts of information on the international psychoanalytic movement. However, one must remember that this was a left-wing minority group, whose aim was to promote opposition within the IPA. But many of the statements issued by Fenichel's anonymous friends help to clarify that there were not only racial but also political conflicts inside the Berlin Institute, even among its Jewish members. There were hostilities between Benedek and Jacobsohn, for instance (Mühlleitner & Reichmayr, 1998, pp. 37–46). These *Rundbriefe* are, of course of enormous importance in that they also help one to understand Reich's position. At a certain point Reich seems no longer to have been welcomed by Fenichel and his friends because he had gone his own way and had set up a leftist movement of his own.

    In a *Rundbrief* written in March 1933, some of Fenichel's friends, who were still in Germany at the time, anonymously informed him of what was happening in Berlin, including the terrible conflicts between the remaining Jewish analysts and their Aryan colleagues. They mentioned their plans to leave the Society now that it was under Boehm, to whom they referred on several occasions as *"der neue Führer"*—the new Führer of German psychoanalysis— and whom they described as a weak and anxious man, devoured by ambition and by conflicting loyalties towards Freud.

6. An echo of these tensions seems to filter through Jones's words at Lucerne:

    "Nor unfortunately can it be maintained that our Association is entirely free of national and even racial prejudices which we so deplore in the world around us and which have engendered there such dire consequences. Throughout the history of our Association I have fought, and at times fought hard, for a simple principle in this matter. While respecting the social conditions and laws of the particular country in which it is our lot to live, I have urged that our common interests, as those of every body of scientific workers, are strictly international or rather supranational in character, and that the intrusion of local prejudices is in every way to be deprecated. We all I imagine should give intellectual assent to this principle and yet it is often violated in practice. Emotional influences of just the kind we see acting so balefully in the world of politics seem to infect at times individual analysts or even whole societies. Yet never more than now, when we are faced with such hard circumstances, has the need for union been so great. For our own sakes, in our own interests, and for the work we have so much at heart, we need to make a very great endeavour to sink these national prejudices and to unite together in a common bond of friendly co-operation." [*International Journal of Psycho-Analysis, 15,* 1934, p. 485]

7. Had I had more space at my disposal, I would have liked to have examined more fully the rhetorical implications of Jones's opening speech—that is, what he inferred, and what he did not mention. This would have proved an interesting exercise, as would a close examination of the contents of the speech he gave at the Marienbad Congress in 1936, not least what he said at the IPA's final, and very dramatic, Congress held in Paris in 1938.

8. It is revealing that in his speech Jones does not mention explicitly either Nazism or Hitler, nor does he say anything about the persecution of the Jews. See, by way of comparison, the statements contained in Fenichel's *Rundbriefe* (Mühlleitner & Reichmayr, 1998). Further extracts of Jones's opening speech at the Lucerne Congress are quite informative. At one point, after having mentioned Ferenczi's death, he says:

   "This thirteenth Congress, however, takes place at yet another fateful conjuncture in the history of psychoanalysis. I refer, of course, to the disturbing blow that has been dealt it in one of its longest and best established centres. . . . It would be very easy to register a protest at the fashion in which these political activities have hampered the work of many of our colleagues, but such a course would be assuredly futile. Moreover, it would be to descend from our own position and participate in the emotional turmoil of others. It will be more dignified, and also more profitable, to contrast this sort of politics with the attitude of Science. When Science is attacked its best answer is simply to restate its tenets. . . . To interfere under any pretext whatsoever with the freedom of scientific workers is the same thing as to impede the progress of Science itself. . . . In so far as any Government embarks on, or permits, such interference it assuredly weakens the basis of civilization, primarily in its own country and to a lesser extent in the whole world. . . . We can, however, also learn from the present state of affairs a lesson for ourselves. We see once more that Politics and Science do not mix any better than oil and water. We know, as psychologists, that the motives impelling men to change a given social order are of the most varied kind, a medley of laudable and ignoble impulses in which the desire to ascertain the truth seldom plays any but the most subordinate part. So that anyone engaging in such activities must necessarily be impelled by motives other than scientific ones. The master of our school, though well-known to be strongly imbued with humanitarian desires for the betterment of human life, has always known how to keep these strictly apart from his scientific work, which has therefore never suffered in its purity. In this, as in so many other respects, he has set us an example we should do well to follow. There are not wanting among us signs of impatience with social conditions and eagerness to engage in the changing of them. *From what I said it follows that whoever yields to such impulses becomes by so much the less a psychoanalyst. And to attempt to propagate his particular social ideas in the name of psychoanalysis is to pervert its true nature, a misuse of psychoanalysis which I wish firmly to denounce and repudiate.*" [emphasis added]

9. See also Brecht et al. (1993, p. 137), which quotes some very disturbing correspondence between Jones, Erich Fromm, and Müller-Braunschweig concerning loans that the Jews who had left the German Society had to pay back. Müller-Braunschweig had asked Fromm, who at that time was not aware of

the decision to exclude Jews from the Berlin Institute, to pay back his loan. In his letter to Fromm dated 25 March 1936, Jones informs him that Jews were not being excluded from the Berlin Institute, but that it had been decided that its Jewish members would resign, and that it was in everyone's interest that they did so. Jones then offered Fromm direct membership of the IPA.

10. Curiously enough, the German Psychoanalytic Society was to remain a member of the IPA up until 1938.

CHAPTER FIVE

1. From Jacobsohn's arrest in October 1935, until her release in late 1937, *Die Rundbriefe*, edited by Fenichel (Mühlleitner & Reichmayr, 1998), gave details of her situation, what was being done and what was not being done to help her, etc. See also Brecht (1987) for documents concerning E. Jacobsohn.

2. I would particularly refer the reader to Brecht et al. (1993, pp. 132–137) for a careful reconstruction of these events. This work also contains other very important documents on these matters.

3. However, see Fenichel's *Rundbrief* of 31 December 1933 on this whole issue (Mühlleitner & Reichmayr, 1993) and his *Rundbrief* dated 27 January 1936, where he gives an account of the way the Jews in Berlin were being treated by Boehm (pp. 313–314).

4. On the various meetings held between Müller-Braunschweig, Boehm, and the Freud family, see Brecht et al. (1985, pp. 67, 132). At the opening ceremony of the 1936 Marienbad Congress (in the *International Journal of Psycho-Analysis, 18*, 1937, p. 73), Jones again spoke, somewhat contradictorily, as follows:

"The well-known difficulties analysts have to contend with in Germany have increased rather than diminished; though it may perhaps be said on the other side that they have in some way less reasons for anxiety than they appeared to have two years ago. Political intervention has restricted their cooperative work by dictating the kind of colleagues with whom they may foregather for scientific purposes. Last Christmas the Jewish members of the German Society found it necessary to resign their membership. Availing myself of the privilege bestowed on me by the Lucerne Congress I have granted direct membership of the International Association to all those who asked for it."

After referring to the increased number of emigrants from Germany and the fact that they could be helped, Jones, in a rather optimistic and "Hegelian" manner, stated: "What Germany has lost, other countries have gained" (p. 73)—and, if one overlooks the personal suffering and the problems encountered by the émigrés in this process, these statements are not far from the truth.

It is interesting that Jones should more or less repeat these same statements in his Report to the Executive Committee of the IPA, of which he was Chairman: "The difficulties of the German Society have, as was to be expected, continued, though they are at least becoming more defined." Having explained the difficulties experienced by the Jewish analysts and the fact that they had had to resign from the Society, Jones added: "This is the first time, and we all pray it may be the last, that such arbitrary considerations have forced themselves into the scientific field of psychoanalysis." Then, in speaking of the British Society, he added: "The immigration from Germany has continued and we have now some fifteen or sixteen analysts from that country. Some of them are overflowing from London into the large provincial towns of England and will doubtless form nuclei of Study Groups" (p. 75).

5. See, for instance, Anna Freud's *Rundbrief* dated 7 May 1935, where she reported that Jones had been to Vienna at Easter and that he had given a lecture at the Vienna Psychoanalytic Society, during which he had explained all the theoretical differences between Vienna and London. Anna was, of course, referring to Melanie Klein! In her *Rundbrief* she stressed that Jones had been extremely clear, and that his paper had been well received. She even went so far as to say that in the period following Easter, "*Die Wiener Vereinigung unter den Weichen 'London in Wien' gestanden hat*" [the Viennese Society had been under the sign "London in Vienna"]!

6. The Archives of the British Psycho-Analytical Society contain a very interesting letter from E. Kris to J. Rickman, dated 10 November 1936, in which Kris discusses his views of Rickman's theory of creativity inspired by Melanie Klein. His letter is very kind and open-minded, as Kris was not against Klein as such, although he does confess that he cannot understand her. Together with the reparative role, the creative process was, for him, characterized by the creator's attempt to revive, in a sublimated way, the omnipotent magical thinking of the infantile period.

7. Boehm's report (*International Journal of Psycho-Analysis, 18,* 1937) gives an idea of the strange atmosphere reigning in Germany at the time. By this time Boehm was Director of the Clinic of what had been the Berlin Psychoanalytic Institute, and his report concerns the activities of the German Psychoanalytic Society. Boehm points out that many analyses had been discontinued because of the emigration of Jewish analysts, but that the waiting list at the new institute in Berlin had been reduced (pp. 359–360). He also stresses that a new method of psychic guidance, particularly as far as child analysis was concerned, had been introduced. His following comments deal with something that, curiously enough, would later become common practice even at the Hampstead Clinic in London:

> "Our experience is that, when parents themselves bring their children for treatment, it is almost essential to see parents themselves more than once and to explain where they have made mistakes in the bringing up of the children. *It often turns out that either the father or the mother or possibly both must be treated psychoanalytically if the child is really to get well.*" [emphasis added]

CHAPTER SIX

1. Jones's activities are extremely well documented by Molnar (1992), who has used Jones's personal diaries for the purpose. The Archives of the Freud Museum hold copies of a number of documents from the Public Record Office that tell of the lengths Jones had to go to in order to travel to Vienna on 15 March. These documents also give an account of the pressures he had to put

on the Foreign Office, via Lord de la War, Sir W. Bragg, President of the Royal Society, E. F. Lindley Wood, Lord Halifax, and others, to ensure that arrangements were made for Freud and his family to obtain emigration permits to leave Austria. Particularly interesting are the notes, telegrams, and letters exchanged between the Foreign Office and Sir N. Henderson, the British Ambassador in Berlin, who, together with the American Ambassador, was invited to contact von Ribbentrop to persuade him to allow Freud and other illustrious Austrian scientists to leave Austria. See telegram Classified C 2912, 12 April 1938, from Henderson: "As regards Freud I am informed by United States Ambassador that he has been authorised to leave and will do so as soon as his health permits." (See also letter of Sir W. Bragg to Lord Halifax, dated 25 April 1938, concerning Freud, E. Schrödinger, and E. Mak.) A telegram concerning Freud had been sent to Hitler by the American President, Theodore Roosevelt, but Hitler had not replied.

Yet there is also a curious hand-written note, dated 30 March 1938, from the Prime Minister's Private Secretary, which highlights the prudent and detached approach of British diplomacy. A telegram had been sent to the Prime Minister by Mr J. Pope with a request for "instant news of Professor Freud". The handwritten note, Classified 380 IQ 3401, reads as follows:

"A past or a future? patient! A Dr. Ernest Jones went out to Vienna to see whether he could get news of Professor Freud; but we do not know whether he had any success. I am inclined to agree that we should ignore this peremptory request; but if it is thought that a reply should be sent, we can only say that no information is available here. Private Secretary."

The note refers to Jones's journey to Vienna, which was supported by telegram Classified 289 R 2890, 15 March 1938, from the Foreign Office to the British Embassy in Vienna, asking them to help Jones find out about Freud's situation. See also Jones's letter, dated 23 March 1938, Classified 291 Index, to Lord Viscount Halifax of the Foreign Office, in which Jones thanks him for the help he received.

It might interest the reader to know that on 14 April 1938, at the House of Commons, Commander R. Locker Lampson proposed a Bill to extend Palestinian Nationality to the Jews, who, first in Germany and now in Austria, were being victimized by ever-increasing persecution. In his speech he mentioned Freud, saying: "In spite of Freud being old and dying, the Nazi monsters have deprived him of liberty." The Bill was not passed because there was fear that it would have aroused anger among the Muslim populations then living in Palestine (Documents of the House of Commons, pp. 943–944).

2.   But see also Freud's extremely moving letter to M. Eitingon, dated 6 February 1938, in reply to one from Eitingon, who had asked Freud about the situation in Austria, as it seemed to be quite serious, according to the newspapers. Freud, however, began his reply by saying that it was incredible how newspapers could lie. And after having commented, still in a rather positive mood, about what was going on in Austria, and that "*Unsere in ihrer Art brafe und tapfere Regierung*" [our in its own way courageous and good government] was energetically warding off the Nazis as it had done before, he very sanguinely informed Eitingon of the operation H. Pichler had just performed, adding that another operation would be required—but, he reassured Eitingon, he would not suffer, as it would be performed under anaesthetic. The letter ends with

one of those marvellous literary quotations with which Freud could so graphically describe a situation. He said that one was almost forced to think of Meister Anton, a character in one of Hebbel's dramas. At the end of Hebbel's script, Meister Anton states: "*Ich verstehe diese Welt nicht mehr*" [I cannot understand this world any longer]. "Have you read", Freud asked Eitingon, "that the Jews can no longer give German names to their children in Germany? The Jews could answer with the request that the Nazi renounce their loved first names, such as Johann, Josef and Maria."

3.   We will shortly also see Alexander's comments to Jones on this matter.

4.   Apart from the correspondence I have already quoted between Jones, van Ophuijsen, and Eitingon, it is interesting to refer to the *Bulletin of the International Psycho-Analytical Association*. See Jones's opening speech at Marienbad on 2 August 1936:

> "Political intervention has restricted their cooperative work [Jones was referring to the German analysts] by dictating the kind of colleagues with whom they may foregather for scientific purposes. Last Christmas the Jewish members of the German Society found it necessary to resign their membership. Availing myself of the privileges bestowed on me by the Lucerne Congress I have granted direct membership of the International Association to all those who asked for it." [*International Journal of Psycho-Analysis*, *18*, 1937, p. 73]

5.   In the *Internationale Zeitschrift für Ärztliche Psychoanalyse* and in the *International Journal of Psycho-Analysis* (*18*, 1937, pp. 346–358). *Bulletin of the International Psycho-Analytical Association*. General Meeting of the International Training Commission. At one point Eitingon claimed:

> "It is really astonishing that we of the Council of the ITC which is after all only the seismograph of psychoanalytical development and the organization which systematically keeps it in mind of those analysts responsible for the training of candidates, should have incurred the suspicion of the rebels wanting to lay down rigid rules and to lord it over the world of analysis. No, that has most certainly not been our intention. . . . But we do not think that it could possibly be a good thing for the movement to develop independently in the various countries. . . . The ITC is intended to be a framework within which development can take place." [p. 353]

6.   See, for instance, the cable Eitingon sent to Jones on 25 April 1937; the letter Oberndorf wrote to Jones, dated 26 May 1937; the very worried letter from A. Freud to Jones, dated 3 June 1937; the kind and prudent letter from Jones to Lewin of 5 June 1937; Eitingon's letter to Jones, dated 7 June 1937; Jones's to A. Freud, dated 29 May 1937; A. Freud's letter to Jones, dated 9 June 1937; etc.

7.   See particularly Daniels' letter to Jones, 30 October 1937, which read very much as an ultimatum. Matters were quite out of hand, as the New Yorkers had become very despondent and the Europeans could not understand their intentions. In a letter to Anna dated 26 December 1937, Jones enclosed a letter he had received from Daniels dated 21 December 1937, stating: "I find this letter as remote from human dignity as any I have ever seen in my life from an official person." See also A. Freud to Jones, 16 November 1937; A. Freud to Jones, 18 November 1937; Eitingon to Jones, 21 November 1937; Eitingon to Lewin, 6 December 1937; Lewin to Jones, 3 November 1937; Daniels to Jones, 21 December 1937.

8. See *International Journal of Psycho-Analysis*, 19, 1938, pp. 287–289.
9. The situation in the United States would explode two years later.
10. See Mühlleitner and Reichmayr (1995). Of the Austrian analysts, 62 were successful in emigrating to the United States. Another 26 emigrated to Britain, 11 of whom had left for the United States by 1941. The Relief Committee of which Kubie was Chairman until 1943, when it was disbanded, helped 149 people to obtain work by helping them with affidavits, etc. Yet one should remember some of the principles on which this Committee was founded. The Committee had been created to:

> "study all problems arising in connection with the emigration of analysts from Europe to this country [the United States of America]. . . . The primary functions of the Committee were to restrict and control immigration, to direct it *to communities not already overcrowded* [remember some of the statements contained in the correspondence between Jones, Brill, and Oberndorf during the early 1930s, and remember what Alexander had said in his letters to Jones of April–May 1938] and to keep the teaching of analysis centered in the hands of our recognized teaching institutes."

11. Notwithstanding all the problems, Alexander continued to reassure Jones that there were plenty of opportunities for refugees emigrating to the United States. For instance, in his letter of 10 May 1938, he told Jones that he was in constant contact with Kubie and the Committee on Relief. He also informed Jones that, on the recommendation of O. Pötzl and Dr Bibring, he had found a good job for Dr G. Pisk, a young medical candidate from the Vienna Psychoanalytic Society, with the Elgin State Hospital, of which Dr A. Read was head, adding: "I am sure that many such possibilities for young men with good medical background do exist in this country, if only one knew of them. I am doing my best to get information about them."
12. Kubie concluded his letter by giving Jones the news that Dr Rubinstein, a Viennese analyst, had written to him about emigrating, and that he was relieved to have had news of the Wälders, who were now in Geneva and to whom he would soon be writing to help them to emigrate to America.

    Much more flexible than Kubie was Alexander, who was President of the American Psychoanalytic Association. He tried to distance himself and the Chicago Psycho-Analytic Society from New York, for instance. There was "too much emotion" in New York, he wrote to Jones on 28 May 1938, in congratulating him for his efforts in helping the Freuds leave Vienna. "I really do not know what would happen without your help to many of the Viennese refugees", he had added. However, he was also very clear that he would have wished to have been of more help, but "*as you know the lay question here binds our hands to a considerable degree*" (emphasis added).
13. In fact, after various unsuccessful attempts to save it, the Viennese Society ceased to exist and was formally absorbed into the German Society on 1 October 1938. (For a full account of these events, see Mühlleitner & Reichmayr, 1995, pp. 105–111.)
14. Müller-Braunschweig went to Vienna to sign the document. It was also signed by A. Freud, E. Jones, H. Hartmann, M. Bonaparte, E. Hitschmann, R. Wälder, and others, with Freud's agreement, of course. A photographic copy of the document, signed and dated 20 March 1938, was published in the *International Journal of Psycho-Analysis*, 19, 1938, p. 374.

15. Also worth noting is the moving letter Freud wrote to Jones on 28 April 1938, a few days after Anna's to Jones:

> "I am sometimes disturbed by the idea that you might think we believe you simply do your duty, without our valuing the deep and honest feeling expressed in your activity. I assure you that this is not the case, that we recognize your friendship, rely on it and fully reciprocate it. This is a rare expression of feeling on my part for among beloved friends much should be taken for granted and left unsaid." [Freud, 1993, p. 772]

16. In his letter to Jones of 28 April 1938, Freud had also commented on his proposed emigration to Britain, and had expressed his concern that his departure risked being delayed for months as financial and property matters had still to be settled. And he had then added:

> "In general one has to be patient and still wait for weeks, perhaps months. At the moment emigration applications are not being processed at all. Kris's application was returned unprocessed after four weeks. Our application could not be filed until Monday (25th)." [Freud, 1993, p. 772]

17. Having gone to Liverpool and found the situation there very difficult, the Isakowers later emigrated to the United States. See O. Isakower's letter to S. Payne dated 13 April 1940. For the role he was to play in America, see Kirsner (2000).

18. In a warm letter dated 23 April 1938, Freud had also recommended Steiner to Jones: "Among the many who have turned to you concerning entry into England is also Dr. Maxim Steiner. I beg you to take up his case. I cannot claim he is important as an analyst", Freud added, explaining that Steiner nevertheless was a specialist in dermatology and "an old special friend of mine . . . and moreover is one of the oldest, i.e. earliest members of the *Vereinigung*" (Freud, 1993, p. 761).

19. Langer and Gifford (1978) report that when the President of the New York Psychoanalytic Society was asked for sponsoring affidavits for Viennese colleagues, he refused, claiming "what in the world would we do with all those additional analysts" (p. 42; see also Kirsner, 2000).

20. The correspondence between the IPA and the Americans provides us with some idea of what happened. From May to July—that is, in the months immediately preceding the Paris Congress—the Americans appeared to be in a very combative mood, and, as I said earlier, this hindered, at least in part, the efforts that were being made to find the refugees a new home in the United States. It is interesting that Alexander, who had previously maintained his objectiveness with regard to the disputes between the New Yorkers, the IPA, and the Europeans, should write to Jones on 12 July 1938 to say that, notwithstanding the differences, he agreed with those colleagues who considered the International Training Committee, as it stood then, to be a "paper institution". He reminded Jones that psychoanalysis in the United States was increasingly becoming associated with the medical profession and that young American analysts no longer felt their roots to be with the IPA. There was a strong desire for local autonomy as far as training was concerned, although no one wanted to question the authority of the IPA as such. Nevertheless, the problems stemmed from the IPA having granted "membership at large" to the German refugees first, and now to the Austrians! Alexander had found that this membership at

large "in a few instances here was only a source of trouble and dissent". Training analysts and analysts from Europe had to be affiliated to local American Societies if they wanted to practise. Furthermore, the goodwill of the Americans toward any well-trained European medical analyst meant that membership at large was not only unnecessary, but to grant it meant that the Europeans and the IPA were interfering with American training. Alexander, however, recognized that lay analysts were a problem. In reality there were only a few, but they needed all the help they could possibly get, because they were much more exposed than the medically trained immigrants. *Moreover, regulations in the United States prevented them from practising.* Their membership at large was not therefore a guarantee in America, where psychoanalysis as a practice could *only survive and develop "as a medical speciality"*. Alexander offered to give as much help as he could to find "academic and research positions in the different fields of applied psychoanalysis" for those Austrian and other lay analyst refugees who came to America. But, he insisted, "We cannot however authorize officially their therapeutic work."

On similar lines, but expressing an even greater eagerness to help, is a very long letter from Kubie to Alexander and to Jones, dated 15 July 1938. Kubie agreed in principle with the decision taken by the American Association regarding their autonomy. However, he wanted to make sure that the decisions taken by New York would not be construed as having been plotted by Rado in person. Kubie broached the problem of European lay analysts by suggesting that as there were very few of them and as most of them were prominent personalities, they could perhaps be considered the honorary guests of the various U.S. societies. What he wanted to avoid was that, should they be excluded by the Americans, they would then form a group among themselves and *create their own association, thus increasing the number of trained lay analysts much more than "if they are working with us within the general structure of our organization"*. Another of Kubie's proposals was to keep the Viennese Society alive, notwithstanding the fact that its members would be scattered all over the globe; this would give the Americans more time to find a better solution for lay analysts. Kubie stressed that it would be a folly to leave lay analysts out of the IPA, but he wanted to make it clear that he thought that many of the decisions concerning lay analysis in the United States should be taken independently of all the problems connected with the emigration of German, Austrian, and Central European analysts, for lay analysis in the United States was essentially an internal problem.

It is, of course, impossible to go into all the details of this voluminous correspondence, but a few of the letters must again be referred to. For instance, there is a letter from Kubie to Jones dated 20 July 1938, in which Kubie explains his views on how best to solve some of the problems regarding European lay analysts. In this letter he makes no attempt to disguise how badly he feels about some aspects of this tormented issue, which he describes as "the inhospitability of the formal action of our American societies towards the older established lay analysts from abroad". Kubie insists that this is due to the "measure of the wave of anxiety which afflicted part of our membership when they envisaged a huge flux of countless hordes of Continental lay analysts in the American scene". Some of the problems, in Kubie's view, stemmed not so much from Rado as from Nunberg and his behaviour, which had served to complicate further the immigration issue and the relationship between the New York Society and Vienna and the Europeans (Kubie to Jones, 20 July 1938).

Another very revealing letter is one from Alexander to Kubie, dated 25 July 1938. Alexander writes that he hopes that "in the fall after the sentiments have calmed down" they would find a proper solution to the problem of lay analysis. But he insists on the fact that psychoanalysis in the United States is strictly linked to the medical profession, saying, "*it is both fortunate and unavoidable that psychoanalytic therapy is becoming a medical speciality here*" (emphasis added). This was principally the result of the ever-increasing knowledge in psychosomatic diseases, which made it necessary to integrate psychoanalysis with medicine. At some time in the future it might have been possible to create a non-medical Society, for applied psychoanalysis—"The fact with which we have to cope, lay analysis had its origins in the early phases of psychoanalysis." But Alexander reiterates that they ought to try to help as much as was possible "our older colleagues who have devoted their lives to psychoanalytic therapy".

Indeed, by November 1938 the situation seemed to have improved. For example, in his letter to Jones dated 21 November 1938, Alexander informs him that emotions have calmed down and that the administrative independence of the American Association is now taken "as a matter of fact", and they are very keen to help the refugees. He then gives Jones news of Kubie, tells him of the efforts that had been made to help E. Weiss in Chicago, of the help that had been given to Dr S. Polacheck and to the Eisslers. He also informs Jones that Landauer had been invited by Dr K. Menninger to Topeka, and that Dr F. Grotjahn was now working in Chicago after having been in Topeka. He had even tried to help Federn. But his concerns were now for his colleagues in Budapest, as the immigrant quotas had been cut. It would now be very difficult to "get anybody in from Hungary". "I still hope", concluded Alexander, "that Hungary will remain faithful to its old traditions"—but this was to remain an impossible wish-fulfilment.

There are other letters, mainly concerning the American Psychoanalytic Association, for in spite of all the efforts made by the Europeans to calm the waters, not all matters had been settled satisfactorily. It is true that the problem of lay analysis no longer appeared to be as serious. After all—as Kubie wrote to Alexander on 10 January 1939—only six lay analysts had arrived from Europe. He did, however, reiterate that he was opposed to membership at large, as he feared that these Europeans would set up their own institute with different standards from those controlled by the Americans. And in a letter to Jones and to Glover on 12 January 1939, Kubie informs them that in the following 12–18 months every analyst physician who arrived from Europe would be elected a member of the society closest to where he settled, provided he was accepted, of course. However, in a letter to Jones dated 11 February 1939, Alexander rather harshly insists that, as far as the Americans were concerned, the IPA should be no more than a scientific platform—no longer a tightly knit professional organization. In this same letter, he also tells Jones of some difficulties concerning Weiss in Chicago and Federn in New York, where the New York Society seemed to have adopted a *numerus clausus* policy because they were "afraid of an overcrowding of psychoanalysts".

In a desperate attempt to settle the matter between the IPA and the Americans, Jones wrote to Alexander on 1 March 1939 to suggest that he and Glover should visit the United States to discuss the problems concerning the status of psychoanalysis as a medical profession and the relationship between the American Psychoanalytic Association and the IPA.

A full description of the situation within the American Association of Psychoanalysis, of its problems with the IPA, the emigrant problem, and the way Kubie's Relief Committee worked may be found in many of the *Rundbriefe* contained in the second volume of Fenichel's *118 Rundbriefe* (Mühlleitner & Reichmayr, 1998). For instance, his exceedingly long *Rundbrief* No. IIL gives a very detailed account of the situation within the various local American psychoanalytic societies and institutes; also very informative are the other *Rundbriefe* contained in Volume II (1998).

21. Interestingly, further evidence of this can be found in the letters Freud wrote at around the same time to Minna Bernays, for instance, on 14 May 1938: "*Ich bin in dieser Woche zweimal ausgefahren um vom Wien Abschied zu nehmen*" [I have been out twice during this week, to take my leave of Vienna]; and on 28 May 1938: "*Heute sind wir auf die Hohen-Strasse gefahren*" [Today we went through Hohenstrasse].

22. Again, see this extremely moving extract from a letter Freud wrote to Minna Bernays on 2 June 1938:

> "*Anna: sie hat keine Hilfe, die ihr einmal etwas abnimmt und dabei wird sie von Freunden noch immer bedrängt und belästigt am ärgsten von Steiner und Federn die freilich in sehr bedauerlicher Lage sind. Es war unrecht Anna so allein zu lassen. Ich bin natürlich ganz unbrauchbar.*"

> [Anna: She has nobody to help her, who could take anything off her shoulders and at the same time she is still being bothered and troubled by strangers. The worst are Steiner and Federn who are of course in a very pitiable situation. It was a mistake to leave Anna so alone. I am of course completely useless.]

23. See also Freud to Bernays, 25 April 1938. It is interesting to note that Freud used almost the same images as his daughter. His comments on the uncertainty of the political future of Austria, and the world in general, emphasize the confusion felt by Freud's family and also show just how difficult it was for one to make up one's mind during those months. It is well known that, until the last possible moment, many Jewish and non-Jewish refugees remained undecided as to whether or not to leave Germany and Austria.

> "*Man spricht viel von drohen der Kriegsgefahr aber es scheint dass nichts daraus werden wird obwohl die abscheulichen Zeitungen nicht aufhoeren zu hetzen. Bullitt in Paris soll erklärt haben wie wir lesen, dass die U.S.A. den Konflikt nich für aktuell halten. . . . Alles ist in gewissen Sinn unwirklich, wir sind nicht mehr hier und noch nicht dort. Die Gedanken flattern hin und her zwischen Berggasse und Elsworthy Road.*"

> [There is a lot of talk about the danger of war, but it looks as if nothing will come of it even if the atrocious newspapers are continually agitating the danger of war. Bullitt in Paris is supposed to have stated, so we read, that the U.S.A. doesn't consider the conflict likely to happen. . . . In a certain sense everything is unreal. We are no longer here and not yet there. Our

thoughts flutter back and forwards between die Berggasse and Elsworthy Road.]

(Die Berggasse was the street where Freud lived in Vienna; Elsworthy Road was the address he first stayed at when he came to London.)

24. The immigration quotas set by the British Government prevented the Hungarians from entering Britain. Nevertheless, one has to say that Jones may even have been unwilling for them to settle in Britain, as he did not want to disturb the delicate balance of the British Psycho-Analytical Society.

    As we saw from the correspondence between Jones and Brill (see chapters two and four), the Americans had also set up a fund to assist the refugees. We also saw that, in the United States, an Emergency Committee, chaired by L. S. Kubie, was set up to help those psychoanalysts who wished to emigrate to the States. It also arranged for funds to be made available should the refugees have been unable to enter the United States for any reason. Analysts from Hungary, therefore, had to apply to this Committee for assistance. In Britain, apart from the two Committees set up by the British Society, a third Committee called the War Committee (later changed to the Ernest Jones Rehabilitation Committee) was set up. Jones helped the Hungarians to settle in South Africa, New Zealand, Australia, India, etc.—in other words, in the Colonies, where it was still possible to send refugees. Money, visas, affidavits, useful addresses were all part of the help that was given the refugees. Even those Hungarian analysts who wanted to emigrate to the United States had to send their documentation (curriculum vitae, etc.) to London in the first instance.

25. Unfortunately I was unable to find this letter of Rickman's.

26. Later on the Róheims were in correspondence with Rickman again—see, for instance, the letter from Ilmka Róheim, dated 17 February 1941, from New York, where they had managed to emigrate. In this letter, Ilmka informed Rickman of their situation: "We have a very bad life here. Sometimes I think one cannot bear it any longer." This was a rather common statement; it can be found in many letters from Central European psychoanalysts and refugees of those years, as we already know and as I will further document.

27. One should remember that at that time Hungary had not yet been invaded by the Nazis, nor had it been occupied, as Austria had. But the anti-Jewish legislation in 1938–39 had become very severe, according to information given to me by relatives of mine.

28. In the Archives of the British Psycho-Analytical Society, there is an unsigned letter addressed to E. Kubie, concerning Gyömröi, dated 27 April 1938 and probably written by Fenichel, which urgently requests Kubie to obtain an affidavit for Gyömröi. Fenichel had telegraphed Kubie from Prague to tell him that Gyömröi was in danger because she had been a Communist in her youth, and at the time that Ferenczi had the Chair in Psychoanalysis, courtesy of the left-wing government, Gyömröi had been involved in politics. There was fear that the Nazis would come to power in Hungary too, and it was "most desirable that there should be no members of the Society who have been in any way in the past engaged in Left Wing political activity". Fenichel stresses that it is in the interest of the Hungarian group that she be helped to emigrate—she had not been involved in politics since her youth. But the records of her past were still available, and this is what made the situation so dangerous. In concluding his letter, Fenichel states:

"This is another instance of the saying which is on everybody's lips in Central Europe now 'Gestapo never forgets'. Once a person has been on their black list or on somebody's black list that they have taken over, that person is hounded and everyone connected to the person is in danger. The courage of the Budapest Group in facing what seems to me to be an inevitable and frightful fate commands one's highest admiration. The Government is trying to stop migration out of the country perhaps through fear of losing doctors for the war which at least in that part of the world seems to be imminent and because they are afraid of Jews taking money out of the country. As feeling runs there, or at least as it did less than a week ago, by the time you get this letter the frontiers may be practically closed to anyone wanting to leave permanently."

It is also interesting to note what Fenichel said at the end of his letter, after he had thanked Kubie for his help on behalf of the Hungarian analysts: "In passing through Vienna on the way back I saw Professor Freud and he was in astonishingly good health and spirits."

29. The original of this letter from Gyömröi has a note typed on it, either by Jones or his secretary, which records that Gyömröi's letter was acknowledged on 29 December 1938, and that a cheque for £100 was sent to Miss Popper on 2 January 1939. (Miss Popper was the person mentioned by Gyömröi in her letter who would have cashed the money for her.)

30. Unfortunately, we do not have a copy of Jones's reply.

31. There is further evidence of Gyömröi's vicissitudes. The Archives of the British Psycho-Analytical Society hold an incredibly moving and telling letter she wrote to E. Rosenfeld on 19 June 1945, when the war in Europe had just ended, in reply to one she had received from Rosenfeld, in which Rosenfeld had asked her whether she could pay back her debt of £100, as the money was needed in England to help other analysts. In her letter, Gyömröi apologizes for the delay in paying back the debt, and says she will do so immediately. Things had not gone very well professionally in Ceylon, either for herself or for her husband. Having made her apologies, and given various other information, she then asks Rosenfeld whether she would write to let her know "all what you know about the fate of the Continental analysts". Showing what would later become a typical syndrome of those who had survived the concentration camps, Gyömröi expresses her deep worries and a sense of guilt for having survived. Could Rosenfeld tell her about those colleagues who had remained in Vienna and in Budapest during the war? Gyömröi had had news of Eitingon, Balint, Fenichel, Lázár, and others. But being so isolated in Ceylon . . . what about the others . . . she was very worried about Dr. Hollos, and Mrs. K. Levy, and Lillian Rotter. Had they survived? She was planning to leave Ceylon in 15 months' time. She wanted first to go to Palestine and then "to try to use the time to find out what had happened to my people, though I start to give up every hope for the survival of my father and my son". It is here that the letter becomes even more moving and revealing, both of Gyömröi's personality and of the survival syndrome, which, as I said, would characterize so many people later on. "I am reluctant to go about in the world as tourists do, visiting places of devastation while everybody I care for is in utter misery. I am anxious to use this year to do some work and to try to help wherever I can. No doubt there will be lots that a psychoanalyst could do, organizing homes for

destitute children, help the army of adults who must be mentally injured after what they had to go through." She did not know where to ask for information. Could Rosenfeld put her in touch with someone? She then adds: "I do not care *where* I could be useful. I am speaking Hungarian, German, French and English, so wherever there is a place for me and use for what I can do, will be right for me. . . . It is absolutely incompatible with my usual attitude towards life that I should sit here in safety without lending a hand in order to help while everybody else is in trouble." The letter enclosed a draft for £100. It is also worth noting the reply E. Rosenfeld sent her from London on 23 September 1945. After thanking Gyömröi for the cheque, Rosenfeld tells her that they know "very little about the Continental analysts". The diaspora, one could say, had achieved its sinister results! But she knew that "Kata Levy is safe. There is naturally still no communication with the Continent", Rosenfeld added, "so that hope is not lost that many more of our colleagues will be traced." Then Rosenfeld suggests that Gyömröi "fix up some social work for yourself when you are here and have really recuperated. There are 1000 orphaned children from concentration camps all over the Continent collected now in Windermere, North England. Every helping hand is needed, I know that", she concludes—reassuring Gyömröi that once she was in England, she would find plenty to do!

Gyömröi also wrote something similar to John Rickman, probably in 1944 or 1945. After having told him that she had remarried and that things were much better for her after the death of her husband, and having given him information about her relatives, she added: "We will have a year free which we can use for whatever we like and we hope to be able to offer our services for the benefit of those who are in need in any of the countries which suffered under the war."

The Archives also contain a letter from Balint to S. Payne, undated, but written probably during the same year, in which Balint informs Payne of the fate of the Hungarian analysts, some of whom had died, some of whom were in Budapest, now facing new difficulties as a result of the economic and socio-political situation, and that Jones and the British Society were being asked to help them. And with this, and E. Rosenfeld's above letter to Gyömröi, the story of the Hungarian emigrants comes to an end, at least as far as the documents of the Archives of the British Psycho-Analytical Society are concerned. There would be another chapter to this story in 1956, and although it has many analogies with this earlier one, that would obviously have to be the subject of another book.

CHAPTER SEVEN

1. On the apprehensions they caused, etc., see below. One such example, discussed earlier, would be the difficulties that were created by some of the more troublesome of *"Sorgenkinder"* during the first emigration wave.
2. For a detailed account of the relationship between Reich, Fenichel, and friends, their disagreements on how the relationship between psychoanalysis and Marxism should have been interpreted, and the subsequent break-up of this

relationship, see O. Fenichel's *119 Rundbriefe* (Mühlleitner & Reichmayr, 1998, Vol. I.; see also Vol. II).

3. See also Mühlleitner and Reichmayr (1995, pp. 102–105), in which D. Hartmann, E. Jacobsohn, and Reich give a description of their experiences during this period.

4   The fact that Reich had become politically active in Vienna.

5. Again, I have to stress that these statements have to be understood in context. The disagreements between Freud and Reich had begun much earlier (Chasseguet-Smirgel & Grünberger, 1986; Roazen, 1985; Sharaf, 1983; Sterba, 1982). Whether or not Reich was actually a fanatical believer in a totalitarian form of Marxism did not interest Freud and his circle. The situation was so difficult and so confused, the anxieties so deep, that it was practically impossible for Freud to see Reich's political beliefs as separate, and the discord between him and Reich became even greater. Anna Freud's statements would seem to be confirmed by Boehm's account of events in Germany in 1933, where he says that Freud told him *"befreien Sie mich von Reich"* [free me from Reich] (see *Abschrift* dated Berlin 21 August 1934, in Brecht et al., 1993, p. 119; see also Reich's letters in appendix two).

6. It is important to remember that when Brill heard of Reich's situation from Jones, he said that he had no wish to help Reich to emigrate to America (Brill to Jones, 7 June 1934): "The Jews have so much trouble already with radicals *that we would not want him here"* (emphasis added).

7. In fact, Reich had been trained in Vienna and had moved to Berlin in the early 1930s.

8. Yet in his inaugural speech at the Lucerne Congress, Jones would condemn Reich, without mentioning him by name. This shows the difficult situation Jones would find himself in at times, and how on occasion he would have to contradict himself, because of pressures from Freud and because of the complex political and institutional situation of psychoanalysis in Germany and Austria at the time.

9. Pearl King has also confirmed that this was the case (personal communication).

10. For an account of the situation with the Berlin Institute, see Brecht et al. (1993). In this work the reader will also find letters written in 1935 by Boehm and Müller-Braunschweig to Jones (pp. 126–130) and Boehm's report, dated 4 December 1935, on the events in Berlin (pp. 132–133). A much more judgemental version of these events is contained in Fenichel's *Rundbriefe* (in particular, see *Rundbrief* No. 22, dated 27 January 1936, in Mühlleitner & Reichmayr, 1998, Vol. I, p. 313). In this *Rundbrief* Fenichel acknowledges Jones's efforts but at the same time emphasizes that unfortunately many people had connected Jacobsohn's case to the fate of the German Psychoanalytic Society. He also underlined the *"Angst"* of *"Einmischung der Politik und die Psychoanalyse"* [the anxieties caused as a result of politics interfering with psychoanalysis] that this case had produced, particularly in Vienna.

That politics in psychoanalysis was a serious issue is also quite evident from other documents. A letter dated 4 January 1935 (incorrectly dated, in my opinion, as the year should read 1936) by H. Hoel, a Norwegian analyst who had trained in Berlin, gives Jones details of what happened to E. Jacobsohn, and then states that, in Jacobsohn's case, as in Reich's, the principal concerns of both Freud and his daughter Anna were to ensure that psychoanalysis was preserved in its purest form possible. Hoel adds that Freud and his daughter condemned Jacobsohn for having put Boehm in a very difficult position in his dealings with the Nazi authorities. "Anna Freud did say that analysis had to go before all things", Hoel stated at one point, disagreeing with Anna's views. This letter would merit closer reading, as it is an extremely courageous attempt to raise the issue of the relationship between analytical neutrality and a particular political situation, in this case the Nazi totalitarian regime, and what this implied in terms of the integrity and the impartiality of psychoanalysis.

Jacobsohn's situation is also discussed in letters exchanged between Jones and A. Bucholtz in June 1936. Bucholtz, now in Oslo, had been a patient of E. Jacobsohn, and on 5 June 1936 she wrote to analysts of every nation to protest about the fact that after eight months Jacobsohn was still in prison. She accused Boehm and Müller-Braunschweig of having badly influenced "Die Internationaler Psychoanalytiker", who had initially been very eager to help Jacobsohn. Jones wrote back to Bucholtz on 18 June 1936 to deny her claims, and he assured her that he and his friends, together with Jacobsohn's lawyer, were doing their utmost to help Jacobsohn. However, note Fenichel's comments in his Rundbrief No. 2712, of June 1936, where he defined Bucholtz's plea as "eine Kinderei" [childish nonsense]. He also wrote to Jones, saying that "I do not need to assure you that I have nothing to do with this affair, doubtlessly well meant, but ridiculously made up and quite useless" (Mühlleitner & Reichmayr, 1998, Vol. I, p. 433).

A full account of Edith Jacobsohn's story can be read in Fenichel's Rundbriefe, which tell of her arrest in October 1936, of her escape from the sanatorium to Prague, and of her successful endeavours to reach the United States. Note the delight with which he opened his Rundbriefe No. IIL, dated Los Angeles, 25 June 1938, announcing that Jacobsohn had managed to escape the Nazis: "Edith ist in Prag" [Edith is in Prague] (1998, Vol. II, p. 877).

11. In a letter to Anna dated 2 December 1935, Jones reiterates his wish to help, but at the same time his letter also reflects the cautiousness with which he moved in this case. He does, however, emphasize that if matters went according to plan, the Stadtsanwalt would release Jacobsohn, and he adds that this would also be thanks "to English influence". None of this, of course, happened.

CHAPTER EIGHT

1. It might also be important to note Fenichel's comments concerning the situation in Vienna during those months. In his Rundbrief No. XLIV (Mühlleitner & Reichmayr, 1998, Vol. I, p. 741) he stresses how, immediately after the Anschluss, the panic reaction of the Viennese psychoanalysts resulted in their spreading the word that there was to be "Nicht emigrieren" [no emigration]— the reason being that it was thought that the collapse of the Viennese Group would mean the collapse of psychoanalysis altogether. The general opinion was that the group should therefore stay together for as long as possible (p. 741).

2. I have already referred to Klein's letter to Jones, written in the late spring of 1941, where she commented on the way Jones had handled the Freuds' and

that of the other Viennese move to London. It should be noted that Klein took part in the discussions that decided on the analysts and candidates who would be settled in England.

There are also other documents that help to further clarify what went on in the British Psycho-Analytical Society in those years—Fenichel's *Rundbriefe* (Mühlleitner & Reichmayr, 1998) among others. Some of Fenichel's closest friends and collaborators—Kate Friedländer, B. Lantos, and others—had emigrated to London in the mid-1930s, and some of Fenichel's *Rundbriefe* were written with information that was sent to him by Friedländer, although her name does not appear on them. These letters give a very interesting and amusing account of life at the British Psycho-Analytical Society, the role that was played by Klein, and the way in which other members of the Society would react to her views. They also contain reports of meetings between Melanie Klein and S. Bernfeld, who was still in London at the time. Nor does Jones escape criticism. This collection of *Rundbriefe* would, of course, deserve a more careful study, as they help us to acquire a better understanding of the events that eventually led to the Freud–Klein Controversial Discussions (during which Anna Freud received the full support of both Friedländer and Lantos). One must add, nevertheless, that Fenichel was not totally opposed to some of Klein's findings—or "*das Kleinienische*", as he called them! (See his comments on Wälder's visit to London, and the paper he gave in 1935—*Rundbrief* No. XXI, 11 December 1935, Vol. I, pp. 293–294; see also his comments on Klein's "*profunden Funden*" or "deep findings", *Rundbrief* No. XXX, 23 October 1936, p. 505.) On Bernfeld's presence in London, the part he played in Klein's seminars, and the child seminar arranged by those Germans who had emigrated to London, see *Rundbrief* No. XXXV, 28 April 1927, pp. 571–572, and *Rundbrief* No. XXXVI, p. 583. Here one also reads that there was a wish on the part of "*den Engländern*" to make contact with the views of both Bernfeld and the Berliners (p. 582). Very important and interesting is the letter written by E. Kris to Fenichel and reported in *Rundbrief* No. XXXVII, 29 June 1937, concerning the situation in London. Kris was very critical of Klein, Riviere, and their "mystic tendencies", but he thought they could not be influenced by others' views. He also reported that there was some opposition to Melanie Klein inside the Society by people such as N. Searl and J. C. Flugel. The strongest opposition came from Glover and M. Schmideberg. According to Kris, who had been in London to give a paper, "*Jones selbst steht unter dem Bann der neuen Mystik, aber beurteilt sie offenbar mit wechselndem Gefühl. Es is möglich dass er zurückgewinnen wäre*" [Even Jones is under the spell of the new mystic but he judges it obviously with ambivalent feelings. It is possible that he might be won back] (1998, p. 676).

Kris, incidentally, was one of Anna Freud's closest friends at the time, and one can well imagine what he must have reported to Anna on the situation in London! I cannot, of course, quote from all of the *Rundbriefe* in which London is mentioned, but again of particular interest is the *Rundbrief* in which Fenichel reports on the situation in London after having visited there in January 1938. He thought that Melanie Klein's star was in decline! He described the way Klein had reacted to his paper, the problems caused by Klein's difficult relationship with her daughter Melitta, and the role that was played by Glover in opposing Klein. He also claimed that Jones was gradually extricating himself from Melanie Klein's influence and that he would listen to the Viennese more and more often (*Rundbrief* No. XLIII, 14 February 1938, pp. 722–723). Even once Fenichel emigrated to the United States some months later, he continued to write reports on the British Psycho-Analytical Society, using Kate Friedländer, B. Lantos, and Dorothy Burlingham as his informers. There are a few more letters which I think I ought to mention. One *Rundbrief* (No. LIII, 30 December 1938, Vol. II, p. 1009), contains a marvellous description of the contrasting ways in which the British Psycho-Analytical Society and the Viennese functioned, and it also provides an extremely interesting analysis of the differences in culture between the two, including the geographical differences between the cities of London and Vienna—something that had created such enormous discrepancies as far as contacts between analysts, students, seminars, etc. were concerned. The anonymous "informer" on whom Fenichel relied claimed that since the Viennese had arrived, those members of the British Psycho-Analytical Society who were opposed to Klein had become more courageous. The dissensions would become greater as the Viennese began to feel more at home in London.

In Fenichel's *Rundbrief* No. LIV (6 February 1939, Vol. II, p. 1064) he remarks that for years people had not spoken so much about sexuality as they were doing at the moment, all due to the presence of the Viennese. But probably the most interesting *Rundbrief* is No. LXI (15 October 1939, Vol. II, pp. 1204–1205), written after Freud's death and thus after the Second World War had begun (both mentioned very briefly). The "informer" had told Bernfeld about a child seminar they had attended, and at which Anna Freud, Melanie Klein, Susan Isaacs, and others were also present. Dorothy Burlingham's paper "Phantasie und Wirklichkeit in einer Kinder analyse" ["Phantasy and Reality in a Child Analysis"] had been discussed. Apparently Klein had gone on and on, insisting on the importance of the internal object, supported by Susan Isaacs. But the Viennese had claimed that Klein's statements had nothing to do with the case. The atmosphere was very tense. The one who seemed to have suffered the most had been Anna Freud; Jones in the Society was always on the side of "*der Melanieser*" [Melanie's people]. The two groups around Klein and Anna Freud were referred to by Fenichel's "informer" as the "*Welfen*" [Guelfs] and the "*Gibellinen*" [Ghibellines]. The controversies were hopeless and the aggressiveness of "Melanie's people" quite alarming. . . . Kris and the Bibrings thought one ought to wait: time would allow "*die richtigen Ansichten*" [the right views] to penetrate the British Psycho-Analytical Society. Moreover, not all members of the Society followed Klein. And besides, their Central European colleagues working in Manchester (the Balints) were much more optimistic. . . . And I could go on quoting, but I think I have given a good-enough idea of the way the situation was viewed by Anna Freud's friends in that first year in London, and what their presence meant for Melanie Klein.

3.   Rubinstein had originally applied to emigrate to America, as we have seen in a letter Kubie wrote to Jones. However, he eventually remained in England, in spite of the reservations expressed by Jones and others.

4.   The Archives of the British Psycho-Analytical Society contain two interesting documents that refer to the meetings Jones mentions in his letter to Anna Freud dated 29 April 1938.

The first document, signed by B. Low, is called "Hospitality Committee for Colleagues from Austria" and gives an account of the decisions that were taken on 30 March 1938 at a special meeting of the British Psycho-Analytical

Society. The Committee was composed of Miss I. Grant Duff, Miss B. Low, Dr Hilde Maas, and Dr M. Schmideberg. The document was circulated to all members of the British Psycho-Analytical Society, with the request that they should reply in good time what they or their friends were able to offer in the way of hospitality for their colleagues arriving from Austria. The form enclosed was very detailed: it asked Members to let the Society know about a number of matters: (1) hospitality in own home (if only for a few days); (2) daily hospitality (e.g. meals or any other support); (3) hospitality for children without adults (town, country); (4) introduction to friends; (5) any share in consulting-rooms. Under this heading the Members were even asked to provide information as to the possibility of "Meeting colleagues with motor, either at their port of debarkation or at London terminus".

The second document refers to the same special Meeting but, interestingly, mentions the problem "of settling our Psychoanalytical Colleagues from Vienna", adding "(and elsewhere)". It is signed by E. Glover, who also stressed the urgency of the information requested. The information concerned the possibility of relocating the refugees in provincial towns or in densely populated provincial centres, where there would be psychiatrists interested in analysis who might be able to find temporary or permanent posts for those English-speaking refugees trained in psychiatry. It also asked whether members had any "contact with doctors holding permanent consulting or official positions in the provinces, who might be able to help in securing posts or providing posts in (a) Psychoanalysis; (b) general psychotherapy; (c) general medicine." Glover also asks his colleagues: "Have you any contacts with University or College officials at Oxford, Cambridge or any provincial centre?"

The arrival of the Viennese seems to have mobilized the caring side of the British Psycho-Analytical Society to quite a noticeable degree (!), particularly when one considers the difficult circumstances, the restrictions on immigration quotas, and the laws on emigration and immigration in Britain at that time. Indeed, also reflected are the difficulties of this process, for Glover reminds his colleagues that "the individuals in question not possessing an English medical degree could only have the status of (for example) a Clinical Clerk. Also whatever the situation provided, it would be necessary for them to have time to study for an English medical qualification."

5.   Stengel, for instance, would eventually settle in Leeds.
6.   Jones wrote to Eitingon again on 21 October 1939 to keep him informed of the situation of Freud's family following Freud's death:

"The three women left in the house have all suffered a serious reaction since. Frau Professor, who had been a such younger and gayer person since coming to London, has now very much aged. . . . Anna is losing weight and also looks much older. Tante Minna, who in any case has very poor health, has perhaps felt the blow most of all."

He then informs his colleague that the British Psycho-Analytical Society has discussed "a suitable memorial, and we all agreed that this could only take the form of a Collective Edition of his work in English". He continues by giving Eitingon an account of what was being done in this regard and ends with Jones speaking about his day-to-day life, saying "I am living in the country where a few patients still attend . . . ", but for his colleagues in London "the situation is of course extremely difficult".

In another letter dated 28 November 1939 Jones informs Eitingon that Anna's health has improved, but that "she told me yesterday that she would like to retire from her analytic practice and devote herself to helping with the Collected Edition of her father's work in English. . . .". It is interesting to note his comments on the Viennese refugees: "All our foreign analytical friends are now free from restrictions. They are however in a serious financial position, as are our English colleagues, because practice has dwindled to a minimum."

7.   In this letter Jones appears to have wanted to comfort Eitingon in some way, for he again talks about himself and the Freud family, saying:

> "Anna is in good spirits and a tower of strength to all her friends. She refused three offers to go to America, including to professorships of Psychoanalysis. The old people are also very brave, though of course their life is very empty since the Professor's death. It is evident that he did not miss much in dying when he did."

He then gave Eitingon news of the immigrants: "Eidelberg, Isakower and Witt have gone to America and also a young Dr. Geleerd, a Dutch candidate of A. Freud. Kris is also going this week, but on a temporary secret mission." He also gave the latest news on Lampl, Landauer, Marie Bonaparte, and R. Laforgue.

It is important to note his concluding remarks:

> "We are confident on repelling any German invasion. Perhaps after all it might not come, and our enemies may turn their attention to the Balkans and Africa. *I still think it will be a long war and that other nations will become involved before it is finished.*"

8.   See also Anna Freud's letter, dated 28 August 1938, to Dr McCord, a friend of hers, in which she expresses her feelings about England:

> "England indeed is a civilized country and I am naturally grateful that we are here. There is no pressure of any kind or in any direction and there is a great deal of space and freedom ahead. Of course it is strange still and I wonder whether an immigrant in England will ever be anything but an immigrant."

9.   Sterba (1982, p. 160) added that at this point Freud said, "with one exception", referring affectionately to him, who was not a Jew. Of course, as we know, Sterba felt so identified with his colleagues that he left Vienna too.

APPENDIX TWO

1.   The term *"Gleichschaltung"*, for which possible English translations are "co-ordination" or "forcing into line", was indeed "the most modern expression" in the spring of 1933. It was the term used for the political, social, and cultural centralization carried out in Germany by the Nazis after the passing of the Enabling Act of March 1933. It involved an end to the federalism of the Weimar Republic and the coordination of all institutions in German society to the Nazi cause.

REFERENCES AND BIBLIOGRAPHY

Anderson, P. (1968). Components of the national culture. *New Left Review*, 50: 3–57.

Ash, M. G. (1991). Central European emigré psychologists and psycho-analysts in the United Kingdom. In: W. E. Mosse (Ed.), *Second Chance: Two Centuries of German-Speaking Jews in the United Kingdom* (pp. 101–120). Tübingen: Mohr.

Benda, J. (1927). *La trahison des clercs*. Paris: B. Grasset.

Benjamin, W. (1970). Theses on the philosophy of history. In: *Illuminations, 9*. London: Fontana.

Besserman Vianna, H. (1997). *N'en parlez à personne ... Politique de la psychanalyse face à la dictature et a la torture*. Paris: L'Harmattan.

Bloch, M. (1954). *The Historian's Craft*, transl. P. Putnam. Manchester: Manchester University Press.

Boehm, F. (1934). Abschrift. Ereignisse 1933–34. Archives of the British Psycho-Analytical Society.

Boehm, F. (1937). Report dated 27 February. *International Journal of Psycho-Analysis, 8:* 359–360.

Botz, G. (1980). *Wien von "Anschluss" zum Krieg: Nationalsozialistische Machtübernahme und politisch-soziale Umgestaltung am Beispiel der Stadt Wien 1938–39*. Vienna: Jugend & Volk.

Brecht, K. (1987). Der "Fall Edith Jacobsohn" Politischer Widerstand: ein Dilemma der IPA. In: L. M. Hermanns & K. von Bomhard (Eds.), *PSA Info., 28*, March.

Brecht, K., Friedrich, V., Hermanns, L. M., Kaminer, I. J., & Juelich, D. H. (Eds.) (1993). *Here Life Goes On in a Most Peculiar Way*. London: Kellner.

Breitman, R., & Kraut, A. M. (1987). *American Refugee Policy and European Jewry (1933–1945)*. Bloomington, IN: Indiana University Press.

Breslaw, Nachman von (1987). *I racconti*. Milan: Adelphi.

Bunzl, J., & Marin, B. (1983). *Antisemitismus in Österreich: Sozialhistorische und Soziologische Studien*. Innsbruck: Inn-Verlag.

Carsten, F. L. (1986). *The First Austrian Republic, 1918–1938: A Study Based on British and Austrian Documents*. Aldershot: Gower.

Chasseguet-Smirgel, J., & Grünberger, B. (1986). *Freud or Reich? Psychoanalysis and Illusion*. London: Free Association Books.

Cocks, G. (1985). *Psychotherapy in the Third Reich: The Göring Institute* (2nd ed.) New York/Oxford: Oxford University Press, 1997.

Cohn, N. (1967). *Warrant for Genocide*. London: Eyre & Spottiswoode.

Coser, L. A. (1984). *Refugee Scholars in America: Their Impact and Their Experiences*. New Haven, CT/London: Yale University Press.

Dawidowicz, L. (1975). *The War Against the Jews, 1933–45*. London: Weidenfeld & Nicolson.

Dawidowicz, L. (1981). *The Holocaust and the Historians*. Cambridge, MA/ London: Harvard University Press.

Dyer, R. (1983). *Her Father's Daughter: The Work of Anna Freud*. New York: Jason Aronson.

Eco, U. (1979). *The Role of the Reader: Explorations in the Semiotics of Texts*. Bloomington, IN/London: Indiana University Press.

Eickhoff, F. W. (1995). The formation of the German Psychoanalytical Association (DPV). Regaining the psychoanalytical orientation lost in the Third Reich. *International Journal of Psycho-Analysis, 76* (5): 945–956.

Eisold, K. (1998). The splitting of the New York Psychoanalytic Society and the construction of psychoanalytic authority. *International Journal of Psycho-Analysis, 79*: 871–885.

Federn, E. (1990). *Witnessing Psychoanalysis: From Vienna back to Vienna via Buchenwald and the USA*. London: Karnac Books.

Fermi, A. (1968). *Illustrious Emigrants: The Intellectual Migration from Europe 1930–41*. Chicago, IL/London: University of Chicago Press.

Fleming, D., & Bailyn, B. (Eds.) (1969). *The Intellectual Migration: Europe and America 1930–1960*. Cambridge, MA: Belknap Press of Harvard University Press.

Foulkes, E. (Ed.) (1990). *S. H. Foulkes. Selected Papers: Psychoanalysis and Group Analysis*. London: Karnac Books.

Fraenkel, J. (Ed.) (1967). *The Jews of Austria: Essays on Their Life, History, and Destruction*. London: Mitchell.

Freud, A. (1938). Unpublished letter to Dr. McCord, dated 28 August. Sigmund Freud Museum, London.

Freud, A. (1979). Paper read at the meeting to celebrate the centenary of Jones's birth. *The Scientific Bulletin of the British Psycho-Analytical Society* (November): 1–17.

Freud, S. (1900a). *The Interpretation of Dreams. S.E. 4–5.*

Freud, S. (1938). Unpublished letters to M. Bernays, dated 14 May; 25 May; 2 June. London: Sigmund Freud Museum.

Freud, S. (1970). *The Letters of Sigmund Freud and Arnold Zweig*, ed. E. L. Freud. London: Hogarth Press & The Institute of Psycho-Analysis.

Freud, S. (1993). *The Complete Correspondence of Sigmund Freud and Ernest Jones 1908–1939*, ed. R. A. Paskauskas. Cambridge, MA/London: Belknap Press of Harvard University Press.

Friedlander, S. (1993). *Memory, History and the Extermination of the Jews of Europe.* Bloomington, IN: Indiana University Press.

Friedman, L. J. (1990). *Menninger: The Family and the Clinic.* Lawrence, KS: University Press of Kansas.

Friedman, L. J. (1999). *Identity's Architect: A Biography of E. Erikson.* New York: Scribner.

Frosch, J. (1991). The New York psychoanalytic civil war. *Journal of the American Psychoanalytic Association, 39*: 1037–1064.

Gardner, S., & Stevens, G. (1992). *Red Vienna and the Golden Age of Psychology 1918–1935.* New York/London: Praeger.

Gay, P. (1988). *Freud: A Life for Our Time.* New York: W. W. Norton.

Gedye, G. (1947). *Die Bastionen fielen: Wie der Faschismus Wien und Prag überrannte.* Vienna: Danubia Verlag.

Gilman, S. L. (1985). *Difference and Pathology: Sterotypes of Sexuality, Race and Madness.* Ithaca, NY/London: Cornell University Press.

Glaser, E. (1981). *Im Unfeld des Austromarxismus: Ein Beitrag zur Geistesgeschichte des Österreichischen Sozialismus.* Vienna/Munich/Zurich: Europaverlag.

Goldhagen, D. (1996). *Hitler's Willing Executioners.* London: Little Brown.

Granoff, W. (1975). *Filiations: L'Avenir du complexe d'Oedipe.* Paris: Éditions de Minuit.

Grinberg, L., & Grinberg, R. (1984). *Psicoanalisis de la Migración y del Exilio.* Madrid: Alianza Editorial.

Grosskurth, P. (1986). *Melanie Klein: Her World and Her Work.* London: Hodder & Stoughton. Reprinted London: Karnac Books, 1989.

Hale, N. G. (1978). From Berggasse 19 to Central Park West: The Americanization of psychoanalysis 1919–1940. *Journal of the History of the Behavioral Sciences, 14*: 299–315.

Hale, N. G. (1995). *The Rise and Crisis of Psychoanalysis in the United States: Freud and the Americans 1917–1985.* New York/Oxford: Oxford University Press.

Harris, B., & Brook, A. (1991). Otto Fenichel and the Left opposition in psychoanalysis. *Journal of the History of the Behavioral Sciences, 27*: 157–165.

Higgins, M. Boyd (1994). Introduction. In W. Reich, *Beyond Psychology: Letters and Journals 1934–39*, ed. M. Higgins, transl. D. Jordan, I. Jordan, & P. Schmitz. New York: Farrar, Strauss, & Giroux.

Hilberg, R. (1985). *The Destruction of the European Jews, Vols. 1 and 2*. New York: Holmes & Meier.

Holmes, C. (1979). *Anti-Semitism in British Society, 1876–1939*. London: Edward Arnold.

Huber, W. (1977). *Psychoanalyse in Österreich seit 1933*. Wien: Geyer.

Huber, W. (Ed.) (1978). *Beiträge zur Geschichte der Psychoanalyse in Österreich*. Vienna: Geyer.

Jacoby, R. (1983). *The Repression of Psychoanalysis: Otto Fenichel and the Political Freudians*. New York: Basic Books.

Jahoda, M. (1969). The migration of psychoanalysts: its impact on American psychology. In D. Fleming & B. Bailyn (Eds.), *The Intellectual Migration: Europe and America (1930–60)* (pp. 420–445). Cambridge, MA: Belknap Press of Harvard University Press.

Jeffrey, W. D. (1989). After the Anschluss: the Emergency Committee on Relief and Immigration of the American Psychoanalytic Association. *The American Psychoanalyst, 23* (2): 19–37.

Jelavich, B. (1987). *Modern Austria: Empire and Republic 1815–1986*. Cambridge: Cambridge University Press.

Jones, E. (1910). Unpublished letter to Freud, dated 19 June. Freud Archives, Colchester.

Jones, E. (1933). Unpublished letter to Freud, dated 10 April. Freud Archives, Colchester.

Jones, E. (1934). Opening speech at the Thirteenth International Psycho-Analytical Congress, Lucerne, 26–31 August 1934. *International Journal of Psycho-Analysis, 15:* 485–488.

Jones, E. (1937). Opening speech at the Fourteenth International Psycho-Analytical Congress, Marienbad 2–8 August 1936. *International Journal of Psycho-Analysis, 18:* 72–74.

Jones, E. (1938). Photographic copy of document regarding the dissolution of the Vienna Psychoanalytic Society. *International Journal of Psycho-Analysis, 19:* 374.

Jones, E. (1939). Opening speech at the Fifteenth International Psycho-Analytical Congress, Paris. *International Journal of Psycho-Analysis, 20:* 122–126.

Jones, E. (1940). Unpublished letter to Melanie Klein, autumn. Melanie Klein Archives at the Wellcome Institute, London.

Jones, E. (1953–57). *Sigmund Freud: Life and Work, Vols. 1–3*. London: Hogarth Press.

Jones, E. (1957). *Sigmund Freud: Life and Work, Vol. 3*. London: Hogarth Press.

King, P., & Steiner, R. (1992). *The Freud-Klein Controversies, 1941–1945* (2nd ed.). London: Routledge.

Kirsner, D. (2000). *Unfree Associations*. London: Process Press.

Klein, H. (1995). Sandor Rado and the founding of the Columbia Center. *American Psychoanalyst, 28* (4): 3a–8a.

Klein, M. (1940). Unpublished draft of a letter to Jones (autumn). Melanie Klein Archives at the Wellcome Institute, London.

Klein, M. (1944). Unpublished circular letter, 25 January. Melanie Klein Archives at the Wellcome Institute, London.

Kurzweil, E. (1989). *The Freudians: A Comparative Perspective*. New Haven, CT/London: Yale University Press.

Kurzweil, E. (1995). "USA". In: P. Kutter (Ed.), *Psychoanalysis International: A Guide to Psychoanalysis Throughout the World* (2 vols.). Stuttgart: Frommann-Holzboog.

Lacina, E. (1982). *Aber bei uns zu Hause war es besser*. Stuttgart: Klett Cotta.

Langer, M. (1989). *From Vienna to Managua: Journey of a Psychoanalyst*, with E. Guinsberg & J. del Palacio, transl. M. Hooks. London: Free Association.

Langer, W., & Gifford, S. (1978). An American analyst in Vienna during the Anschluss 1936–1938. *Journal of the History of the Behavioral Sciences, 14*: 37–54.

Le Goff, G., & Nora, P. (Eds.) (1974). *Fair de l'histoire* (3 vols.). Paris: Gallimard.

Lockot, R. (1985). *Erinnern und Durcharbeiten: Zur Geschichte der Psychoanalyse und Psychotherapie im Nazionalsozialismus*. Frankfurt-am-Main: Fischer Verlag.

Lockot, R. (1994). *Die Reinigung der Psychoanalyse: Die Deutsche Psychoanalytische Gesellschaft im Spiegel von Documenten und Zeitungen (1933–51)*. Tübingen: Diskord.

London, L. (2000). *Whitehall and the Jews, 1933–1948: British Immigration Policy and the Holocaust*. Cambridge: Cambridge University Press.

Lorand, S. (1969). Reflections on the development of psychoanalysis in New York from 1925. *International Journal of Psycho-Analysis, 50*: 589–595.

Meisel, P., & Kendrick, W. (Eds.) (1986). *Bloomsbury/Freud: The Letters of James and Alix Strachey*. London: Chatto & Windus.

Molnar, M. (Ed.) (1992). *The Diary of Sigmund Freud 1929–39: A Record of the Final Decade*, transl. M. Molnar. London: Hogarth Press.

Morse, N. D. (1968). *While Six Millions Died: A Chronicle of American Apathy*. New York: Random House.

Moser, J. (1975). Die Verfolgung der Juden. In: *Widerstand und Verfolgung in Wien, 1934–45: Eine Dokumentation, Vol. 3*. Vienna: Österreichischer Bundesverlag für Unterricht, Wissenschaft und Kunst.

Mühlleitner, E. (1992). *Biographisches Lexikon der Psychoanalyse, die Mitglieder der Psychologischen Mittwoch-Gesellschaft und der Wiener Psychoanalytischen Vereinigung, 1902–1938*. Tübingen: Diskord.

Mühlleitner, E., & Reichmayr, J. (1995). The exodus of psychoanalysts from Vienna. In: P. Weibel & F. Stadler (Eds.), *Vertreibung der Vernunft: The Cultural Exodus from Austria* (pp. 98–121). Vienna/New York: Springer Verlag.

Mühlleitner, E., & Reichmayr, R. (Eds.) (1998). *Otto Fenichel 119 Rundbriefe (1934–45), Vols. 1, 2*. Frankfurt-am-Main/Basel: Stroemenfeld Verlag.

Neuringer, S. M. (1980). *American Jewry and United States Immigration Policy, 1881–1953*. New York: Arno Press.

Pauley, B. F. (1981). *Hitler and the Forgotten Nazis: A History of Austrian National Socialism*. London: Macmillan/Chapel Hill, NC: University of North Carolina Press.

Peball, K. (1974). *Die Kämpfe in Wien im Februar 1934: Militärische Schriften reihe helft 25*. Vienna: Österreichischer Bundesverlag für Unterricht, Wissenschaft und Kunst.

Peters, U. H. (1985). *Anna Freud: A Life Dedicated to Children*. New York: Schocken Books.

Pulzer, P. G. J. (1964). *The Rise of Political Anti-Semitism in Germany and Austria*. New York: John Wiley.

Pulzer, P. G. J. (1981). *Storia e vita culturale in Austria*. Roma: Bulzoni.

Roazen, P. (1976). *Freud and His Followers*. London: Allen Lane.

Roazen, P. (1985). *Helene Deutsch: A Psychoanalyst's Life*. New York: Anchor Press-Doubleday.

Roazen, P., & Swerdloff, B. (Eds.) (1995). *Heresy: Sandor Rado and the Psychoanalytic Movement*. Northvale, NJ/London: Jason Aronson.

Scholem, G. (1973). *Sabbataï Sevi: The Mystical Messiah*. London: Routledge and Kegan Paul.

Schur, M. (1972). *Freud, Living and Dying*. London: Hogarth Press & The Institute of Psycho-Analysis.

Schwager, E. (1984). *Die Österreichische Emigration in Frankreich 1938–45*. Vienna: Bohlau.

Sharaf, M. (1983). *Fury on Earth: A Biography of Wilhelm Reich*. London: Deutsch.

Sherman, A. J. (1973). *Island Refuge: Britain and Refugees from the Third Reich, 1933–1939* (2nd ed.). London: Elek, 1994; Ilford: Frank Cass.

Spira, L. (1981). *Feindbild "Jud": 100 Jahre politischer Antisemitismus in Österreich*. Vienna: Löcker.

Steiner, R. (1985). Some thoughts on tradition and change in psychoanalysis. In: *International Review of Psycho-Analysis, 12*: 27–71. [Also in: *Tradition, Change, Creativity: Repercussions of the New Diaspora on Aspects of British Psychoanalysis*. London: Karnac Books, 2000.]

Steiner, R. (1993). Introduction: In: *The Complete Correspondence of Sigmund Freud and Ernest Jones, 1908–1939*, ed. R. A. Paskauskas (pp. ii–xxxix). Cambridge, MA/London: Belknap Press of Harvard University Press.

Steiner, R. (2000). *Tradition, Change, Creativity: Repercussions of the New Diaspora on Aspects of British Psychoanalysis*. London: Karnac Books.

Steiner, R. (in preparation). "The future as nostalgia".

Stengel, E. (1939). On learning a new language. *International Journal of Psycho-Analysis*, 20: 471–479.

Stepansky, P. E. (Ed.) (1988). *The Memoirs of Margaret S. Mahler*. New York: Free Press.

Sterba, R. F. (1982). *Reminiscences of a Viennese Psychoanalyst*. Detroit, MI: Wayne State University Press.

Strauss, H. A. (1983). Social and communal acculturation of German-Jewish immigrants of the Nazi period in the United States. In: J. B. Maier & C. I. Waxman (Eds.), *Ethnicity, Identity and History: Essays in Memory of Werner J. Cahnman* (pp. 227–248). New Brunswick, NJ/ London: Transaction Books.

Tartakower, A. (1967). Jewish migratory movements in Austria in recent generations (pp. 285–310). In: J. Fraenkel (Ed.), *The Jews of Austria: Essays on Their Life, History, and Destruction*. London: Mitchell.

Tomlinson, C. (1996). Sandor Rado and Adolf Meyer: a nodal point in American psychiatry and psychoanalysis. In: *International Journal of Psycho-Analysis*, 77 (5): 963–982.

Wachtel, N. (1974). L'acculturation. In: G. Le Goff & P. Nora (Eds.), *Fair de l'histoire*, 1: 174–202.

Walk, J. (1981). *Das Sonderecht für die Juden im N-S Staat: Eine Sammlung der gesetzlichen Massnahmen und Richtlinien*. Heidelberg: Müller.

Wallerstein, R. (1998). *Lay Analysis: Life inside the Controversy*. Hillsdale, NJ: Analytic Press.

Wasserstein, B. (1979). *Britain and the Jews of Europe, 1939–45*. Oxford: Clarendon Press. [New edition Leicester: Leicester University Press, in association with the Institute for Jewish Policy Research, 1999.]

Witmann, E. (1982). *Zwitschen Fascismus und Krieg: Die Sozialitische Jugend internationale 1932–1940*. Vienna: Europa Verlag.

Wyman, D. S. (1984). *The Abandonment of the Jews: America and the Holocaust 1941–1945*. New York: Pantheon Books.

Young-Bruehl, E. (1988). *Anna Freud: A Biography*. London: Macmillan.

INDEX

Abraham, G., 49, 53
Abraham, H., 36–37, 39–40, 49, 53, 171
Abraham, I., 36–37, 39–40, 49, 53, 99, 171
Abraham, K., death of, 39, 57, 139, 172
Adler, A., 46, 149
Adorno, T., 11
Aichhorn, A., 73, 138
Alexander, F., 18–19, 61–62, 109–110, 183–186
  and Benedek, T., 80
  in Chicago, 62, 67, 168
  and Jones, E.:
    appeal to for financial assistance from, 96–97, 99
    correspondence with, 101–102, 109, 182, 185–186
  and Kubie, L. S., correspondence with, 109–110, 184–185
  on opportunities for immigrants in U.S.A., 96–97
American Association of Psychoanalysis, 170, 173, 184–186
American Medical Association, 168
American Psychiatric Association, 60–61, 96, 168, 169
American Psychoanalytic Association, 28, 92, 96–97, 110, 167–168, 182, 185, 186
Anderson, P., 11, 138
Anschluss, 1, 8–10, 26, 28, 87, 95, 191
anti-Semitism, 44, 53–54, 78, 81, 171
  in Great Britain, 7, 11, 12
  ideological history of, 11
  in North America, 7
Argentina, 22, 134
Ash, M. G., 105

Association of Socialist Doctors, Copenhagen, 158
Australia, 5, 6, 114, 121, 122, 123, 187
Austria, *passim*

Bailyn, B., 10
Balint, A., 116, 143, 193
Balint, M., 82, 116, 143, 188, 189, 193
Benda, J., 81
Benedek, R., 20, 79, 131, 176
Benedek, T., 79, 80
Benjamin, W., xi
Berlin, *passim*
  Clinic, 33
  Group, 24, 128, 151
  Psychoanalytic Institute, 15, 77–84, 131, 190
    and Boehm, F., 70, 74, 179
    and Eitingon, M., 36
    and Jewish members, 128–129, 176, 178,
    and Jones, E., 47, 54, 70–75, 77–84, 128–129
    and Ophuijsen, J. H. W. van, 33–34, 39, 47–48
  Psychoanalytic Society, 56, 79, 89, 139
Bernays, M., 110, 186
Bernfeld, S., 39, 82, 97, 127, 161, 162, 192, 193
Besserman Vianna, H., 134
Bibliographical Centre (London), 98
Bibring, E., 82, 86, 95, 111, 140–142, 182, 193
Bibring, G., 82, 111, 140, 141, 193
Bloch, M., 2
BMA (British Medical Association), 12, 13, 121, 123